HOUSEPLANTS

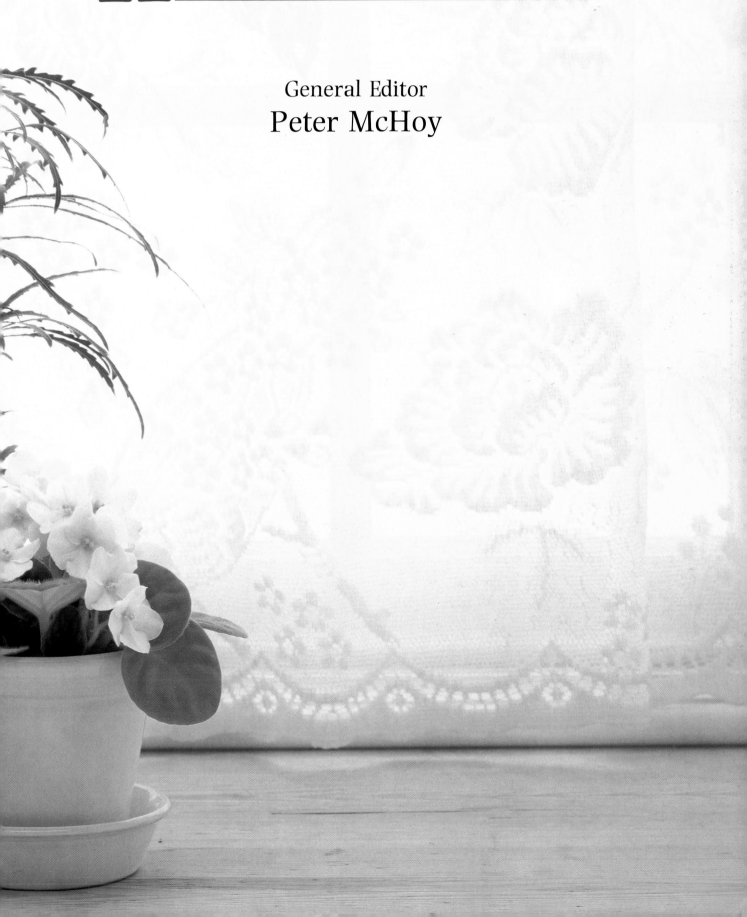

HOUSEPLANTS

General Editor
Peter McHoy

CONTENTS

This edition first published exclusively in paperback for
Marks and Spencer p.l.c.
in 1982 by Octopus Books Limited
59 Grosvenor Street,
London W1

© 1981 Hennerwood Publications Limited

ISBN 0 906320 10 0

Produced by Mandarin Publishers Limited
22a Westlands Road
Quarry Bay
Hong Kong

Printed in Hong Kong

Houseplants was first published
in hard cover in 1981
by Octopus Books Limited

INTRODUCTION

Indoor gardening has all the excitement, challenge and pleasure of outdoor gardening – but with the bonus of comfort. Whatever the weather you can tend and enjoy your plants.

Houseplants also make it possible for everyone to experience the joys of gardening – whether they live in a high-rise flat in a city or in a country home with a large garden. Even the disabled can have the satisfaction of tending pot plants or an indoor miniature garden. And as with most hobbies there are many rewards that are not always obvious before one becomes involved – delightful though they are, the ubiquitous rubber plant (*Ficus elastica*) and busy Lizzie (impatiens) do little justice to the vast range of wonderful plants waiting to be grown in the home.

Only two ingredients are necessary for a more colourful and more interesting home: imagination and the will to try new plants.

The only restraint on the use of houseplants is imagination – provided the right plant is chosen for a particular situation, you can have them standing on the floor, window-sill, mantelpiece and hearth (provided there is no fire), climbing round the window frames, cascading from indoor hanging-baskets or pots suspended in macrame holders, or even climbing up poles or trellises as a kind of living room divider.

No room with a window is unsuitable for a plant of some kind: bedrooms, bathrooms and loos can all be enhanced by a well-chosen plant. Even halls and stairways – frequently inhospitable places in older homes – can take an ivy (*Hedera helix*), a grape ivy (*Cissus rhombifolia*, syn. *Rhoicissus rhomboidea*) or an aucuba. In warm, light halls the scope is widened of course – although it would be unwise to try anything that might object to icy blasts when the front door is opened in winter.

Always try to build a collection of plants with a plan in mind. Decide clearly on the role the plants are to play – whether they are to be a focal point or merely decorative objects.

Try to buy plants to fulfil a particular need, and endeavour to resist the temptation to buy plants requiring conditions you cannot provide.

The ideal is to have a greenhouse or conservatory, or a growing room equipped with special lighting, in which plants can recuperate between spells of duty in the home. If such conditions can be provided there is every chance that even the more difficult plants can be grown successfully, otherwise it is best to settle for those kinds likely to thrive with the conditions and attention you are able to offer them. By all means buy the more difficult plants if you are prepared to regard them as expendable – if bought in good condition they will probably provide many weeks of pleasure and enjoyment before becoming weak or sickly – but as a rule knowing your limitations is most of the secret of success with houseplants.

DECIDING ON THE PLANTS

One of the fascinations of gardening is the constant challenge of growing difficult plants, especially when experience has been gained; but nothing is more certain to snuff out the flame of enthusiasm at the beginning of this hobby than to start with tricky ones. To simplify the choice for beginners and experienced houseplant enthusiasts alike, all the plants mentioned in the main alphabetical section of this book (pages 50 to 131) have been graded by stars according to their ease of cultivation. One star indicates a good plant for the beginner – undemanding and easy to grow, and requiring no special treatment other than providing basic conditions such as the right amount of light and moisture. A two-star plant is more difficult and should only be tried once experience has been gained with easier plants. Three stars indicate a difficult plant, often requiring high temperatures and humidity, and considerable care. Never buy the plant first because it takes your fancy, and wonder where to put it when you return home; either decide on the type of plant you need for a particular situation, or check that the plants you like in the shop can be accommodated. In a good shop the plant will have a label listing basic requirements – an excellent innovation that must have saved many a plant from an untimely death – otherwise the assistant should be able to advise.

GETTING OFF TO A GOOD START

A good houseplant will be an object of beauty and interest in the home for many weeks and months – probably for years, if looked after carefully. Buying one should therefore not be approached with the casualness of purchasing a bunch of flowers, which you know will only last a short time. If a plant is in ill health or been subjected to adverse conditions, no amount of nursing and coddling is likely to revive it sufficiently to make a strong, healthy plant.

Houseplants are inexpensive if they give you months or years of pleasure, which most of them will do, but costly if the failure rate is high. It should also be borne in mind that the effort involved in looking after a poor plant is just as great, often greater, than it is looking after a healthy starter.

Quality is as important in plants as in any other commodity – do not be tempted to go for the cheapest unless you know it is good value. Be prepared to shop around – you will frequently find an amazing difference in price and quality from one type of outlet to another. And remember, going to a garden centre is no guarantee of good plants – they may be subjected to as much mal-treatment there as anywhere else.

Learn to discriminate, watch for tell-tale signs of good care, and take the plants home and acclimatize them carefully. Then you can be certain of getting off to a good start with your houseplants – which is most of the way to success.

Where to shop

Gardeners acquire plants in many ways – from jumble sales and bazaars, and exchanging with friends, to ordering from nurseries specializing in particular plants. But most of us buy from shops, nurseries or garden centres, and these are likely to provide all the houseplants the average enthusiast is likely to require. Only when a special enthusiasm for a particular group of plants has been generated will it be necessary to go to more specialized sources, where the less common houseplants will be stocked.

Houseplants can be chosen to suit a variety of positions, from desktops to darkened corners and bright windows.

The excellent growing conditions in this modern garden centre are a sure indication of strong, healthy plants, and good advice.

Anyone who starts to grow houseplants is likely to fall victim to the charms of a particular group of plants, however, and that is the time to join one of the specialist societies. If your interest lies with cacti, bromeliads, ferns, saintpaulias, or orchids, you will find a society that can offer a shared interest, plants or seeds, and information on nurseries supplying some of the less usual species.

For most of us who just want a collection of beautiful and dependable houseplants, it is best to use ordinary shops, florists, horticultural sundriesmen or garden centres. At any one time none of them is likely to stock more than a small selection of the plants mentioned in this book, but part of the fun of collecting houseplants is to keep an eye open in your favourite shops for any new plants that take your fancy, or that you have been looking for.

Far more important than the type of outlet is the way the plants are treated and displayed. It is on this, and not the number or range of plants, that a plant seller should be judged.

What to look for

How the plants are displayed is important. Avoid any shop that displays its houseplants outside – even in winter some sellers stand their plants on the pavement or on market stalls, which makes an attractive display but does nothing for the well-being of the plants. Cold draughts can be fatal to a plant, many of which may have come straight from a warm greenhouse. No matter how attractive they look, or how cheap they may be, do not buy.

Inside the shop, the way the plants are displayed will also indicate how well they have been cared for. Irregular watering can also cause problems, and plants wrapped in paper can hardly be receiving adequate water. If they are standing on trays or on shelves with nothing beneath the pots for water, it is another indication that they are not likely to be receiving proper attention.

Ideally, they should be displayed in trays containing a capillary mat – a thin black or green felt-like material, which is kept moist and from which the compost in the pots is able to extract some moisture. Although such mats should not be swimming in water, beware if they are bone dry – watering has been neglected. Apart from whether the soil is too moist or too dry, there are other tell-tale signs:

Lift the pot and look underneath. If there are many roots coming out of the drainage hole, the chances are it should have been potted-on (given a larger pot) earlier and may now be starved of food; even if it looks in good health, you want to avoid the need to pot-on too soon after getting it home, as it is important to get it acclimatized with as little disturbance as possible before subjecting it to any shock. Wilting could be a sign of excessive watering, too little watering or diseased roots – whatever the reason the plant is best left in the shop. The same goes for any plant with leaves browning at the edges or that are yellowing or distorted. In short, the foliage should be strong and fresh-looking, with no sign of injury.

Pests and diseases should also be left in the shop, so look carefully – not only for any kind of creepy-crawlies but for eggs too. These may not be visible to the naked eye, so it is best to avoid all plants in the shop if you find adult pests. Diseases will usually be manifest as mottled, blotched, or mouldy leaves, and obviously these must be avoided.

Houseplants are sometimes offered for sale ready wrapped, with just the head of flowers or foliage clearly visible, or they may have a transparent sleeve or collar as protection. Don't take such plants at face value. They may be perfectly fine specimens, but unless you remove them from the sleeve or wrapper, you'll never know until it's too late. With cyclamen in particular, the fine upstanding plant may turn out to be weak and straggly. If the seller objects to you inspecting the plant properly, you should take your custom to a more professional source.

Plants are sometimes offered for sale in specially designed sealed bags. These are in effect miniature Wardian cases – the forerunners of today's bottle gardens. Provided they are not displayed in full sun, which could produce an excessive temperature in the bags, these plants should fare well. The bags are designed in such a way that you can see exactly what you're buying, and you should not open the bag to inspect the plant – if you don't buy it the special environment will have been destroyed. But do check that the one you buy has a fully inflated bag – if it is not firmly expanded the plant will probably have suffered.

It is necessary to be clear about the type of plant you want – whether it is to provide a brief but spectacular display, or a more subdued but pleasant show, probably of foliage, for many months, or even years; whether you want a small plant for the window-sill or table, or a large specimen to stand in a tub on the floor. Sometimes it is worth paying for a brilliant or spectacular flower even if you know the plant may have to be discarded afterwards – all-the-year-round chrysanthemums are an example of flowering pot plants that make an attractive but unrepeatable show (they will have been specially treated with chemicals and grown under strict lighting conditions to induce flowering in a pot out of season), but you can plant them outdoors and they may produce flowers at the normal time and on tall plants in future years. Nevertheless they make such a good show that they are still much cheaper than most cut flowers to provide blooms over the same period, and there is something infinitely more satisfying about observing a growing plant develop from tight buds to full and glorious bloom.

Whether small specimens or large ones are bought it is largely a matter of patience . . . and price.

Large specimens are always the most imposing, but they are naturally more expensive – they have had to be grown for very much longer in the nursery (and naturally that costs money). If you want to build an extensive collection of houseplants, and are prepared to wait for the results, small specimens are the answer, for they are naturally less expensive. On the other hand, if money is no obstacle, the large specimens that

can be bought from good suppliers will probably be healthier and more robust than you are likely to achieve yourself in the home, for they will have been growing in greenhouse conditions, which can never really be matched indoors. On the other hand, there is nothing more satisfying than to have grown a large and mature specimen plant from a young seedling or cutting by your own care and skill over the years. That is something no bought superplant can bring.

The journey home

Always ask the assistant to wrap the plant well, if this has not already been done, making sure the paper or bag completely covers the plant. A suitable carrier-bag often offers the best protection from cold winds, and makes the carrying less of a balancing act.

It naturally makes sense to buy your plants at the end of a shopping trip, so that they do not have to be carried round longer than necessary – which not only puts them at risk from temperature fluctuations, but increases the chance of physical damage.

Don't leave plants in the boot or interior of a car which is parked for long periods in hot weather. The temperature can very soon soar to a level that is unacceptable even to tropical plants.

It is also common sense not to travel with them in the boot if there is any risk of them toppling or being crushed. It is always best to hold or carry them.

When you get the plants home, acclimatize them gradually; and pamper them a little bit more than you would normally. If the compost is dry, water it immediately, otherwise wait until it needs it (see page 16). Place the plants in a warm room, out of draughts and scorching sunshine during this period. Maintain a humid atmosphere by spraying the plants with a fine mist at least twice a day.

After a week or two, when you are confident that they have overcome the shock of transition from greenhouse to shop and finally home, you should be able to place the plants in the position you intended.

Remember, in many cases they will have been in a warm, humid greenhouse in good light only a few days before, although if they have been in a florist's shop they may have become partially acclimatized.

Far left: Pot chrysanthemums.
Below left: A garden centre display with a begonia protected for travel.

Below: Foliage and flowering plants can be used to complement each other.

HOUSEPLANT CARE

GENERAL CARE

By definition a houseplant should grow and thrive in a house, and with a little care most will do so for many years. But it must be remembered that the home is a very alien environment for plants, far removed from the tropical rain forests of South America, the arid deserts of Mexico or Arizona, or many other parts of the world from which our house plants originally came.

Even if we keep our homes warm they lack the natural humidity and light that most exotic plants require, and it is these two factors that prevent many good greenhouse plants being grown in the home for long periods.

It is impossible to match natural conditions, and our efforts must inevitably be aimed at a compromise. This is not always a bad thing, for we don't want our rubber plants as high as a house or cacti as tall as a man – sizes which they might achieve in the wild.

If a greenhouse or a conservatory is available, many houseplants will benefit from a spell in these more amenable conditions from time to time – but that is no substitute for providing the best conditions within the home. Light, temperature and humidity are all important, but compost, feeding and watering are equally vital and due regard must be paid to all of them if you want healthy and thriving plants.

COMPOST

Compost does more than anchor the plant – it holds reserves of food and moisture and keeps the roots aerated. It is also host to many micro-organisms, some of which are beneficial.

Compost is not essential – hydroponic units use only water and fertilizers and an inert aggregate – but this is a specialized method of growing plants and it has taken many years of laboratory research to reach the stage where we can easily achieve with water and chemicals what the soil does naturally. Even then it would be totally wrong to suggest that all plants can be grown successfully in nutrient solutions.

For the vast majority of houseplants, a good compost is essential, and the choice will lie between a traditional loam-based type or one of the peat-based composts. There is much to be said for each kind, and it is likely that both will continue to be used.

Loam-based composts are best made to the John Innes formula. This is not a proprietary compost and anyone can make it, though the amateur is advised to buy it ready mixed.

The main ingredient is good quality sterilized loam, which gives the compost substance and weight (important for plants with heavy top growth, which may become unstable in a light compost). It is also less prone to dry out so completely and as rapidly as a peat compost, and there is a better reservoir of plant food. And because it has been sterilized, harmful organisms have been removed. Most plants will grow equally well in John Innes compost or a loamless type, but a few plants such as the shrimp plant (*Beloperone guttata*) seem to prefer the John Innes mixture.

Peat-based composts are light and pleasant to handle, and for plants such as African violets (*Saintpaulia ionantha*) are a superior growing medium. Their drawback is that plants set in them need feeding sooner after potting than would be the case with John Innes, and watering is more difficult to control accurately. The compost can dry out suddenly, and be difficult to moisten thoroughly. Also, it is less easy to judge visually whether the compost is in need of water, and more emphasis must be placed on weight, (see page 16). Large plants may topple when they become heavy, and for plants of some stature a loam-based compost is best.

Provided they are watered and fed properly, however, peat composts can produce extremely gratifying results.

No matter how useful standardized composts are, there will always be the need for special mixtures for particular groups of plants – bromeliads, orchids, and lime-hating plants all have their particular needs. Where a particular compost is required this will be explained in the relevant part of the book, but where no special mention is made it can be assumed that either John Innes or a peat-based compost will be suitable.

Potting on

Never be in too much of a hurry to pot on a plant into a larger container. Growing plants indoors has to be a compromise between providing the roots with sufficient soil and nutrients and the need to avoid root disturbance. No plant appreciates having its roots unsettled, and any damage to them will result in some check to growth.

Never repot a houseplant merely as a matter of routine – say on an annual

---

PLASTIC V. CLAY?

Just as there are devotees of loam-based and peat-based composts, so there are gardeners who will only use clay pots or plastic pots. But, as usual, there are pros and cons for both, and each has its place.

The vast majority of plants purchased will be in plastic pots, which is good enough evidence that commercial growers find them satisfactory. They are clean and easy to handle, look attractive, are easy to keep free of green algae, and are comparatively inexpensive.

Most plants also grow well in them; they retain moisture better and the compost is less likely to dry out so rapidly (particularly useful if peat composts are used).

With all these benefits, why use clay pots? Firstly they are likely to be longer-lasting – surprising though it may seem, most plastic pots are more easily broken than clay ones. Short of dropping a clay pot on the floor from a height it is unlikely to break, but plastic pots can become very brittle and even a slight knock or scuff is sometimes sufficient to cause a

crack and break them.

With a heavy plant a clay pot may be needed to provide a stable and more substantial base than a plastic pot could offer. The extra weight can be especially useful if a peat compost is used.

A clay pot should always be soaked for several hours before use, otherwise it may absorb too much moisture from the compost.

basis. Some plants may require potting on annually, but many others will not and to do so could affect flowering.

Be guided by the specific information in the A-Z of Houseplants (pages 50 to 131), and by the state of the roots. If the pot is full of roots (you can check this by inverting the pot, supporting the plant, and giving it a sharp tap on a hard edge to release the soil-ball), and they are coming through the drainage holes in the bottom of the pot, then repotting is probably necessary.

Don't be misled by a few fibrous roots coming through the drainage holes, however. If the plants have been grown on a capillary bench or mat – the roots are naturally attracted to the source of water. And it is quite normal for some roots to run round the side of the pot – only if there is a solid mass of roots will it qualify for potting on.

A few plants need very little soil – bromeliads, for instance, use their roots principally for anchorage.

Some plants do not have an extensive root run and are best grown in half-pots instead of pots – cacti are typical of this group. Half-pots have the diameter of conventional pots but not the depth.

Plants in 7.5cm (3in) pots are normally potted on into 12.5cm (5in) size, and from that size to 15cm (6in) pots, and so on in 2.5cm (1in) increments.

To repot a plant, either use the technique illustrated on the right, or use the method described below. Both methods produce equally satisfactory results.

Start by placing a piece of broken pot over the drainage hole of a clay pot, or just fibrous material such as peat over the base of a plastic pot (always avoid crocks if capillary mats are to be used). Place a little dampened compost over the base material, then insert the existing pot (or empty one of the same size) inside the larger one, ensuring the level of the soil surface will be about 12–25mm ($\frac{1}{2}$–1in) below the top of the new pot when filled. Pack compost firmly between the inner and outer pot, so that it leaves a mould when the inner pot is removed.

Always use the same type of compost as that in the existing pot, ensuring that both it and the soil-ball are uniformly damp – not dust-dry, but not too wet.

Knock the plant out of the old pot by tapping it sharply on a hard surface while supporting the plant. The root-ball will fit snugly into the depression in the new pot and compost, and it can be firmed into place with a further sprinkling of compost. Firm well using the fingers or a suitable piece of wood. Finally, water well and keep out of full sun for a few days.

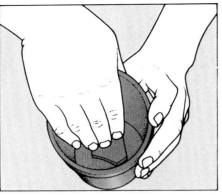

Always pot on into a pot only slightly larger than the existing one. Place broken crocks over the drainage hole.

Place some compost in the bottom of the pot, insert the root-ball and add more compost round the sides.

Finish by levelling the compost off with the fingers, allowing at least 12mm ($\frac{1}{2}$in) of space for watering.

Moisten the soil-ball in the old pot before knocking it out and transferring it carefully to the new container.

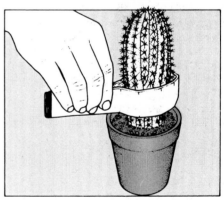

Press the compost firmly down round the sides of the pot, without actually over-compressing it round the roots.

Prickly cacti are difficult to handle but this is easily overcome by using a thick strip of folded paper.

FEEDING

Give your plants the right compost, temperature and light, water them regularly, and they will survive. But it is proper feeding that makes the difference between a plant that just survives and one that thrives. Never underestimate the importance of feeding your houseplants, for it can make a tremendous difference to their well-being.

It is best to use a special houseplant fertilizer, not because their requirements are very different from those of most outdoor plants, but because the dilution rate is more practical for home use – a few drops to a pint (litre) perhaps.

Most loam-based composts will contain sufficient reserve of the minor or 'trace' elements such as boron, molybdenum and copper, to make it unnecessary to worry about these – but plants in pots soon run short of the three major plant foods: nitrogen, phosphates and potash. These will be found in adequate proportions in all houseplant foods or in a good general fertilizer.

Whether you use a liquid concentrate or a soluble powder makes little difference to the plants, but for say a pint of diluted fertilizer a liquid is probably best as it is difficult to measure the powders accurately at this level; but if you are likely to use about 5 litres (1 gallon) or more at a time, it could be as easy to use a soluble powder and there could be savings if you choose one that can be used for the garden too so you can buy a large size. There is little merit in using foliar feeds as it usually means the plants have to be moved to a place where overhead spraying is not likely to wet furnishings.

Fertilizer tablets have the merit of being easy to apply (just press into the compost), but are not the best method if a capillary system of watering is adopted.

When to feed

Feed regularly during the active growing season – every week or fortnight (be guided by the manufacturer's instructions). Feed only infrequently (perhaps once a month) if a plant is growing during the winter, but not at all during a resting period. Obviously plants vary in this respect – and although feeding is best done on a regular basis it should not be undertaken according to the calendar regardless of the state of the plant.

As a general guide, most plants will need feeding from late spring until autumn. Plants that make a lot of growth may need more than those of more restrained habit. Bromeliads and cacti do not need much food, and in the case of most bromeliads it is necessary to apply it to the central vase (see page 155).

Most plants will need feeding when you buy them – the food reserves in the compost are not great and if established and well-rooted plants are purchased they will probably be ready for supplementary feeding.

Peat composts in particular can run short of plant food quite suddenly. Although they have a long-life fertilizer added when they are made, they lack the natural reserves possessed by loam.

Plants growing in a hydroculture unit will require feeding about every six months, if an ion-exchange fertilizer is used (see page 30).

WATERING

Probably more houseplants are lost through errors in watering than from any other cause. And ironically, it is usually too much rather than too little water that causes the problem.

Unlike plants growing outdoors with a large reservoir of soil, houseplants have very little ability to withstand extremes of drought or waterlogging. There is usually no ultimate soakaway for the water, and any surplus simply sits in the saucer and the compost remains waterlogged unless there is a suitable gap.

Conversely, because of the small volume of compost in a pot, it tends to dry out quickly in warm weather: clay pots are more prone to this than plastic pots. And though most plants will wilt – even drop a few leaves as a natural way to conserve moisture and reduce water loss through transpiration – they will normally revive. But there comes a point of no return for any plant, and to leave them unattended for more than a week in warm weather is inviting losses.

The ability to judge when a plant needs water is a combination of experience and observation.

The traditional way to determine when a clay pot requires water is to tap the outside with the knuckle or something like a cotton-reel on a stick. If the pot and soil-ball are dry the pot will produce a hollow ring, and the plant will need water; but if they are still moist the pot will produce a dull tone and no water should be given. The difference soon becomes obvious with a little practice. The knuckle method is fine for one or two plants, but if you have a large number of pots it becomes a little hard on the skin, and an improvised 'hammer' is the best solution.

Tapping only works with clay pots, and as most plants are sold in plastic containers nowadays it is most unlikely that it can ever be the complete answer.

A rather laborious but very accurate method is to weigh the pot. By placing the plant on a spring scale when it requires water and weighing it again once the compost has been moistened sufficiently, the two weights can be noted. It is not unusual for the difference for a small plant in a peat-based compost to be about 50g (2oz). Once this has been done it is always possible to ascertain the moisture requirements of the compost (although as the plant grows it will be necessary to repeat the 'before and after' exercise occasionally).

Unfortunately, life is not long enough to enable many plants to be watered in this way, but it can be useful for a few plants that will not be likely to suffer damage as a result of regular handling for the weighing operation. Its greatest merit is as a means of providing the beginner with the necessary experience to judge the state of the compost by sight and touch. After a few weeks of weighing, a natural judgement will be acquired and the need for such precise measurements will diminish.

It is possible to buy meters having a probe which is pushed into the compost to give a reading of the moisture level in the compost. They hardly look elegant sticking out of the compost, and constantly pushing the probe into the soil is likely to damage the roots. As an aid to learning to judge the visual signs, however, they can be useful.

Unless one of the 'automatic' systems is used it is going to become necessary to learn to depend on judgement; and this has the advantage that it makes you observe the plants more closely.

Most plants will tell you in no uncertain terms that they need water – by wilting. But that stage should never be reached –

Regular watering, feeding and good humidity are necessary for healthy houseplants. The wick method is one way of watering while on holiday.

16

it means you have failed to notice the more subtle indicators.

The compost itself is the best guide, but never go by surface appearance alone: if you give it just a dribble of water the surface will appear moist, but the compost at root level could still be dry.

Loam-based composts are the easiest to judge and to water. It will be clear from the lighter appearance of the surface that it is drying out, and it will be drier to the touch. Even so, discretion must be used – if the plant was only watered the previous day the chances are that only the surface has dried and the compost beneath may be damp. Do not be in too much of a hurry to water, as loam-based composts tend to dry out gradually.

Peat-based composts are more difficult. They can dry out very rapidly once allowed to become too dry and when that happens it is much more difficult to moisten them evenly again. Because the colour difference between moist compost and dry is less pronounced than it is with traditional composts, it is more difficult to determine when water is needed. But because dry peat is very light, the weight of the pot and plant is a good indicator (there is no need to place the pot on scales; the difference will be so marked that you will soon be able to judge).

Never water by the calendar – if the weather and home environment were as predictable as the date there would be some merit in watering on a particular day of the week, but that is not the case. Also, some plants will need watering more frequently than others, and at certain times of the year most plants will require a resting period when they should be kept almost dry. This makes it necessary to judge each plant on its merits before watering.

There is something to be said for 'watering days', provided you do not water everything regardless of its needs. By watering on say Mondays and Thursdays, the plants are not likely to be forgotten and they will be inspected at least twice a week. It also makes feeding easier to remember – you can apply a suitable fertilizer perhaps every Monday, or every-other Monday, depending on recommendations, the plant, and the time of year.

How to water
There are two simple rules – water generously but ensure the pot does not remain standing in surplus water.

It is no use simply splashing the surface of the compost with water and then going on to the next plant. Pour steadily until the gap between the compost and the rim of the pot is full, then wait until it drains through. If it's all absorbed, apply more water and again wait until it runs through. If it runs through immediately, the compost has probably become so dry it has shrunk from the sides of the pot (or in the case of a peat-based compost, the peat has dried out). If this has happened it will be necessary to place the pot in a bowl of water until the compost is thoroughly moist again. This is the best way of watering plants growing in a very peaty compost, such as azaleas.

A self-watering pot with a visual gauge showing the water level.

For plants with a low rosette of hairy leaves, such as saintpaulias, or corms that may rot, such as cyclamen, it is best to add water to the saucer and allow it to be taken up by capillary action. This may take a little time.

A good watering-can specially designed for indoor use is essential. Choose one with a long, narrow spout so that the water can be controlled accurately. If the spout is too short and the diameter too wide there will be a tendency for the water to shoot forward when the can is tipped, making it difficult to control, resulting in water over the window-sill and furniture as well as the plant.

Because you don't want the plants to stand in water, it is quite likely that surplus will have to be emptied from the saucer or container. However, a small bonus for this extra effort is that if a liquid fertilizer is being used, it may be possible to reuse some of the run-off water and so economize.

There are two situations where the excess water may be left with safety – if the pot is standing on a layer of pebbles and the water is not in direct contact, or if the plant is one of the rare exceptions that will tolerate wet feet. The umbrella grass (*Cyperus alternifolius*) is naturally adapted to marshy ground, while the Indian azalea (*Rhododendron simsii*) and mind your own business, *Soleirolia soleirolii* (better known as *Helxine soleirolii*), are examples of plants that will thrive in wet conditions.

'Automatic' watering

Hydroculture units apart (see page 30), there are self-watering containers available that will take much of the guesswork out of watering. Individual systems vary, but most use wicks to transfer water from a reservoir to the compost. Even so, you still have to look at the water level indicator periodically and top up the unit as directed.

There are many attractive plastic self-watering containers, but if these do not appeal there are also glazed pottery containers with a porous compartment that is filled with water which gradually seeps into the compost.

Self-watering containers are useful for anyone with little time to spare, or if short stays away from home are a frequent problem, but they should not provide an excuse for neglect.

Capillary mats are frequently used in greenhouses and good shops selling houseplants, and can also be bought for home use. These mats are most useful where many plants are grouped together on a tray but this is not how plants are generally arranged in the home. Capillary mats are, however, useful for placing in the long trays that can be bought for standing plants on a widow-ledge. If such a mat is used, it should not be assumed that regular checking is not required – the mat can dry out just as easily as the pots – but it does ensure that the pots receive a steady amount of water. The mat should be kept evenly moist, but not swimming in water, and the pots should be pressed well into the mat's surface to ensure good contact.

Type of water

As long as the water is not too hard, most houseplants will be perfectly healthy if given tap water. If you live in a particularly hard water area it is best to use a water softener or to boil the water first – but allow the boiled water to cool before use. Rainwater can be used, but an adequate supply is not always available, and unless it is kept as clean as possible it is likely to introduce and spread diseases. Rainwater is best reserved for those plants that respond adversely to lime, such as camellias, azaleas and blue hydrangeas.

Hydroculture plants grown with an ion-exchange fertilizer, however, must be watered with tap water as the calcium is necessary to trigger the chemical reaction that will release the nutrients.

Going on holiday

Houseplants can be almost as much of a problem as pets at holiday time – knowing what to do with them for a week or two is always difficult.

If the holiday is brief – less than about five days – it should be sufficient to water them well before you leave. In all except the hottest weather no permanent damage should be caused, although it makes sense to remove plants from a hot sunny window-sill to a cooler and more shaded environment.

Hydroculture units and self-watering devices can be left for a fortnight without worry provided there is sufficient water in the reservoir. This is one instance where 'topping up' may be advisable if the level is getting low (but be sure to let the roots of hydroculture plants dry a little upon your return).

Most cacti and succulents will survive a week or two without water if absolutely necessary, but alternative watering arrangements simply must be made for all other plants.

There may be a temptation to put some plants outside, on the basis that most of those outdoors manage to survive with the rain that nature provides. But there is no guarantee that it is going to rain at the right time, and nature does not have plants growing in pots raised above the ground. Even if the pots are plunged in damp soil, most houseplants will not be able to withstand the sudden shock of being placed outdoors even in high summer. Try only those plants that the A-Z of Houseplants (pages 50–131) suggests can stand outdoors in summer – and even then provide a sheltered spot. The best solution is to arrange for an understanding neighbour or relative to care for your plants in your absence. If this is impossible you will either have to arrange your holiday to coincide with the resting period of most of your plants (winter) or prepare them to last the siege as well as you can, in which case there are various techniques that can be tried. Group the plants together in a light place out of direct sunshine (or in a shady place for shade-loving plants), and arrange a reservoir of water at a slightly higher level (a large ice-cream container is suitable). By using wicks, which you should be able to buy from a good horticultural sundriesman, a steady supply of water can be applied to the pots. An alternative method is to run wicks from a reservoir and stand the pots on the wicks, allowing capillary action to transfer water to the pots. Always have a trial-run first, however, to be sure you have a system that works.

If damp peat can be packed round the pots, so much the better.

Do not apply a stronger dose of feed before you leave the plants, to compensate for not feeding while you are away. It is better to miss a feed than to risk damage through over-feeding.

HUMIDITY

Plants are much more sensitive to humidity – or rather the lack of it – than humans. They lose water constantly through their leaves in the form of vapour transpired through minute pores, and if the atmosphere is dry the rate of loss will increase and often cause stresses within the plant.

Obviously, plants vary in their tolerance and while cacti are well adapted to a dry atmosphere as well as dry roots, other plants from the rain forests of Peru and elsewhere, such as fittonias and philodendrons, need humidity.

Humidity produces a buoyant growing atmosphere that is immediately sensed as soon as one enters a greenhouse full of healthy plants.

Modern living, with its ever-increasing central heating and tendency towards a dry atmosphere, is unfortunately not conducive to this environment, and it is a constant battle of balance between an atmosphere that is right for the plants and one that is comfortable for us.

A start can be made by using humidifiers over radiators or near other forms of heating (taking into account safety aspects), which will prevent the air becoming excessively dry. Failing anything more sophisticated, a few bowls of water will help.

There is no way that we can recreate the steamy atmosphere of a warm greenhouse in the living-room as a whole, so efforts are best concentrated on providing a localized environment.

It is quite easy to provide moist air around small plants, by standing the pots on gravel or similar small stones to hold the bottom of the pot above the water in the base of the container.

Another method sometimes used is to pack moist peat or moss between the pot and the outer decorative container. This is effective in producing a good micro-

Excessively dry air has a damaging effect on plants, and a humidifier, particularly in centrally heated homes, can help maintain a more humid atmosphere. They work by evaporating water.

climate, but it is not easy to judge whether excess water is standing in the bottom – the consequences of which can be an overwatered and ailing plant.

Spraying the leaves with a fine mist of water is very effective, but also time-consuming and not always good for the wallpaper and furnishings. In a bathroom it is simply a matter of placing the plants in the bath for their daily syringe, but in other rooms it may involve removing them to a more suitable place. It is a technique probably best reserved for those plants that will benefit immensely from this treatment, such as ferns, selaginellas and fittonias.

By grouping plants together the local humidity is increased and the plants tend to thrive better than they would as individual specimens.

Never place a plant over a warm radiator or fire – apart from the safety aspect, the warmth will do them no good if the dry air kills them.

TEMPERATURE

It surprises many beginners to learn that temperature is frequently less important than light and moisture. Certainly many plants we now grow in our homes were regarded as 'stove' plants not many years ago, and it is only comparatively recently that it has been realized how hardy some of our houseplants really are. Great heat used to be thought necessary for vrieseas, for instance, but we now realize that most species will grow happily at 10°C (50°F). It is not that the plants have suddenly adapted, but false assumptions were made by previous generations of gardeners.

If we look at an average collection of houseplants it is quite likely to contain philodendrons from the tropics of South and Central America, the rubber plant (*Ficus elastica*) from tropical eastern Asia, a kangaroo vine (*Cissus antarctica*) from Australia, aspidistras from China and Japan, cacti from places such as Mexico and Texas, and ivies (*Hedera helix*) from Britain. The amazing thing is that they will all grow happily together in the same home – and it demonstrates the adaptability of plants regarding temperature.

Very few houseplants will tolerate frost, however, and great care will have to be taken in selecting plants for rooms where the temperature is likely to drop below 7°C (45°F). At that temperature, most houseplants will live, provided they are kept very dry at the roots (some plants, including most cacti, appreciate a cold spell and will flower better for it). Raise the minimum temperature to 10°C (50°F) and most plants will thrive.

A winter night temperature of 15°C (59°F) may be required for a few plants, but there is a danger that there will be insufficient light to support good growth during the winter months if the plants are stimulated into too much growth. Examples of houseplants that need 15°C (59°F) are caladiums, dieffenbachias, codiaeums, and fittonias.

Although a few houseplants will grow well in a temperature range from 7°C (45°F) to 15°C (59°F) – the sweetheart vine (*Philodendron scandens*) is one – most prefer a higher temperature, and this should be met as far as possible. Do not assume that extra warmth is always good, however – plants from temperate zones, such as ivies and × *Fatshedera lizei* will not grow very well if kept too warm in winter.

A resting period is vital to many plants, and during this time they should not be stimulated into growth by too much water or warmth. A spare bedroom or light garage with a good window are suitable for resting plants that need a cold period, such as most cacti and succulents, provided there is no danger of exposure to frost.

Modern homes tend to allow a wider range of houseplants to be grown than was possible 20 years ago. They have larger windows, which means lighter rooms, and better, more evenly controlled, heating. Even so there are still dangers if the heating system is used only during the day, with the consequent drop in temperature at night. Obviously some drop in temperature is perfectly acceptable – it happens in nature – but with artificial heating in winter the difference can be quite dramatic. And the large windows that are so beneficial from a light aspect can permit a large heat-loss, to the detriment of plants placed on the window-sill. This can be especially pronounced if they are trapped between drawn curtains and the window.

If your home is likely to cool drastically at night, bring your plants into the room and draw the curtains early to retain as much warmth as possible.

Both windows and doors can be a source of draughts, which can be extremely harmful to houseplants, not only because they lower the temperature in these areas, but because the turbulent air removes excessive moisture from the leaves in comparison with still air. Draughts may cause leaves and flower buds to drop.

LIGHT

The reason so many plants grow much better in a greenhouse than the home has more to do with light than temperature or humidity.

All houseplants need light – those we grow in shady or dull spots are simply more tolerant of poor light by reason of natural adaptation.

Shade-tolerant plants usually have plenty of green chlorophyll to take advantage of any light they do receive. But even these plants are likely to become drawn and leggy unless the light is of sufficient quality.

Plants with variegated or brightly coloured leaves almost always require good light, and the colour intensity will be diminished if it is not provided. With a few plants new leaves may emerge green if kept in heavy shade, but produce the variegation if transferred to good light (but don't confuse this with shoots that have 'reverted' – these must be removed otherwise the whole plant may gradually go back to the unvariegated state). Good light does not necessarily mean direct sunlight. Magnified through glass, fierce summer sun can be too strong for many plants – that's why shading is often provided for greenhouses during the summer months.

Be especially careful with fleshy-leaved plants, which may suffer from sun scorch. This is particularly likely to happen if the plants are placed beside a sheet of decorative glass – of the type often found in entrance halls and front doors. A pattern of circles, for instance, may act as a magnifying glass and irreparably damage the leaves. A plant that has thrived happily in an adjoining window of plain glass for years may be scorched within a day if placed besides decorative glass in the same aspect in strong sunlight.

Light intensity falls off very dramatically even a short distance from the window. This can be demonstrated most effectively with a light meter of the kind used by photographers. The same device will also emphasize the strong directional effect of the light. This will lead plants with a strong light requirement to turn towards the source and consequently produce drawn or uneven growth.

Even plants on the window-sill may benefit from a quarter of a turn of the pot each day, to encourage bushy, symmetrical growth. But don't do this with plants just coming into flower as it may cause bud drop.

Some groups of plants, such as bromeliads (see page 150) and orchids (see page 170) naturally live perched among forest trees or in other situations where they receive only filtered light. Because

Large plants like this *Dizygotheca elegantissima* are ideal subjects for self-watering containers – the water level indicator is on the left.

they are naturally adapted to these conditions, they can be grown away from direct light for most of the year.

Other groups, on the other hand, revel in as much sun as they can get – the terrestrial cacti and succulents being good examples.

As a general rule, flowering houseplants need more light than foliage plants. This is because good light is needed to produce a hormone responsible for flower initiation; the hormone, called florigen, is only produced in sufficient quantity when the light intensity and certain other factors are right for the particular species. Some plants, such as a few of the desert cacti, have never ever flowered in this country because the light intensity is never great enough to initiate flowering in those species. If a plant is failing to flower, it may benefit from more light; if an African violet (saintpaulia) is not flowering well, for instance, it may bloom more prolifically if placed in better light.

It is not only the quality of the light that affects flowering, but also the length of time for which it shines. With many houseplants this is not critical and they will bloom regardless of the day length, other factors having a stronger influence on flowering. But some other popular houseplants, such as the Christmas cactus (*Schlumbergera × buckleyi*), kalanchoes and chrysanthemums, are profoundly influenced by day length.

All-the-year-round chrysanthemums only flower as the days shorten and nights lengthen – a phenomenon commercial growers can use to produce blooms at will at almost any time of the year. By using artificial light at certain times and enforced darkness at others, the plants can be hoodwinked to flower out of season.

For this reason, and because a growth retardant is also used to keep them dwarf, all-the-year-round pot chrysanthemums can not be kept to flower in the same way for the next year. They can, however, be planted outside to grow into taller plants and to bloom at their natural time.

It is not normally practicable to advance flowering by artificially increasing the dark period at home, but it might be worth experimenting with kalanchoes, which can be induced to flower earlier by covering them with black polythene at the right time. Being short-day plants they normally flower in winter, but can be induced to flower in mid or late autumn if covered to ensure the plant only receives nine or ten hours of daylight during early and mid summer. Try to avoid the temperature rising above 15°C (59°F).

As most people want their Christmas cactus to flower at Christmas, the problem is usually one of ensuring that flowering is not delayed. Artificial light in the evening is going to delay flowering – even though it may only be switched on for a short time it will be sufficient to affect flowering. For that reason it is often best to keep the plant in a garage or spare room where artificial lighting is likely to be used infrequently, until the buds start to form.

At the very first sign of flower buds, move it to its flowering position *then leave it undisturbed*. The flower buds will grow in relation to the light source, and turning or moving the plant will cause them to attempt to readjust – and almost certainly drop in the process.

Artificial light

Most domestic lighting is perfectly satisfactory for working and reading by, and even for displaying plants effectively, but ordinary light is not so suitable for *growing* plants. For efficient photosynthesis and healthy growth, plants need a different type of light.

Fortunately, lamp manufacturers produce special fluorescent tubes that produce light of the right quality, and these can be obtained from good electrical shops or from aquarists' suppliers (they are used to illuminate aquariums, where light of the right type is necessary for healthy growth of aquatic plants). These can be used to grow plants in otherwise unsuitable places.

GROOMING

It is not sufficient just to feed and water your plants and expect them to look their best. A little grooming can make all the difference to the appearance of a plant – particularly one in bloom or a foliage plant that tends to be leggy.

There is a very good reason for removing dead flowers from a houseplant – not only does it look better but it also reduces the risk of moulds forming on leaves on which the dead flowers have fallen. It is for that reason that flowering plants are not used in sealed bottle gardens.

The more floriferous the plant the more of a problem dead flowers become – *Begonia semperflorens* is an excellent pot plant, flowering for months, but each morning there will be a mass of dead flowers around the pot. Remove these daily and you have a highly desirable plant and a clean home – neglect them and you soon have a sorry-looking sight. Leggy plants, with bare and etiolated stems, look equally sorry for themselves, and frequently end up being banished from the home. Yet a little judicious pinching and pruning can usually improve these plants.

Tradescantias are attractive trailers, but may look ungainly with sparse stems a metre (yard) or more long; the polka dot plant (*Hypoestes phyllostachya*, normally sold under the name *H. sanguinolenta*) will rapidly become spindly even in good light – and the popular busy Lizzies (impatiens) often become gross and lank – yet all can be transformed into bushy plants by carefully pinching back any long or weak shoots.

Sometimes, plants such as *Philodendron scandens* and ivies (*Hedera helix*) tend to make small-leaved sickly growth in winter, and this should also be cut back to healthier growth in spring.

'Stopping' the plant like this encourages the growth of sideshoots, and these in turn can be 'stopped' to make an even bushier plant.

Only treat plants in this way when they are growing actively (usually late spring and summer).

Turning plants

To achieve even growth and a symmetrical plant, turn the pot occasionally. A couple of times a week may be adequate for most plants, but where shape is important, such as a nicely rounded pelargonium or a charm-type chrysanthemum, an enthusiast would give the pot a quarter of a turn each day.

Be careful about turning plants in bud or flower, however, as it may cause some plants to drop buds. Much depends on the plant – chrysanthemums would come to no harm but it could be quite disastrous for, say, a Christmas cactus (*Schlumbergera × buckleyi*) once the buds are well developed.

During the summer when the heating is switched off, most plants will benefit from a lighter window position. Larger plants on the floor also help to soften the stark lines of the radiator.

Staking

Staking should always be done with discretion – it is easy to end up with the support being more conspicuous than the plant.

Some philodendrons, particularly *P. laciniatum* and *P. erubescens* and the Swiss cheese plant (*Monstera deliciosa*) are effective grown up moss poles.

Although it is possible to buy moss poles from garden centres and horticultural sundriesmen, it is not difficult to make your own. Select a stout tube (wood or plastic) or a stick about 5cm (2in) in diameter and of sufficient length for the pot and plant in question. Apply a thick layer of damp sphagnum moss (this is usually available at garden centres in spring, when hanging-baskets are being made, but you should be able to obtain it at any time of the year from a good florist); this can be fixed to the pole by wrapping a piece of green plastic netting round it, tying in at regular intervals with green twine or nylon thread.

Ordinary bamboo canes are not very satisfactory indoors – they are usually conspicuous and obtrusive, and unless the pot is a large one it is difficult to fix them firmly enough to hold a plant with heavy top growth. For plants such as *Cissus antarctica*, however, they can be perfectly satisfactory as these plants produce plenty of dense growth to hide the cane. Split canes are more successful and can be used in conjunction with rings to hold plants such as *Campanula isophylla* upright. You can also buy split canes dyed green.

Climbers of moderate proportions can be supported on pot trellises or cane spirals – black-eyed Susan (*Thunbergia alata*), and some of the slow-growing ivies can be grown this way. For climbers of more substance and more twining habit, this may not be adequate. Small specimens can be wound round wire loops – the Madagascar jasmine (*Stephanotis floribunda*) is often sold like this and looks delightful.

Once a climbing plant reaches a stage where a self-contained support within the pot is not practicable, the decision must be made whether to propagate new plants and start afresh with a small specimen, or to incorporate the large plant into the decor as a more permanent feature (see page 39).

Cleaning leaves

Even in the best-kept household, dirt and dust lurks, and it is as likely to settle on the plants as elsewhere.

To attempt to dust all the leaves on your plants each time you dust the furniture is obviously pointless and impractical, but a periodic dusting will certainly not come amiss.

Plants with shiny leaves that have a natural gloss, such as the rubber plant (*Ficus elastica*) and the sweetheart plant (*Philodendron scandens*) are naturally easy to clean. If you want to put a real shine on them you can use a proprietary leaf cleaning fluid, but it may appear to put too much of an artificial gloss on the leaves; a wipe with a moist soft cloth will be perfectly satisfactory.

There is no way that a plant with hairy leaves, such as a gynura, or a spiny cactus, can be wiped with a damp cloth. The next best thing is a dusting with a soft brush – a pastry brush kept for the purpose is ideal.

Remember, not only will the leaves look better for being dust-free, they will also be more effective to the plant, as dust and grime can block the openings through which plants transpire and breathe as well as cutting down light.

DISPLAYING FERNS

If you think of ferns as just being bracken on a piece of common land, you are very mistaken. They are some of the oldest plants in the world, and their variety and delicately shaped and textured fronds are fascinating. And they are adaptable to many places and several different methods of display, from the confines of a totally enclosed glass case to being suspended in the air as a focal point of interest.

Glass fern cases:

Specially-made cases have a sloping glass roof to enable the condensation produced through the respiration of the plants to run freely back into the compost. Narrow cases are best, as they allow a long row of small ferns to be set at the front with a backcloth of tall ones. These cases are adaptations of the old Wardian cases (see page 167).

Bell jars set on a stand can be used for small ferns, and can make excellent centre-pieces for hall tables.

Fern balls:

Fern balls can be suspended from ceilings, and are well suited to conservatories. Ferns such as *Davallia canariensis* and *Humata tyermannii* are ideal for training this way. Form wet sphagnum moss into a ball kept in shape with florist's wire, and set the roots of the fern in the centre of it. As the long rhizomes (root part) grow to the outside of the ball of moss, they are tied around the ball until it is entirely covered by the fern fronds (see right).

It is essential to keep the ball of ferns and moss damp, and for a few hours after watering the moss it may be necessary to place a drip-tray underneath it. Fern balls are best placed in a conservatory with a stone floor. A better way of watering is to place the whole ball in a bucket of water for five minutes, then hang it up and allow the water to drain away.

Fern columns:

This is a novel way of growing and displaying ferns under a glass dome. A tube of wire-mesh netting, about 10–12.5cm (4–5in) in diameter is formed by winding the netting around a piece of stiff card rolled to form a column. Wind a couple of layers of netting around it, winding the loose end-pieces around each other, and remove the

cardboard. The bottom of the netting can then be secured to a base, and a moist peat-based compost added in stages to the inside of the netting. At the same time, small ferns are planted through the netting, so that the roots are in the compost and the fronds on the outside. When planting is complete, syringe the column thoroughly and place it under a glass dome.

Suspended ferns:

Many ferns look at their best when suspended from a firm support. This is usually most practicable in a conservatory where, perhaps, drips from the plants will not be too much of a problem. *Nephrolepis exaltata*, known as the ladder fern, is well suited for suspension in a basket. The tapering fronds hang around the baskets.

The stag's-horn fern, *Platycerium bifurcatum* (*P. alcicorne*) is naturally an epiphyte and is ideal for growing attached to a piece of wood or cork with the roots growing in moist sphagnum moss. When established, the main fronds can be up to 75cm (2½ft) long, and the whole plant becomes very heavy. This is a fern that can also be fixed against a wall, where it will produce a natural 'face' side outwards.

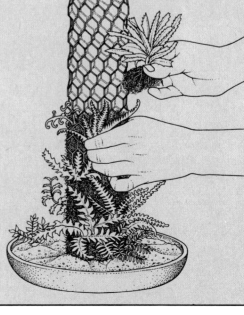

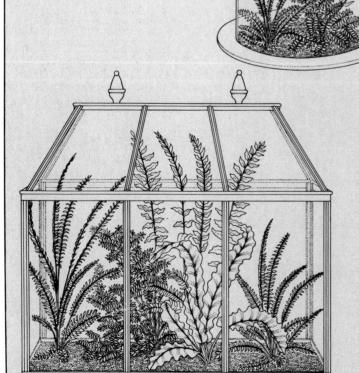

PESTS & DISEASES

Houseplants are usually relatively free of pests – and provided they are properly looked after little difficulty should be experienced with diseases or disorders either. But even well cared for plants fall victim to problems sooner or later.

The difficulties that can beset a plant in the home may look formidable, but remember that the chances of most of them troubling your plants is remote. The important thing is to be able to recognize the first signs of distress, and to act quickly. Troubles spotted and treated at the earliest symptoms are much easier to control and cure.

Most of the things that go wrong with houseplants are due to cultural mistakes, and these are easy to put right by attention to detail. Once pests and diseases take hold, however, it is almost inevitable that chemicals of some kind have to be used. Select the right treatment, and use it strictly according to instructions, then you can be assured that plants, people and pets are not put at risk. Treat all insecticides and fungicides used in the home with even more respect than you would in the garden.

USING CHEMICALS INDOORS

There are many chemicals besides those mentioned in this chapter that will kill pests and diseases of houseplants – but some are totally unsuitable for use in the home. A few could be particularly dangerous to humans as well as pets if used in the confined and enclosed environment of a room; some also have a most unpleasant smell that would be highly undesirable indoors; others may mark or damage furnishings.

If it is necessary to use an ordinary garden chemical on houseplants, take the plant outside to be sprayed, and do not bring it back indoors until the spray has dried. The problem is that for more than half the year the weather is going to be totally unsuitable for this simple course of action.

An alternative worth considering, even for sprays designed for use in the home, is to place the plant in a large plastic sack or clean dustbin, apply the spray while outdoors then seal or cover – and then if the weather is bad place it in a shed or garage. Leave the plant sealed in for 15 minutes, then ventilate to disperse any unpleasant fumes before returning the plant to its rightful place – hopefully completely cured.

Watering the plant with a systemic insecticide may seem a good idea, but it renders the plant toxic for some time and it is not worth the risk if you have pets or young children as they may try to eat the leaves.

Undoubtedly, aerosols are the most convenient form in which insecticides can be bought for indoor use – there is no mixing, if only one plant is affected there is no waste with unused solution, and they are extremely easy to use. Those designed for home use are generally safe, normally containing natural substances such as pyrethrum. Some sprays can be

THE DISPENSARY

Common chemical name (may be in small print)	Pest or disease controlled	Notes
BENOMYL	wide range of fungus diseases, including leaf spot	Systemic
DIMETHOATE	aphids, whitefly, red spider, mealy bugs, scale insects	Systemic. Do not use on cinerarias, fuchsias, hydrangeas, impatiens, calceolarias, primulas or chrysanthemums
MALATHION	whitefly, aphids, red spider, thrips, leaf miner, mealy bugs, scale insects	Do not use on ferns, poinsettias, crassulas, pileas or petunias
PIRIMIPHOS-METHYL WITH PYRETHRINS	whitefly, red spider, aphids, mealy bugs, scale insects (crawler stage)	Do not use on cacti and succulents
MANCOZEB	leaf mould, leaf spots, rusts, downy mildew	
RESMETHRIN AND PYRETHRUM	whitefly, aphids, thrips, red spider	
ROTENONE (DERRIS)	caterpillars, beetles	
THIOPHANATE-METHYL	fungus diseases, including powdery mildew, leaf mould, grey mould	Systemic

Leaf miner damage on chrysanthemums.

An infestation of mealy bugs.

White flies on a fuchsia.

harmful to fish, so the aquarium must be protected. Care is also needed in the way the aerosol is used – always hold the can at least 45cm (18in) away from the plant, otherwise the propellant may damage the foliage. And avoid spraying a plant standing on a polished surface (don't spray directly on to fabric either). Some sprays should not be used on open flowers. Read the label – and *take seriously any advice* that it contains.

Only use indoors those products clearly marked for use in the home – 'use only as a garden insecticide' means just that: only in the garden.

Some of the indoor insecticides may need to be applied several times (perhaps every three days when dealing with whitefly) to achieve a total kill, but this is preferable to using anything stronger. Another possibility, if there is a stubborn problem and more potent chemicals have to be resorted to, is an insecticidal dip. If the solution, of say malathion, is placed in a suitable container (kept for the purpose, always rinsed out, and stored in a safe place), a small plant can be inverted by holding one hand over the soil-ball in the pot while supporting with the other, and the foliage dipped into the solution. *Always* wear rubber gloves if doing this as many poisons can be absorbed through the skin. And even if gloves are used, wash your hands well afterwards – and don't touch the plant again until the insecticide has dried.

Fungicides are not normally formulated as indoor sprays, so these should be sprayed or watered on outdoors.

HOW TO DIAGNOSE THE PROBLEM

If your plant looks sick, track down the problem by using the simple key below. By answering the questions a process of elimination will leave you with the most probable cause of the problem – and the suggested remedy.

Start by answering the first question, then follow the steps until a probable cause is identified.

1 Are symptoms manifest primarily on the leaves?
YES answer next question.
NO answer question 43.

2 Can you see insects on the leaves (look closely – some may look more like scales and will not be mobile)?
YES answer question 30.
NO answer next question.

3 Are the leaves yellowing?
YES answer question 22.
NO answer next question.

4 Are coloured or variegated leaves losing original colour?
YES answer question 17.
OR: Are the leaves wilting or falling without discolouring?
YES answer question 18.
OR: Are the leaves obviously blemished or supporting some form of growth?
YES answer next question.

5 Do the leaves have brown spots or blotches, or brown edges or tips?
YES answer next question.
NO answer question 10.

6 Is the browning confined to the tips and edges of the leaves?
YES probably due to draughts or a dry atmosphere; may occasionally be due to too much lime in the compost or water (if the plant is sensitive). If plant is fed frequently or in strong concentrations, could also be due to build-up of salts in the soil.
REMEDY: remove from draught and increase humidity (see page 19). If this does not seem the likely cause, try watering with rainwater; if the plant has not been fed regularly, apply a liquid feed (but not during a resting period). If it could be due to overfeeding, soak the pot and root-ball, allow it to drain, and do not feed so often.
NO answer next question.

7 Are straw-coloured, brownish or orange spots or blisters visible?
YES answer question 9.
NO answer next question.

8 Are there brown roughly circular patches, soft in appearance?
YES: probably fungal spots, especially if hederas (ivies), dieffenbachias or dracaenas are affected, and atmosphere is very humid.
REMEDY: if just a few leaves are affected, pick off as soon as noticed; if more severely attacked, spray with benomyl or thiophanate-methyl.
OR: Are there large pale brown patches, sometimes papery in appearance?
YES: probably sun scald, especially if plant has suddenly been placed in strong sunlight. African violets (saintpaulias) are among the plants particularly susceptible.

9 Are there tiny straw-coloured or brown blisters or scales, not surrounded by dead tissue, mainly on the undersides of leaves but occasionally on the upper surface?
YES: probably scale insects (see 41 for control).
OR: Are there rusty-coloured outgrowths, sometimes surrounded by an area of dead tissue?
YES: probably rust disease, especially if on cinerarias or pelargoniums.
REMEDY: remove and destroy infected leaves or stems, then spray with mancozeb.

10 Is a whitish powder or mould visible, or are the leaves (and possibly stems) visibly rotting?
YES answer question 20.
NO answer next question.

11 Are pale-coloured wavy lines and blisters visible on the leaves? (If silver streaking is present, turn to 16).
YES probably leaf miner, especially if on cinerarias or chrysanthemums.
REMEDY: if only a few leaves are affected, just remove them. If badly affected, remove the most blemished leaves and dip the plant into a malathion solution, taking the necessary precautions. Remove scarred leaves when plant has grown sufficient new ones.
NO answer next question.

12 Are the leaves twisted or contorted?
YES examine them carefully, especially the undersides beneath folds or wrinkles. If there are signs of insects the problem is probably due to aphids (see 42).
If there are no signs of insects but the leaves are also mottled or yellowing, a virus could be responsible (see 29).
NO answer question 14.

13 Are there sticky patches on leaves; insects present, or recently present (examine plant closely)?
YES probably 'honeydew' (secretions from aphids).
REMEDY: control aphids (see 42) and dip plants into a solution of mildly soapy water if necessary (and only with smooth-leaved plants).
OR: Are there black sooty patches?
YES probably due to sooty mould, following attack by aphids.
REMEDY: as above.

14 Are there holes in the leaves?
YES most probably due to slugs or snails, but very occasionally caterpillars may attack a few indoor plants. See also earwigs (39) and vine weevils (40).
REMEDY: if due to caterpillars these will be seen if the leaves are examined carefully; remove by hand and destroy. If slugs or snails are responsible, use a slug pellet only if there are no young children or pets – hand control is best indoors (look beneath the pot).
NO answer next question.

15 Are there sticky or black patches on the leaves?
YES answer question 13.
NO answer next question.

16 Are there spots or white marks or rings visible, sometimes resembling marbling or leaf-miner trails?
YES probably due to physical damage caused by cold water being splashed on leaves (particularly plants with hairy leaves such as gloxinias and African violets) or by aerosol sprays.
REMEDY: avoid cause.
OR: Is there a silver-streaked appearance and sometimes pale papery scars? Trails of black specks may be visible
YES probably thrips (see 37).

17 Are the variegated leaves changing to plain green
YES probably due to lack of light, although if only the leaves on one or two stems are affected it is probably due to reversion.
REMEDY: if whole plant is affected, place in better light; if only a few shoots affected, remove them by cutting back to a variegated section.
OR: Do the coloured but not variegated leaves change to green or lose intensity of colour?
YES probably due to poor light.
REMEDY: place in better light; to intensify the colour, also keep compost fairly dry.

18 Are the leaves falling?
YES probably due to cold draughts, overwatering (although they usually wilt first), or watering with very cold water.
REMEDY: correct probable cause.
OR: Are the leaves hanging limply but not falling?
YES answer next question.

19 Are the leaves hanging limply, but otherwise unblemished; the whole plant wilting?
YES probably due to lack of water if soil is dry and symptoms sudden; probably due to overwatering if compost is wet, and especially if some leaves have started to yellow.
REMEDY: if due to lack of water, soak pot in a bowl of water. If due to too much water, remove soil-ball from pot for a day, and do not water for several days.
OR: Does the plant wilt even though compost is neither too damp nor too wet?
YES probably due to a root pest or disease. An overdose of fertilizer or trauma from repotting can also cause these symptoms.
REMEDY: knock soil-ball from pot and inspect roots for signs of grubs. If present see root aphids and mealy bugs (44), otherwise water with benomyl twice at ten-day intervals. If the cause might be an overdose of fertilizer, repot in fresh soil.

20 Is the mould fluffy and greyish? (if small fluffy spots, answer next question).
YES probably botrytis (grey mould), a disease that may start on dead leaves or flowers but spread to living tissue. Gloxinias, African violets, cyclamen and gynuras are especially susceptible.
REMEDY: remove affected leaves and stems, then spray with benomyl or thiophanate-methyl.
NO answer next question.

21 Are there small fluffy white spots on leaves and often at stem joints?
YES probably mealy bugs (see 41).
OR: Is there a white powdery coating or white fluffy growth covering large areas of leaf?
YES probably mildew. There are two kinds, powdery mildew appears as white dusty areas, while downy mildew has a fluffier appearance. Both are usually the result of too much water and insufficient ventilation.
REMEDY: remove infected parts of the plant, increase ventilation and spray once a week with benomyl or thiophanate-methyl.

22 Is the plant deciduous (not evergreen)?
YES deciduous – answer next question.
NO evergreen – answer question 24.

23 Are leaves yellowing after plant has finished flowering or fruiting?
YES probably entering resting period. See instruction for specific plants in the relevant chapters for details and treatment.
NO answer next question.

24 Are there minute yellow specks visible, sometimes accompanied by a fine webbing on or between leaves or stems?
YES probably evidence of red spider mite (see 32).
NO answer next question.

25 Does the yellowing tend to appear as a mottling or as streaks, or along veins?
YES answer question 29.
NO answer next question.

26 Are the leaves dropping?
YES answer question 28.
NO answer next question.

Signs of red spider mites.

A typical attack of botrytis.

27 Do the leaves turn yellow but not drop?
YES probably due to too much lime in the water or compost for a susceptible plant (check with entry in the A-Z of Houseplants, pages 50 to 131, to see whether it dislikes lime).
REMEDY: ensure a lime-free compost is used (normal composts contain lime, but you can obtain special formulations without it). Use rain-water or boiled tap-water.
OR: Are the leaves pale green gradually turning yellow; plant weak with poor new growth?
YES probably lack of plant food, especially nitrogen, or poor light.
REMEDY: feed, and pot on if necessary; ensure light is adequate.

28 Do the lower leaves slowly turn yellow and eventually drop?
YES probably due to overwatering.
REMEDY: remove soil-ball from pot for a day, then return to pot and do not water for a few days.
OR: Do the lower leaves turn yellow and drop quickly
YES probably due to a sudden drop in temperature or to draughts.
REMEDY: avoid cause.

29 Does the yellowing appear as mottling or in streaks, possibly accompanied by slow or stunted growth?
YES probably due to a virus.
REMEDY: destroy plant without delay.
OR: Is the yellowing mainly along veins; or are leaves pale green gradually turning yellow; plant not fed regularly?
YES could be nutritional deficiency. Try a good houseplant food. Pot on if the roots have filled the pot.

30 Is the colour black or dark grey?
YES answer question 36.
NO answer next question.

31 Is the pest smaller than 5mm ($\frac{1}{4}$in) in length.
NO answer question 38.
YES answer next question.

32 Does the pest resemble tiny red or brownish-red or straw-coloured spiders (sometimes accompanied by 'cobwebbing' on the leaves or leaf joints)?
YES probably red spider mite.
REMEDY: spray with pirimiphos-methyl with pyrethrins, rotenone, or resmethrin with pyrethrum. Because the pest is encouraged by a hot dry atmosphere, increase humidity.
NO answer next question.

33 Do the insects look like small brown blisters or scales or small grey-white woodlice?
YES answer question 41.
NO answer next question.

34 Does it look like either a tiny white fly or small white oval-shaped larva, or a plumpish green insect with or without wings?
YES answer question 42.
NO answer next question.

35 Are there almost microscopic colourless mites feeding among the young folded leaflets of cyclamen, fuchsias, begonias or saintpaulias (possibly with stunted growth and curled leaf edges)?
YES probably cyclamen mite.
REMEDY: difficult to control. Best to burn infested plants.
NO the insects may not be harmful pests, but if they appear troublesome, try an insecticidal aerosol such as pirimiphos-methyl with pyrethrins, and if this does not control it, resort to a malathion dip, taking the necessary precautions.

36 Do small active black flies rise from the compost or plant if disturbed, resembling miniature houseflies on the wing?
YES probably sciarid flies. They are rather gnat-like in appearance.
REMEDY: use a resmethrin, pyrethrum or rotenone aerosol.
NO answer next question.

37 Are there plumpish black insects, with or without wings, resembling black greenfly?
YES probably blackfly.
REMEDY: spray with pyrethrum or pirimiphos-methyl with pyrethrins, or resmethrin with pyrethrum.
OR: Are there tiny black winged insects, with long, narrow bodies?
YES probably thrips.
REMEDY: spray with resmethrin and pyrethrum.

38 Are there caterpillars?
YES see Remedy.
REMEDY: pick off by hand, or spray with rotenone.
NO answer next question.

39 Are there long, narrow, brownish insects with pincers at the rear end?
YES probably earwigs.
REMEDY: set traps, using small rolls of corrugated paper, where the pests will hide. Empty and destroy regularly, until controlled.
NO answer next question.

40 Are there dull black beetles with tiny yellow speckles: margins of leaves eaten?
YES probably vine weevil. Begonias, cyclamen and primulas are among the plants most commonly attacked.
REMEDY: spray with rotenone.
NO if not a slug or snail (control with slug pellets if hand picking is not possible), or woodlice (use a rotenone powder where they are likely to hide), it is not likely to be a serious indoor pest, but try a rotenone powder or spray if it seems troublesome.

41 Are there small insects like tiny whitish woodlice with woolly coats, usually found under the leaves in the leaf axils?
YES probably mealy bugs.
REMEDY: dab with a cotton-bud dipped in methylated spirit or surgical spirit. Alternatively spray with pirimiphos-methyl with pyrethrins, or use dimethoate if necessary.
OR: Are there brown or straw-coloured scale or blister-like insects, most commonly found on the undersides of leaves?
YES probably scale insects.
REMEDY: spray with malathion or dimethoate (taking suitable precautions); pirimiphos-methyl will also control the young 'crawler' stages.
The egg cases, protected by the dead adult's body, may need to be wiped off, as the tough-shelled body will resist most insecticides.

42 Are there tiny white flies, somewhat triangular in shape. And/or tiny oval-shaped white larvae?
YES probably whitefly.
REMEDY: use an aerosol containing resmethrin or pirimiphos-methyl with pyrethrins.
OR: Are there plumpish green insects with or without wings
YES probably greenfly (aphids).
REMEDY: use an aerosol containing pyrethrum, resmethrin or pirimiphos-methyl.

43 Are flowers or fruit (or lack of them) the problem?
YES answer question 45.
NO answer next question.

44 Is the stem or crown rotting at soil level?
YES probably due to a combination of overwatering and low temperature.
REMEDY: If it is possible to cut out affected part and leave some good growth, do so – then reduce water and keep in a warm place.

OR: Does the whole plant seem to lack vitality, and have a dull appearance?
YES could be root aphids or root mealy bugs, or some other root problem.
Remove plant from pot and examine roots. If grubs can be seen around the roots, wash all traces of soil from them and repot in fresh compost if the plant appears able to withstand this treatment, otherwise water the compost with malathion every seven days for three weeks (taking the necessary precautions).
If no insects are visible, try watering with benomyl.

45 Is there a problem with the fruit?
YES answer question 48.
Is there a problem with the flowers?
YES answer next question.

46 Does plant grown for its flowers fail to flower (assuming it is of sufficient maturity)?
YES could be lack of light, shortage of food, or too much nitrogen (indicated by lush, leafy growth), or insufficient warmth.
REMEDY: correct whichever situation seems the most likely cause. Try a high-potash feed.
NO answer next question.

47 Do the flower buds drop without opening?
YES could be due to dry atmosphere, moving the plant or turning it round, to a sudden drop in temperature. Too much or too little water at the crucial time may also cause buds to drop.
REMEDY: correct whichever cause seems the most likely.
Are the flowers of bulbs brown or stunted
YES probably due to insufficient water while the bulbs were developing roots.

48 Is the fruit failing to set on a plant grown for its fruit?
YES probably due to lack of humidity, or dryness at the roots.
REMEDY: in future avoid probable cause, and apply a high-potash fertilizer.
NO answer next question.

49 Do the fruits shrivel and fall?
YES probably caused by temperature being too high or humidity too low. Lack of water at roots.
Are the fruits badly shaped?
YES probably caused by atmosphere being too dry at pollination time. Next time spray the flowers with a fine mist of water.

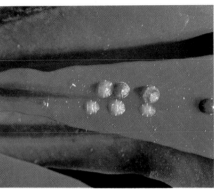
Scale insects on a fern.

A fungal leaf spot on ivy.

Collapse due to root rot.

Aphids attack lush green growth.

HYDROCULTURE

Hydroculture is the technique of growing plants without soil or compost – all the elements for growth being derived from a nutrient solution. The method has made a profound impact on the houseplant scene in recent years – and has gone a long way towards making the growing of houseplants foolproof.

Plants grown by this system are more expensive than those grown in compost, and it may be too costly to grow all your houseplants by this method. But for a special specimen, the cost is well justified by strong, healthy plants that will thrive with the minimum of care.

It is also a highly recommended method for anyone requiring a few superb houseplants but without the time to devote to normal watering and feeding. And in offices, where plants may suffer from irregular attention, they are ideal.

Modern hydroculture units are clean, neat, and trouble-free. Watering is required only infrequently and feeding only about twice a year.

Although there are several variations, all the hydroculture units for home use are based on the same principle: an outer container to hold the nutrient solution; a special inner pot containing the plant; an aggregate (normally expanded clay granules) to anchor the plant and provide the right combination of capillary action and air space; and a suitably formulated fertilizer. A device for indicating water level may be built into the outer container itself or be contained in a tube inserted into the aggregate, which also serves as a topping-up tube.

Containers are usually plastic, the size and shape depending on the supplier, though square and round profiles are naturally the most widely used. Because a hydroculture unit contains within it a reservoir and items such as a water level indicator, as well as the plant holder, it is inevitably a little larger than a conventional pot containing a plant of the same size. Against that is the fact that you have a very presentable container that needs no further disguise before taking its place in the home.

As they all perform well, choice is almost purely a matter of taste.

The clay granules and water-level indicator of a hydroculture unit.

Aggregate plays a vital role, and the type normally used is a special grade of light expanded clay 'pebbles' similar to those used as an aggregate for concrete mixes in the building industry. These are about 12mm ($\frac{1}{2}$in) in diameter, with a dense outer skin but an inner core of a honeycomb structure.

Apart from serving as an excellent anchor, these special clay pebbles have the important ability to absorb water, and this helps to set up a capillary action which keeps all the pebbles in the container moist.

Fertilizer technology has provided the major contribution to making hydroculture suitable for home use. Soil normally acts as a buffer against incorrect feeding, but there is little margin for error when all the plant food has to come from a nutrient solution alone. The real breakthrough has been the introduction of ion-exchange fertilizers, which release just the right amount of food over a long period.

The chemistry of an ion-exchange fertilizer is complex, but the chemicals are bonded to tiny plastic beads and both major plant foods and trace elements are exchanged for impurities in the water, such as calcium, chlorine and fluoride. This exchange goes on at a rate that suits the plants being grown.

The fertilizer comes as a 'battery', which is fitted into the base of a compatible pot, or as loose granules which are spread on the clay pebbles and washed in with a little water. The amount required depends on the size of the container, but if applied at the recommended rate will be sufficient for at least six months.

ROUTINE CARE

Plants grown by this system are notably trouble-free, a periodic check of the water level indicator being the only routine attention required.

Hydroculture plants have the same light, humidity and heat requirements (bearing in mind minimum root temperature) as plants grown conventionally. They will only thrive if provided with these basic requirements. They are also subject to the same pests and diseases as plants grown in compost.

They can be treated with all the usual insecticides used on equivalent plants grown in soil – including systemic types.

Watering is simplicity itself, and removes one of the major causes of houseplant failures. A water level indicator indicates minimum and maximum water levels.

When the indicator registers minimum, *do not water immediately*. Wait two or three days before filling again, to allow air to penetrate between the aggregate. Do not be tempted to keep topping up continually; the roots must have a chance to be aerated.

Always use *tap* water – at room temperature. Rainwater and even soft tap water will not contain the right chemicals to trigger the ion-exchange process. If you have a soft water supply, a few drops of a liquid houseplant food should be sufficient to start the process (it will not need repeating).

It is important to use water at room temperature because the roots can easily become chilled with this method of growing. Chilled roots can be a major cause of failure with hydroculture.

If the water temperature falls much below 15°C (59°F), the leaves may start to yellow and the whole plant deteriorate. With some plants the air temperature may not be so critical, but root temperature is important.

Cross-section of a potted hydroculture plant.

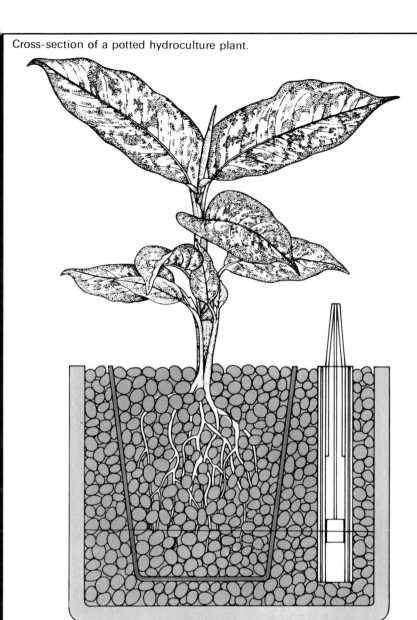

To 'convert' a plant to hydroculture, all traces of compost must be washed from the roots. Care must be taken to cause as little damage as possible.

Above: Special expanded clay granules are packed round the roots.
Below: Keep plants warm and shaded. The bag increases humidity.

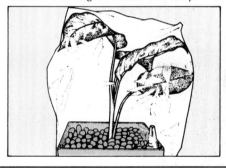

Potting-on

Potting-on will be required only infrequently, as plants grown by this method do not make such an intensive root system and is normally only necessary when the plant becomes out of proportion to the container.

Buy a slightly larger container, and a further supply of aggregate, and a recharge of fertilizer. Wash the aggregate before use, and place a layer in the base of the container. Stand the pot on this, ensuring the rim is about 12mm ($\frac{1}{2}$in) below the top of the container; stand the filler tube in one corner and insert the water level indicator, then pack the aggregate round the tube and the pot until the unit has been filled.

Converting plants

This is not a job for the beginner, but it can provide a lot of interest and much satisfaction for anyone with the inclination to try.

Always start in late spring or early summer, so that the plants have several months of warm weather ahead.

Start by washing the roots free of *all* traces of soil, but do it carefully to avoid damaging them. This must be done thoroughly. Once the roots are clean, pot the plant carefully into a container with open slatted sides (you can buy these from a hydroponics supplier), damaging the roots as little as possible while packing the aggregate granules around them.

The planting pot can then be inserted into the outer container, as already described for potting-on.

From then on two things are critical – warmth and humidity. Keep the plant as warm as possible, but shaded from direct sunlight, to reduce moisture loss by transpiration. To maintain high humidity, spray with a fine mist at least twice a day, or cover with a polythene tent for about a month. During this time try to maintain a minimum temperature of at least 21°C (70°F).

After about a month, possibly up to two, the transition from soil roots to water roots should have been completed.

Suitable plants

Not all plants are suitable, and if you intend to grow your own hydroculture plants, experimentation may be necessary. Ivies, for instance, are not usually successful, but practically all the Araceae family are; fortunately this includes many excellent houseplants, such as philodendrons, scindapsus and aglaonemas.

You can be sure, however, that any plants sold in hydroculture containers will be suitable.

Perhaps surprisingly, some succulents, such as mother-in-law's tongue (*Sansevieria trifasciata* 'Laurentii') do well, although it is essential to ensure an adequate 'dry period' before topping up with fresh water.

PROPAGATION

There is a sound economic reason for propagating your own plants, but just as important is the satisfaction derived in the process. Although it is inevitable that we have to buy many of our houseplants, there is something special about a plant you've raised yourself – whether from seed or a cutting.

Raising your own plants saves money in two ways – those you can grow from seed will probably yield dozens of plants for less than the cost of one grown specimen, and those raised vegetatively will provide plenty of 'barter' material for exchanging with friends.

Most of the plants grown in our homes are easy to propagate, and it should be possible to produce an abundant supply of young plants to give to friends. Indeed, some are so prodigious that the offspring can be an embarrassment.

Some methods of propagation, such as air layering, do not greatly increase the stock, but are a practical way of maintaining fresh, well-balanced plants as the older ones pass their best.

Losses of mature specimens are inevitable at some time, and having a few replacements coming along is always a wise arrangement.

It is perfectly possible to propagate a vast range of plants with no special equipment at all, but a heated propagator will make it all easier and extend the range of plants you can try. A propagator is especially useful for germinating seeds. Even a small propagator will enable you to produce an amazing number of plants, for the warmth is required mainly for germination, and once the seedlings are growing well they will usually tolerate room temperatures.

Cuttings are likely to benefit more from the close atmosphere of a propagator than the warmth (especially as many cuttings are rooted during the summer months), and they will root readily in the high humidity.

The humidity so vital for most cuttings can be provided at less expense by enclosing the pot in a plastic bag, forming a tent. There are various methods: the pot can be placed *in* the bag, which is inflated and sealed with a twist tie; four small sticks can be pushed into the pot and the bag pushed *over* the top and sealed round the pot with an elastic band; or the containers can even be placed in plastic bags and suspended with pegs from a line.

An aid of a different kind comes in the form of rooting hormones. There are many cuttings that will root without these, but with more difficult subjects a rooting hormone will certainly speed root formation and may even make the

Plant propagation is both rewarding and easy – only a few simple tools are needed.

difference between success and failure. A real luxury is a mist unit, which will keep the leaves constantly moist by misting them with a fine spray of water whenever they are about to become too dry. These can be expensive, and are usually used in a greenhouse, but they are equally useful for rooting cuttings of all kinds, whether tender plants or hardy shrubs or trees.

Even the most elaborate aids to propagation will be of limited use unless a suitable rooting medium is used. In the case of seeds this means loam or peat-based seed compost. The brand doesn't matter much – what does, is that it has been formulated for seed-sowing and has been sterilized in the case of loam-based types. Some proprietary peat-based composts are suitable for seeds *or* cuttings, and are very successful provided they are not allowed to dry out. Another excellent rooting medium, because it provides an open texture and plenty of air spaces, coupled with a high moisture-holding capability, is vermiculite (sometimes used for insulating lofts). Failing that, a mixture of equal parts peat and sand is often satisfactory. Because the rooting medium normally contains little reserve of nutrients (sometimes none) it is important to pot up the cuttings as soon as they have formed sufficient roots to be moved safely. This time it is important to use a proper potting compost.

There is always the temptation to root easy plants in a jar of water – it's fascinating to watch, and you know what progress is being made! But it is important to pot the plants while the roots are still tiny, ideally just as they are forming.

PLANTS FROM SEED

Seeds provide an inexpensive and interesting way to raise new houseplants, and most of those widely available germinate easily. A few seeds, however, may need a little help. Some germinate better if prechilled by placing in a fridge, between sheets of damp blotting paper, for a few days before sowing; a few need a period of high temperature to break dormancy, and many with hard seed coats will germinate better if soaked in warm water for 24 hours. Hard coats can also be made permeable by rubbing lightly with sandpaper.

Light can also be important. Begonias require light for good germination, while *Eccremocarpus scaber* needs darkness. Always read the directions on the seed packet before sowing.

Step One: Place drainage crocks at the bottom of the box, fill to within about 18mm (¾in) of the top with a seed compost, and firm gently.

Step Two: Water the compost then sprinkle the seeds thinly over the compost (mix with a little sand if the seed is fine and difficult to handle), or press large seeds into the surface. It sometimes helps to sow in small drills. Cover with enough compost to bury the seeds with their own depth of compost. If the seeds are large, the compost can be watered again from the top using a fine rose. With fine seeds that are lightly covered, sufficient moisture will penetrate from the damp compost.

Step Three: If an electrically-heated propagator is not available, place in a warm position and cover with a sheet of glass or slip into a polythene bag, ensuring the material does not touch the compost, and cover with newspaper. Turn the glass or polythene each day to eliminate condensation.

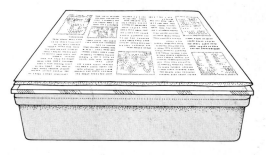

Step Four: As soon as the seeds germinate, give as much light as possible. When the seedlings are large enough to be handled, and before they become too crowded, prick them off into small individual pots, handling them only by the seed leaves (the first to unfold).

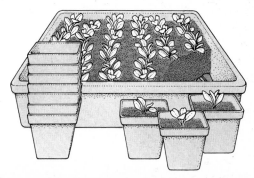

LEAF CUTTINGS

Increasing houseplants by leaf cuttings is quite easy, and from one leaf many new plants can be grown. Mature and healthy leaves should be used. Leaves which are very old and tough will take a long time to form roots. Plants suitable for this form of propagation are streptocarpus, gloxinias and some large-leafed begonias.

Sever the leaf-stalk low down near the base of the mother plant. Then, cut off the stem close to the leaf, and with a sharp knife or razor-blade slit through the veins on the underside of the leaf. Fill a large pot with John Innes seed compost, firming the soil to within 12mm ($\frac{1}{2}$in) of the rim. Thoroughly water the soil and allow the compost to drain. Place the leaf on the compost, with the cut surfaces downwards, and use pieces of bent wire to secure it to the compost.

The pot can be placed in a propagation case or a plastic bag. Three or four canes inserted into the compost will keep the bag off the leaf. When large enough to be handled the rooted plants can be potted individually.

CUTTINGS

Many houseplants root easily and quickly during spring and summer months. Some plants can be increased by having their stems or shoots inserted into a peat-based compost, while others, such as peperomias and saintpaulias (African violets), root easily from the tips their leaf-stalks (the young plantlets appearing at the base of the cut stem once the roots have had a chance to form). The botanical term for this method of propagation is leaf-petiole cuttings and it is an excellent method for suitable small-leaved plants, enabling a number of cuttings to be taken without spoiling the plant.

When increasing plants by this method use only young and healthy leaves. Cut leaves from the parent plant as close to their bases as possible, so that short stems are not left. Then cut the stems to 4cm (1$\frac{1}{2}$in) long.

Dip the end of each leaf stalk in a hormone rooting powder to ensure that roots are quickly formed from the cut ends. It may be necessary to moisten the cut ends to enable the hormone rooting powder to stick to them.

AIR LAYERING

This distinctive form of propagation is useful for giving plants which have become long and leggy – with an expanse of bare stem making them look unsightly – a second life. Codiaeums, cordylines and the rubber plant Ficus elastica benefit from air layering. The Chinese have used this method of increasing plants for many centuries, and since the introduction of houseplants in their millions during recent years it has been employed to regenerate plants which have grown too high to be pleasing or practical in a small room.

Air layering is sometimes called 'ringing', because one method involves the removal of a ring of bark from around the stem. The method most frequently used, however, involves slitting the stem. Eventually, roots grow from the cut and the stem can then be severed from the parent plant.

During the spring and summer, cut a 6mm ($\frac{1}{4}$in) wide strip of bark from around the stem, just below the lowest leaf. A better way, however, is to cut a slit in the stem in an upward direction. Do not cut right through it. This method is better than 'ringing' the stem, as it allows nutrients to pass up the stem to the leaves to keep them in a healthy condition. With 'ringing', the passage of nutrients to and from the roots and leaves is restricted, especially during spring and summer when the plant is growing more vigorously. Before cutting the stem, ensure the plant has been well watered, as those lacking water will not root so rapidly. Avoid air layering in winter.

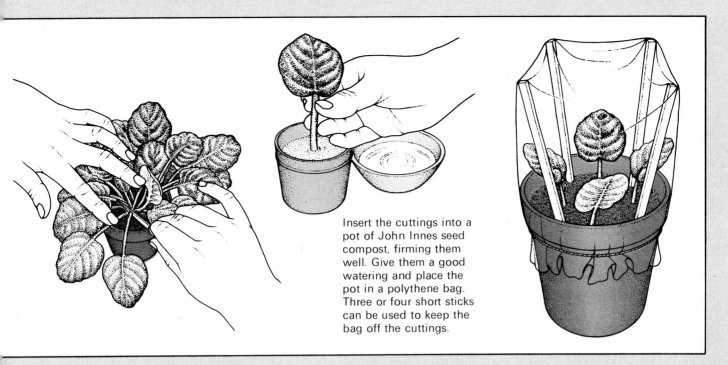

Insert the cuttings into a pot of John Innes seed compost, firming them well. Give them a good watering and place the pot in a polythene bag. Three or four short sticks can be used to keep the bag off the cuttings.

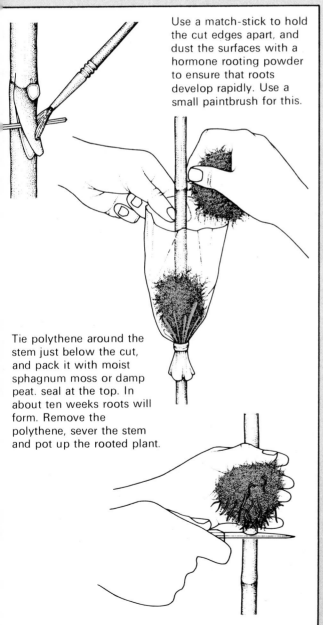

Use a match-stick to hold the cut edges apart, and dust the surfaces with a hormone rooting powder to ensure that roots develop rapidly. Use a small paintbrush for this.

Tie polythene around the stem just below the cut, and pack it with moist sphagnum moss or damp peat. seal at the top. In about ten weeks roots will form. Remove the polythene, sever the stem and pot up the rooted plant.

LAYERING

Many plants can be increased by pegging a stem or shoot, that is still attached to the parent plant, into compost to encourage roots to form.

Saxifraga stolonifera (right) and the small-leaved ivy (below) are two excellent plants for this form of propagation. If the runners are long enough, peg them into pots of John Innes potting compost No. 1. Keep the compost moist. When roots have formed the stems can be severed. Plants such as small-leaved ivies are best set in large plastic trays with compost or a peat-and-sand mixture packed round

them. Trailing stems are pegged into the soil using bent pieces of wire. Once roots have formed the plants are cut from the parent and potted up.

DESIGN & DISPLAY

Decorating the home, to make it interesting, exciting and an extension of one's own personality and identity, is an activity as old as recorded time. Early cave dwellers carved and painted walls, but today, as a result of modern horticultural techniques and the abundant variety of plants discovered by botanists during the last few centuries, it is possible to have a living decor. Furthermore, such is the extensive range of plants now available – as well as illumination aids – that most places in the home, however previously inhospitable to the growth of plants, can now be enriched and made interesting.

The presence of living plants in the house offers the constant ability to change the appearance of the home. The plants can be moved from one place to another, creating new and excitingly different and attractive focal points.

Giving each room a new look every week or month can be easily achieved by swopping plants, and giving new introductions to the home the exact conditions they require. For instance, a cyclamen bought for Christmas decoration will need a cool place in a shaded position, while a poinsettia (*Euphorbia pulcherrima*) will need warmth and good light, but not direct sunlight.

Plants help to create a peaceful and restful atmosphere in a home, aiding in the essential task of combating the hectic pace at which many people live. They also provide a useful foil to the home, helping everything to blend in together. Plants have a further benefit, in that they require personal attention, and therefore it is a welcomed feeling to be needed, an especially valuable and cherished feeling for anyone living alone. And, importantly, plants need attention on a day-to-day basis . . . even to being talked to, some people claim.

Plant psychology is not a new field of study suddenly discovered by a keen research academic. Since the turn of the century many people have investigated the sensitivity and reactions of plants, and there are clear indications that plants do have a form of 'nervous system'. Experts suggest that the reason some people have 'green fingers' and the ability to make plants grow is because they strongly exhibit a sense of love and understanding towards them. Plants have been known – through experiments involving lie-detectors – to react positively on the entry into a room of someone who damaged them on a previous occasion. Music is also said to influence them. It has been claimed that they react more favourably to classical composers such as Bach and Handel than modern rock-type music!

Plants are especially useful in the sick room, offering interest for patients to look at. For anyone in a sick bed, a fresh plant can look very attractive and soothing, and many house-bound gardeners can pursue a worthwhile hobby.

Most people have particular likes and dislikes, and this attitude is often extended to plants as well. But such is the range of plants for the home, that it is inconceivable that no plants could find favour. More traditionally-minded people might prefer the well-established seasonal plants, such as azaleas, cyclamen, hyacinths and poinsettias at Christmas and during the winter, primulas in the spring and early summer, with the home decorated with cut-flower chrysanthemums during the autumn.

THE HISTORY OF HOUSEPLANTS

Many of our world's traditions can be traced back thousands of years to the Chinese, and this is also true with the cultivation of plants in containers. About 5,000 years ago palace gardens were filled with ornamental plants in earthenware pots.

The ancient Egyptians, about a century before the birth of Christ, used pot plants, and even commissioned people to venture into foreign lands to discover and bring back new specimens. King Nebuchadrezzar, a famous Babylonian, used ornamental trees in pots in his Hanging Gardens, and Solomon, King of Israel, employed potted plants in his temple.

The Greeks, in their turn, saw the possibilities of cultivating plants in containers, and used them to decorate their shrines and temples, often setting them in clusters. The early Romans were attracted by the possibilities of growing plants out-of-season and imported plants to be forced into bloom, and encouraged travellers to bring back collections of plants from their journeys. During the Middle Ages in Britain and the rest of Europe the chief gardeners were the monks, who both studied and developed new techniques in growing plants and involved themselves in the searches for plants that would act as medicinal cures and culinary additives. Monastic gardens and, later, cottage gardens and the vegetable growing areas of large houses, began to display a wealth of plants, many of which were grown in containers.

With the advent of easier and safer travel during the 1800s, botanists ventured abroad from England in larger numbers, and the transportation of plants back to England – if the plants were not imported in a dormant state – was aided by Dr Nathaniel Ward who in 1834 discovered that plants would travel well in an enclosed glass case (page 167).

During the mid-nineteenth century, the mania for plants in the home caught the imagination of the people. Elaborate ferneries and palm houses were constructed, and fern-stands became a part of most parlours.

With the advent of large picture windows and double-glazing, the range of plants that can be grown in the home has widened tremendously during the last few decades. Improved mass propagation techniques have relatively reduced the cost of plants and increased their range. Brighter marketing has also made many people more aware of them.

THE MODERN HOME

Plants have benefitted enormously from larger windows, central heating and double-glazing. As a result of double-glazing, the area close to the glass becomes habitable throughout the year for many more plants, and temperature fluctuations both on a daily and seasonal basis are reduced. However, the scorching of tender growth by hot rays of the sun through the glass is still possible during the summer, and at such times vulnerable plants should be removed and ventilation given to reduce the temperature around the plants.

Large foliage plants, such as *Monstera deliciosa* (right) and palms add proportion to a large room.

Radiators are usually placed along the wall under windows, to compensate for the heat loss incurred through windows, and therefore the atmosphere around plants on a window-sill is likely to be dry. It may therefore be necessary to choose the plants very carefully, selecting those best able to tolerate these conditions. Setting the plants in a trough full of damp peat can help to produce a buoyant atmosphere. And remember to use plants which will not be damaged by curtains as they are drawn.

Large picture windows bring both benefits and problems.

The obvious advantage has been a lot more light entering the room, reducing the problems of selecting plants for dark and dreary places. The difficulty with large window areas is that they need larger plants with which to frame them. This problem initiated the introduction of large houseplants, which by their size could be called small trees. Large rubber plants (*Ficus elastica*), Swiss cheese plants (*Monstera deliciosa*), *Ficus benjamina*, and various palms have been used very effectively in this manner.

Changing techniques
Alongside the changes in the home environment there have been radical changes in cultural techniques.

The compost in which we grow our plants has been the subject of much research. In the early days of houseplant growing special recipes were evolved through trial and error and these became part of the mystique of growing pot plants. But the days of special soil mixes for each type of plant have long since gone and are now reserved for a few groups with specific needs. The John Innes loam-based composts became the preferred growing medium for the vast majority of houseplants for several generations, but these have gradually been ousted to a large extent by the newer peat-based composts (see page 14). The convenience and cleanliness of peat-based mixes have had a particular appeal in the home.

The desire to dispense with soil has been carried to a most successful conclusion with modern hydroculture units (see page 30). The technique has progressed from cumbersome systems totally unsuitable for the home, to sleek, compact and totally dependable units that will enhance almost any home.

One advantage of hydroculture containers is that they are attractive in their own right and need no further disguise. Plastic pots have also helped to improve the appearance of many pot plants – they are easier to keep clean and free of green or white growths.

In the days of gas lights only the toughest plants could thrive – rooms were naturally gloomier and many suffered the effects of coal-gas fumes. With natural gas, toxic fumes are no longer a major problem, but just as important is the role modern artificial lighting can play in growing and displaying houseplants.

Apart from light that can be used for display and effect, special fluorescent tubes can be purchased that closely match the quality of natural light. These make it possible to grow many plants in parts of the home previously unsuitable because of very poor lighting conditions.

THE RANGE AVAILABLE
A visit to a houseplant nursery, a florist or a large departmental store soon reveals the wealth of plants available for the home. There are plants to suit the tastes of everyone and the vogue and trends current at any time. There are plants with shapes and colours to blend with every conceivable taste in home decor, from the modern and often highly clinical feeling created by futuristic settings, to the warm and snug atmospheres engendered by cottages with exposed beams, and even to the bizarre and often eye-jolting colours employed by the improvisations of the youth of every decade. For instance, home settings and decors hoping to capture the atmosphere of the future might well use a few narrow-leaved foliage plants such as *Cyperus alternifolius* or dracaenas. While the more closed and often darker environs of an old cottage would welcome tougher green-leaved plants such as ivies and many of the ficus family.

Flowering houseplants
As a result of horticultural techniques introduced during the past few decades, many flowering houseplants which were previously available only during their natural flowering period can now be bought in flower at any time of the year. Perhaps the plant to benefit most in this manner has been the chrysanthemum, which previously was autumn and winter-flowering. Nowadays, chrysanthemums are available the year-round, with compact growth and a neat head of flowers forming a balanced plant, ideal as a table centrepiece. The compact kalanchoe can also be bought throughout the year.

The range of flowering plants is extensive (see pages 50 and 131), and many are trailing or climbing. There are even plants which have both attractive foliage and beautiful flowers, such as the exotic-looking zebra plant, *Aphelandra squarrosa* (see page 57).

Foliage houseplants
Before the 1950s, the houseplant chiefly grown to provide a display of foliage would have been the often despised aspidistra, when it was given comic-song importance which undervalued its tolerance to dark conditions and cold and dreary places, the legacies of so many houses built during the Victorian era. Nowadays, as a result of better home conditions and an increased awareness of houseplants, the range available has widened enormously and there are plants to suit all places in the home.

Because they do not rely on a single flush of colour to provide a display, but more on a continuous array of attractively shaped and coloured leaves, they become permanent features in the home, only being moved or pruned to shape when they outgrow their allotted position. Most foliage houseplants live quite happily in normal interiors, while some, such as the palms and ferns and aspidistra, tolerate shady positions (and there are many other possibilities).

Others, such as the shrimp plant (*Beloperone guttata*) and cacti and succulents, thrive on sunny windows, while the *Dizygotheca elegantissima* (often called *Aralia elegantissima*), prefers a less shady spot where it can be syringed to give a higher level of humidity (see page 19). Information about the cultural requirements of specific houseplants is given on pages 50 to 131.

Small trees

Because so many of the foliage house-plants introduced in recent years are, in their natural environment, large trees or shrubs, it is inevitable that sooner or later they will outgrow their position in the home. Often, they can be moved to an area affording more headroom, such as a stairway, or they can often be sold as mature houseplants to offices wishing to have ready-established large plants.

Large plants demand large pots and amounts of soil, so do remember to place them on a solid-floored base which is well structured to support the plant.

'Trees' add a new dimension to rooms, and that is one of height, and as such affects the overall design concept of a room. A high-ceiling Victorian-type room lends itself to a houseplant with tree-like proportions, but many modern rooms or cosy old and beamed ones would not.

Some trees are symmetrical in shape, while others are trailing and adaptable to corner positions. The beautiful and symmetrical Norfolk Island pine (*Araucaria heterophylla* syn. *A. excelsa*) produces tiers of attractive branches full of pine needles, and as such must be viewed from all sides – as well as being given equal light all round. It is often impossible because of their weight to rotate large plants, so that all sides are in turn given equal amounts of good light. In such cases, it is best to select and buy plants that do not require turning, and have a 'face-side', such as *Monstera deliciosa*.

The weeping fig (*Ficus benjamina*) is another face-sided plant, with shiny and pointed leaves that cascade down in branches. It can be pruned to fit a corner of a room.

A succulent with tree-like proportions, and well suited to a modern home setting is *Crassula arborescens*. It is sensitive to draughts and needs a relatively cool position – perhaps in a hallway but away from the door.

By the time many of our houseplants reach tree-like proportions they become highly treasured specimens, but if as such they dominate a room and become obtrusive, it is best to sell them or to propagate from them.

Above left: Kalanchoes flower throughout the year and as they do not have a 'face' side look splendid on a table. All the plants – even those on the window-sill – should be given a quarter of a turn each day to prevent the foliage turning towards the light and producing imbalanced growth.
Left: *Ficus benjamina* eventually grows into a small tree. It looks best when left in one position and will often grow to suit a specific corner.

Palms

Of all houseplants, the palms are among the most elegant, creating an atmosphere of calm and tranquility. They are plants that demand the correct settings and room proportions to be appreciated to the full. Often they look their best when set in an ornamental pot placed on a plant stand, perhaps 60–90cm (2–3ft) high. At such positions, however, like many other similarly placed plants, they are likely to be knocked over by children or large dogs. Nevertheless, they can be placed in safe positions, perhaps on a shelf or in an alcove.

One of the smallest and easiest palms to grow is *Chamaedorea elegans*, otherwise known as *Collinia elegans* or *Neanthe bella*. It does well in a dry atmosphere, and is therefore suitable for centrally heated rooms. A stately palm, ideal for the corner of a room, where perhaps it is set against a white wall, is *Chamaerops humilis*, with fan-shaped leaves. There are many others to choose from, all stately and offering elegance to the home (see pages 134 to 137).

Ferns

These are exceptionally graceful plants, with a variety of leaf shapes. The bird's nest fern (*Asplenium nidus*) with its long and strap-shaped leaves looks superb on a plant-stand, whereas the more normal ferns with delicately shaped and cut fronds do well in hanging-baskets. Also, they can be set in an empty fireplace during the summer. Although not true ferns, the asparagus fern (*Asparagus setaceus*) and *Asparagus densiflorus*, with long stems covered in fern-like foliage, bring calm and a sense of restfulness. For details of ferns see pages 138 to 139).

Bulbs

There are many bulbs which can be used as houseplants, including hyacinths, tulips, daffodils, crocuses, lilies and lily-of-the-valley which can be 'forced' so that they are in flower out of their normal flowering period. Many small bulbs can be grown in pots, such as snowdrops and bulbous irises, but they do not respond happily to too much heat and therefore are best grown in cool places and brought indoors to some cool position to flower and brighten the room

for a limited period. For details of bulbs, see pages 140 to 145.

With all bulbs, never give them warm conditions when in flower, as the flowering period may be greatly reduced.

Cacti and succulents

These tend to be slow-growing and therefore permanent members of the home. Although they are often grown solitarily, grouping them into a trough or large container helps to create a more spectacular display. They thrive in the hot and sunny conditions of window-sills, although during the winter care should be taken that the low temperatures experienced there, especially if the room is single-glazed and with no central heating, do not damage them.

Large specimens look distinctive, but take care to set them out of the reach of children or animals – the spines can be very painful and difficult to extricate from animal flesh. See pages 158 to 166 for details of these distinctive plants.

Orchids

These delightful plants have a mystique which has grown around them and prevented many people trying them in the home. It is true that many require exacting conditions, but there are a few that will live in the home if given the right conditions. Suitable types are discussed on pages 170 to 175, but principally for good growth they require to be placed where they can receive good light but not direct sunlight, which could damage the leaves.

DISPLAYING PLANTS IN THE HOME

Houseplants require the right setting to display them to perfection. There are many different ways in which to arrange and display plants; all have advantages and disadvantages, and much depends on each plant's habit of growth, whether flowering or non-flowering, size, and so on. Equally, the shape and size of the room into which they are to be placed has an influence.

Grouping plants

By setting plants together, it is possible to create, on a miniature scale, the appearance of plants outdoors. A single plant on its own has architectural value, and is certainly a focal point of interest, but by grouping plants a micro-climate and miniature garden can be created.

Left: Small plants can be grouped together while larger specimens are best displayed on their own.
Above right: Bulbs will flower for longer if grown in cool conditions.
Right: Cacti need a window position.

The number of plants used in each group will, of course, depend on the area to be filled and the size of the plants. Select a range of plants that will give differing height levels, as well as shapes, textures and size of leaves. For instance, the fiddle-back fig (*Ficus lyrata*), the Swiss cheese plant and *Ficus pumila* could be used to give variation, while the introduction to the group of a foliage plant with variegated leaves would add a further dimension and interest.

Formal plants with rigid outlines can be used in pairs or threes where rectangular or round tables need decoration. Flowering houseplants which form a face-side can be introduced to foliage plant settings to give colour during dull months when because of the lack of light plants with totally green leaves are not at their best.

By setting plants in groups, the transpiration of water from their leaf surfaces create a micro-climate that makes the area more acceptable to all of the plants.

Individual specimens

Solitary plants can be used in all room settings, from the clinical and futuristic to the Elizabethan style. Elegant palms, such as *Howeia forsteriana*, form focal points, and a mature *Dracaena fragrans* will be a talking point in any modern setting. Ferns on plant stands or in an empty fireplace can give interest to Victorian-type high-ceiling rooms, while trailing and variegated ivies look at home in low-ceiling and beamed homes.

There are, clearly, plants for everyone's taste, and only a limit to one's imagination reduces their use.

Remember that the height at which a plant is seen is very important. Obviously, those with long stems are best placed on the floor, while bushier and trailing plants will look much more attractive if placed on a table or plant stand.

'Architectural' plants

There are some plants which are so distinctive in shape and size that they need to be displayed on their own or as an integral part of the decor of the house. A large Swiss cheese plant (*Monstera deliciosa*) with its remarkably-shaped leaves forms an 'informal' shape that will blend well in most settings that are not strictly symmetrical, while the formal outline of the Norfolk Island pine (*Araucaria heterophylla*, syn. *A. excelsa*) needs a more symmetrical room. The long-stemmed cordyline reaching perhaps 1.2–1.5m (4–5ft) and with long leaves, can provide a focal point and afford space for young children and animals to walk close to the base.

Screens

Plant screens can be formed from the floor upwards and from the ceiling downwards. Traditionally, a screen of plants would comprise a few plants on the floor with the foliage trained up an open-work screen. However, it can also be formed of plants growing in troughs a foot or so off the floor, with the foliage then interlaced in a screen, or from hanging indoor baskets, well secured from the ceiling, with attractive foliage or flowers cascading towards the floor. Or all three types of screens can be used together.

Plants in troughs

Setting a few plants in a trough is an excellent way in which to reduce the amount of daily attention required for watering. The plants in their pots can be set as they are in a 10–15cm (4–6in) deep trough with moist peat packed around them. This helps to keep the soil in the pots both cool and moist, although individual plants will still have to be watered. Groupings of plants like these are ideal for setting in hallways or on landings, where the floor space is often limited. By setting small plants in troughs which are themselves 30–45cm (12–18in) above the floor, an added dimension can be given to the plants and the room.

Above: Large plants of tree-like proportions have a softening framing effect on large windows while a substantial centrepiece holds a room together.

Far right: This airy kitchen is an ideal growing situation for plants, particularly climbing and trailing varieties.

Below: Plant containers come in all shapes and sizes and the more unusual ones are often the most attractive.

Indoor hanging-baskets

Hanging-baskets, as well as string-made holders for supporting a traditional houseplant, are excellent for displaying some plants. The traditional outdoor hanging-basket, which dripped water everywhere, has now been updated and modified with a drip-tray to prevent water falling on carpets. They are modern in appearance and long-lasting. The vogue for macrame hangers has highlighted the advantages of using what would otherwise be un-utilized space. The woven strings look attractive in their own right, and blend well with many foliage plants.

Baskets or macrame holders if suspended from the ceiling should be attached by fixtures screwed into the joists, and not merely into the plaster-board. The weight of both the plant and wet soil or compost can be very heavy.

Using decorative pots

The range of decorative pots in which to display the clay or plastic growing pot is extensive. Equally wide is the range of colours and materials from which they are made. Imitation pewter and copper, glazed china and earthenware pots, plastic and woven wicker-work baskets with plastic drip-trays, are just a few of the many plant holders available. Each can be selected to suit the texture and colour of the plants, and to blend with the surroundings.

Junk shops and jumble sales often produce excellent holders which in their previous life may have had a more utilitarian existence – from casserole dishes to chamber pots.

43

Plant pedestals

Both compact and trailing plants can be used on these stands, although trailing plants often look best, such as the spider plant (*Chlorophytum comosum*). Ferns such as *Asplenium bulbiferum* are also suitable. The history of these stands can be traced back to the aspidistra of the Victorian era.

Glass cases

The fashion for growing plants in an enclosed environment, like a sealed miniature greenhouse, originated in the mid 1800s with Wardian cases (see page 167). The moisture given off by the plants condensed to provide water for the roots, and it proved possible to keep quite exotic plants this way. Today, the same principle has been extended to terrariums, flasks, bottles and carboys. Terrariums look very much like fish tanks filled with small plants. The word terrarium, of course, is used for a tank used to house small land animals. These small cases are ideal for growing ferns, mosses and small woodland plants. If a high temperature can be given, subtropical and tropical plants of all kinds can be grown.

Large flasks and bottles, such as a large carboy, well established with plants, makes a spectacular focal point in any room, especially if small spotlights are used to highlight the display. The secret of planting a carboy successfully is described on page 168. Because the carboy will be extremely heavy when planted and established, it will need a firm base, either on the floor or, best of all, on a rigid, low table.

DISGUISING BAD FEATURES

Within every room there are good and bad features: those which are best covered up or disguised and others which can be highlighted. Stark outlines can be softened by climbing and trailing plants such as ivies, *Cissus antarctica*, *Ficus pumila*, tradescantia, and so on. While arching windows are best highlighted and filled with 'spot' plants that fill the space and at the same time trail to blend the window with the rest of the room. The blue-flowered *Campanula isophylla* or white *C.i.* 'Alba' could be used, according to the room's decor.

Ferns are ideal for covering unused fireplaces, which can look deadly dull when empty. If a small trivet is not available to stand the pot on, use another pot upturned as a base. This will allow the foliage to hang down around the pot and not be damaged.

Piping, for gas or water, which often adorns the walls of bathrooms and kitchens, can be covered by trailing plants.

However, if the pipe is for hot-water, either lag it or allow a space for air circulation between it and the plant, which could become scorched.

Windows which overlook dreary and dismal places can be improved slightly by setting attractive plants around them. Trailing plants on a ledge above the window and a trough of plants on the windowledge detracts from the view outside. And if the view is that bad, net curtains completely over the window and with an additional shelf for plants half way up the window and completely across will really produce a barrier of colour and interest. The shelf should be removable to enable the window to be cleaned occasionally.

In the same way that bad features can be disguised, the penetration of kitchen smells can be reduced by placing a

Above: Glass cases are ideal for growing ferns and other moisture-loving plants.
Right: Individual plants can make an artistic grouping.

fragrant plant at a strategic position. And remember that a sweetly smelling plant placed near the front door always welcomes visitors and gives a good impression.

The delightfully fragrant *Jasminum polyanthum* is ideal for a cool position. It flowers during the spring and can be grown in a quite small pot and trained over thin split-canes.

Citrus microcarpa (better known as *C. mitis*) has strongly fragrant white star-shaped flowers, and has the additional benefit of producing attractive small oranges. The gardenia is exquisitely scented, but is not easy to grow.

MAKING A BROMELIAD TREE

Bromeliads are very distinctive houseplants and as such demand an unusual and spectacular setting. In nature, they are either terrestrial or epiphytic. That is to say that they grow either on the ground in stony and rocky places (terrestrial), or on trees (epiphytic). However they grow, they do not demand a great deal of soil; their roots serve mainly as an anchor, their leaves and the central 'vase' formed by them absorbing the food they require. Because they do not require much soil, they can be displayed on a 'bromeliad tree'.

This artificial home for them can be formed from a seasoned branch cut from a hardwood tree, such as apple, although this will tend to rot in time. An artificial but very effective trunk can be made from pieces of cork bark fixed to a suitable support. This looks good and is long-lasting. Secure the trunk end of the 'tree' in a small tub or some other container with a wide base and firm bottom. The size of the branch very much depends on the area in which the bromeliad tree will be positioned, but in proportion to the size of the plants a branch 1.2–1.8m (4–6ft) in height is best.

One of the best ways of securing the branch is to place the end in the container, and to pour cement around it. Shingle or small stones can then be placed over the concrete, which gives an appearance of the rocky and stony areas from which some bromeliads originate.

The individual plants are set in the natural crevices of the branch, and these can be found by pouring water down the branch and seeing where it naturally collects.

This preparatory work is obviously best done outside in the garden.

To set the plants in position, remove them from their pots and wrap the root-balls in wet sphagnum moss. Mould the moss around the roots so that it firmly adheres to them. Position the plants, and use green plastic-coated wire to hold each soil-ball together and also to attach it securely to the branch. Water the soil-balls thoroughly, and keep them regularly sprayed so that they do not dry out.

Plants for halls and stairways

The problem with displaying plants in halls and on stairways is the often dark and draughty conditions that too often prevail there. Although during the summer the conditions may be satisfactory, in winter they can be very inhospitable. However, double glazing, central heating and draught excluders around doors can improve matters. Despite their drawbacks, hallways and stairs do offer the opportunity to grow tall or trailing plants – however, much depends on the position of the stairs.

Plants well suited to these conditions are *Ficus benjamina*, *Aucuba japonica*, *Crassula arborescens*, *Monstera deliciosa* and *Grevillea robusta*. They are all plants which have quite sturdy foliage resistant to cool conditions. However, they should not be abused and if they look dejected must be moved to better conditions in order to recuperate.

Palms and ferns are tolerant of low light areas, but if on a ledge will need to be safely secured to prevent them being knocked over. If space is limited, troughs of plants on window-sills or ledges make interesting displays.

If the area is particularly dark, spotlights can be employed to make focal points of specimen plants. They can be most effective at night.

PLANTS IN THE KITCHEN

The kitchen is the work centre of the home, and as such often becomes a hectic and cluttered place. Furthermore, there are severe changes in temperature throughout the day, as well as steam and sudden waves of heat as an oven is opened. It is, therefore, not an easy place in which to keep plants, and much of the skill in successfully growing plants there is in the selection and positioning of them within the room.

Artists' impressions of modern kitchens, with masses of space, are all very well, but in reality many kitchens are often quite small.

However, a few plants in the kitchen can help to make it a nicer place to work in, and give a temporary respite from the pressure of life. Trailing plants, set high up on the tops of cupboards, are ideal brighteners, such as *Setcreasea pallida* (syn. *S. purpurea*), *Zebrina pendula*, *Tradescantia fluminensis* and perhaps *Chlorophytum comosum*. The practicalities of watering these plants should not be overlooked, as if placed on a too high shelf it becomes difficult to judge if watering is necessary. A watering-can also becomes difficult to use.

As well as plants that trail from cupboards, it will be necessary to have at least one plant that grows upright and can be placed on a working surface. This will help to provide interest at eye level. Cacti and succulents do well in trays along the window-sill, and so too, do many flowering plants.

PLANTS IN THE BATHROOM

Many problems of growing plants in bathrooms are quite similar to those prevailing in the kitchen – changes in temperature, hot-water vapour – with the additional hazard of lack of light and the adjuncts to modern living such as aerosols and clouds of talcum powder. There are plants that will survive these conditions, but they do need a great deal of care and attention to ensure that they continue to thrive.

Attractive plants perched on the sides of a bath look very nice in magazines, but are totally impractical in a family bathroom, especially with small children. Far better to select a few tough plants and set them on firm shelves out of direct clouds of hot-water vapour and inquisitive tiny hands of young children.

Flowering houseplants can do well in the bathroom, as they often have a limited life and are then discarded. Foliage plants with tender leaves may need a respite from these conditions, in a first-aid area of the house, before being replaced in the bathroom. If the bathroom is very hot and steamy, use plants with a lot of small leaves, such as *Asparagus densiflorus* and the small variegated ivies, as they can afford to lose a leaf now and again.

The larger the bathroom, the easier it will be to grow plants successfully. Always try to place them near the light and away from hot water vapour and the area in which aerosol sprays are usually used.

PLANTS IN BEDROOMS

Bedrooms, unlike kitchens and bathrooms, are normally much cooler and drier places.

It is often best to select a few choice plants for the bedroom, and to display them in a spectacular way, than to clutter it with many different kinds. Trailing plants, such as ivies and the small trailing ficus, suspended from the ceiling with macrame pot holders look good, especially if they are at a level that is easily seen from the bed.

Unused fireplaces can be enhanced by specimen plants, with perhaps a stately palm against a plain wall. Ferns grow better in bedrooms than in the warmer and drier atmosphere of living-rooms. Flowering plants also do well, such as cyclamen, hydrangeas, kalanchoes, busy Lizzies, plumbago and begonias.

Left: Bathrooms can make nice settings for many plants, but children often preclude a display like this. In any case it would be wise to move them while taking a bath.
Right: Kitchens are easily brightened by tough plants such as ivies, tradescantias and *Cissus antarctica*.

CONSERVATORIES AND GROWING ROOMS

No beginner is going to turn over a complete room to his plants, or dash out to order a conservatory, but once the collecting bug bites the scope offered by the average home seems suddenly inadequate – not only in terms of window space but because of the restrictions that ordinary living places on the creation of a buoyant growing atmosphere. It is that urge to expand one's hobby that has led to many a conservatory being built.

The word conservatory frequently conjures mental images of large Victorian houses with large and lofty glass structures, often quite ornate, built on to the back. There are few homes today able to take anything on this scale – the structure would be out of proportion to most modern homes, and the cost prohibitive for many families. There are, however, some delightful and very tasteful lean-to greenhouses that would enhance any home – they are far removed from the normal purely functional appearance of most greenhouses and would certainly add value to the property. By positioning one of these against French windows the living room can be extended when the doors are open, and you have all the advantages of a greenhouse in your home. Not only will a wide range of plants be happy there, but you will be able to appreciate most of them through the glass.

Often a small washroom or other existing glass-sided or glass-topped lean-to structure can be converted into a conservatory (ensure adequate ventilators are installed), and these can often be made into very pleasant places.

Failing that, there is always the front porch, which should always have a welcome of flowers and plants anyway. By installing a modest heater for the cold weather, and some means of adequate ventilation for the hot days (this should not be overlooked), a wide range of delightful plants can be grown. There are obvious limitations, however, as there is still the problem of icy blasts when the outer door is opened – the surest way to lose the leaves on a croton for instance.

There is another alternative – a growing room. It means devoting a spare bedroom or some other suitable room to your interest, but that applies to many other hobbies. The great advantage is that you can control the total environment – including light.

Setting up a growing room is not cheap. Benches and shelves will have to be installed around the room, and special growing lights used. To grow as many plants as possible in a small space it is usual to arrange some of the shelves in tiers, with the light tubes attached beneath upper shelves to illuminate the plants below. To ensure there is sufficient light each day, the lighting system should be on a time switch.

If existing central heating radiators are not already installed, a thermostatically-controlled electric heater is the answer (provided it is suitable for use in a damp, humid atmosphere). The only other investment, if you have to leave the room unattended will be an automatic ventilator.

Such a room, where plenty of humidity can be created, will have a special 'feel' to it, a buoyancy to the air that makes all the difference to the growth of plants.

PLANTS FOR A CONSERVATORY

A conservatory is like an oasis for many plants – it provides an excellent rest home for those which we try to grow in difficult or unsuitable positions. If used mainly for plants, a conservatory should not be kept at a high temperature; in fact, a minimum winter temperature of 7°C (45°F) is quite adequate.

Most plants that grow in the home will do well in a conservatory, as well as those that like cool conditions in a greenhouse. The A-Z section in this book gives the names of many plants suitable for cool conditions.

Few people are lucky enough to have the Victorian type conservatory, with stone or brick floors and high ceilings. Most have just a lean-to type in which the plants are in separate pots.

Position the plants so that there is interest at all levels, from the floor to ceiling. Large specimens of houseplants, with tree-like proportions, can be grown to give height, with climbing and trailing plants filling in the spaces.

COLOURS AND COLOUR SCHEMES

Too often, that mystical and frequently undefinable thing called 'good taste' in colour selection is nothing more than one person's opinion or particular liking. There are, for instance, colour schemes that clash in one setting, but produce the required effect in another. For example, a teenager's room may be decorated with the most bizarre range of colours that look perfect to its occupant, but would produce nightmares for other members of the family. Similarly, the selection of plants for a particular room is a personal thing.

Strict rules about colour schemes either confuse or inhibit the full use of a person's imagination and natural tendancy to experiment. However, if you should wish to create a particular atmosphere in a room, certain colour schemes can be employed. For example, a room with white walls looks clinical, and needs furniture, ornaments and plants to add a lived in feeling. Whereas a room decorated with delicately flowered wallpaper has a warm atmosphere, with or without the furniture and plants. The type of plant and its effect on a room should be considered with care and although it is a matter of personal taste, the following list will give some ideas.

FLOWERING PLANTS:
Orange and yellow flowers
Begonia × tuberhybrida 'Guardsman': This tuberous-rooted begonia produces large flowers of a deep orange, often 7.5–15cm (3–6in) across. It looks good cascading from a stand or shelf.

Chrysanthemum: There are many varieties with orange or yellow flowers, and all are excellent as centrepieces. They last a long time in flower, especially during the winter.

Citrus microcarpa (syn. C. mitis): For a spectacular display of miniature orange fruits (the flowers are white) this plant has few equals. It does like a humid atmosphere, and should be placed where it can be conveniently misted.

Thunbergia alata: Known as black-eyed Susan, the funnel-like orange and yellow flowers are produced in profusion during the summer.

Red and pink flowers
Cyclamen: These traditionally winter-flowering plants can be obtained in many different colours, including red and pink, and look good as centrepieces for tables in cool rooms.

Impatiens: The busy Lizzie needs little introduction, and lasts in flower for many months. Mature plants tend to lose their lower leaves, so try to place them on a low table where this is not quite so obvious.

Senecio cruentus (cinerarias): These glorious plants produce many heads, bursting with bloom, and can be viewed from all sides. It is best to look down on them slightly, so do not place them on high shelves. They also need plenty of water and therefore must be accessible.

Sinningia: This is the gloxinia, a regular favourite with plant lovers. There are many cultivars, and the blooms appear in summer and autumn. Again, it is nice to look down on the blooms and the buds, which are attractive as they open.

Blue flowers
Campanula: *C. isophylla* and *C. fragilis* are trailing plants, ideal for cascading from a shelf or hanging-basket.

Ipomoea tricolor: This delightful plant, also called *Ipomoea rubrocaerulea*, produces many mauvish-blue flowers. It is a climber, and particularly effective when grown on a trellis and used as a room divider.

Purple flowers
Saintpaulia ionantha: These well known plants are able to live in small pots, relative to the size of the foliage, and produce a good array of flowers. Dome-shaped plants are formed, and these are ideal for table-top decorations.

Streptocarpus: The Cape primrose, as it is known, produces large flowers in autumn or spring, making a good centrepiece for a table. Various shades, mainly purples and blues

Cream flowers
Senecio cruentus: See previous entry.
Chrysanthemum: See previous entry.

White flowers
Chrysanthemums: See previous entry.
Campanula isophylla 'Alba': This is the popular white-flowered form, described on page 64.
Cyclamen: Several white-flowered forms of this plant are available. See page 75 for a full description.
Stephanotis floribunda: This distinctive trailing and climbing plant is a superb addition to any home, with wax-like sweetly-scented flowers. It is ideal for a corner of a room, where it will produce a 'face' side.

FOLIAGE PLANTS:
Orange or yellow foliage
Codiaeum variegatum pictum 'Disraeli': This enchanting croton has yellow patches on the top surfaces of the leaves. Its base may become rather bare, and it is best to stand the plant on the floor so that the lack of leaves is not readily noticeable and the colours of the leaves can be seen to greater advantage.

Coleus: These well-known foliage plants have a wonderful range of coloured leaves, often with patches of orange or yellow.

Dieffenbachia 'Exotica': This has pale yellow markings. If there are children or animals in the house, avoid this plant as the sap is poisonous.

Red or pink foliage
Begonia rex: These popular foliage plants have a range of colours, including pink and crimson.

Cordyline terminalis 'Firebrand': This cabbage palm has highly decorative leaves edged with brilliant red. It is a stately plant, well suited to a low table.

Purple foliage
Gynura aurantiaca: This climbing and trailing plant has eye-catching leaves covered with bright purple hairs. The yellow flowers are best cut off as they have an unpleasant smell. It is ideal for a corner of a room.

Iresine herbstii: This plant needs to be in good sunlight for it to maintain the shiny, heart-shaped purple leaves at their best.

Brown or bronze foliage
Begonia rex: See previous entry.
Coleus: See previous entry.

There are, of course, many other plants with distinctive and coloured foliage. For details of them see pages 50 to 131.

A-Z OF HOUSEPLANTS

The range of plants suitable for the home is vast – more than 600 species or cultivars are mentioned in this book – and deciding which plants to grow is always difficult. Many enthusiasts specialize in a particular type of plant once they have developed an in-depth appreciation and knowledge of a certain group – but for the true houseplant collector there is always something new and unknown to be tried.

This chapter is designed as a quick reference guide to the plants you are likely to encounter in shops and garden centres – plus some that may only be found at specialist nurseries. Even so, there will still be plants offered for sale that are not discussed here – many nurseries grow small quantities of lesser-known or more unusual plants, and in instances where there may be hundreds of cultivars it has only been possible to mention a few of the best. However, the vast majority of houseplants offered for sale will be found in these pages.

To make selection easier, the entries in this chapter have been graded to indicate whether the plant is likely to be difficult or easy to grow. One star indicates a good plant for a beginner – undemanding and easy to grow, and requiring no special treatment other than providing basic conditions such as the right amount of light and moisture, and an adequate temperature. A two-star plant is more difficult and should only be tried once experience has been gained with easier plants. Three stars indicates a difficult subject, often requiring high temperature and humidity, and considerable care in cultivation; these plants may be a challenge to grow well in the home.

Temperature requirement is an important consideration in selecting a plant – many plants will inevitably be sickly if the temperature is inadequate, no matter how well the other cultural requirements are fulfilled. The minimum temperature is indicated for each plant – this will usually occur at night – and it is important to determine the lowest temperature you are likely to be able to maintain. Buy only plants suitable for that temperature range.

Some plants will survive brief periods at a lower temperature, but may receive a severe check to growth – and in some cases the plant may be lost. Much may depend on the moisture level of the compost – there is a better chance of surviving a low temperature if the roots are almost dry.

The range of plants that can be grown successfully is increased if conditions of good light and humidity can be provided, and many subjects will grow much more vigorously and larger if they can be accommodated in a sun lounge or conservatory. But all the plants mentioned will grow in the home, even though some may be less robust than they would be in a less restricted environment.

ABUTILON
* 5°C/41°F

The shrubby abutilons are often called flowering maples, because of their maple-like foliage. The hybrids offered by most seedsmen are particularly good. Sown in March, they will make fine flowering specimens by June and have beautiful veined cup-shaped flowers in a range of colours. Some newer hybrids have the flowers borne erect, so that they point outwards, whereas many older types had more drooping blooms. The plants flower very freely, often continuing well into winter. If the young plants are stopped (the main growing tips removed) they become more bushy, but this delays flowering. Old plants may become very tall and have to be cut back, although it may be best to discard them and sow more. Give the plants good light or slight shade. They are not particularly fussy or prone to any special troubles, and deserve to be more extensively grown as they are very easy.

Quite different is *A. megapotamicum* from Brazil, and it is quite happy in cool places. This plant looks delightful when trained in the roof of a conservatory, but it can be kept compact by growing it up canes or strings. The very attractive, dainty, pendent flowers are contrastingly coloured in red and yellow, and beautifully shaped.

There is a form with green and cream mottled leaves, best bought as a rooted

Abutilon 'Master Hugh'.

cutting in spring. Both are very easy and suitable for either a bright position or slight shade. *A. megapotamicum* can be pruned back to a convenient size in May if it becomes too tall or straggly.

Several other abutilons are worth trying as houseplants. The Brazilian *A. pictum* (syn. *A. striatum*) is a shrubby species that can be kept to about 90cm (3ft) if grown in pots, but will much exceed this if put in a conservatory border. It is rather more tender than *A. megapotamicum*, and has deep green lobed leaves and crimson-veined orange flowers about 4cm (1½in) long from early summer to late autumn. A plant often wrongly catalogued as *A. thompsonii* is actually a form of this species. It has smaller foliage variegated with a yellow mottling. *A. × milleri* can be grown up canes to a height of about 1.2m (4ft) if kept in relatively small pots. Given more root space it will reach at least double this height. It is very similar to *A. megapotamicum*, but again is more tender. The flowers are red veined and orange yellow, rather like *A. pictum* and borne over a similar period. The foliage is large, with green and yellow mottling.

The species *A. vitifolium* will be of interest if you have a cold porch or entrance hall. It is fairly hardy, only suffering damage during severe winters, but in a sheltered place tends to grow vigorously. It can be trained up canes or a wall trellis. The lobed leaves are covered with whitish hairs and the very attractive flowers have widely opening petals about 5cm (2in) across. There are mauvish and white forms.

With the exception of the last mentioned species, which is easier to grow from seed, the abutilon species are easily propagated from cuttings. Abutilons are of special interest because the variegation of the leaves is believed to be caused by a virus, although this is a case of a virus serving a useful purpose and it does not seem to have any harmful effect. Abutilons are not especially prone to troubles, but aphids and whitefly may attack.

ACACIA (*wattle*)
* 7°C/45°F

The best known acacia is the mimosa of the florist's shop. This can be grown from seed to form a pleasing foliage plant useful during its first year. To flower, it needs to be grown in a conservatory or roomy porch and eventually to be given a large pot or small tub. Give plenty of air and light – the plant is hardy outdoors in mild areas and may flower after a kind winter. Seed germinates easily if sown in spring in modest warmth.

Mimosa, *Acacia dealbata*, is also sometimes called silver wattle and can grow to 30m (100ft) in its native Australia. Lesser known, but a far more suitable pot plant, is *A. armata* – another Australian shrub, called the kangaroo thorn. Again, it is almost hardy and likes the same bright, airy conditions. The shrub is prickly and the flowers are similar to mimosa. Established specimens will flower well in April in 20cm (8in) pots. All acacias should be ventilated freely, the year round, and in winter kept only slightly moist. The most likely pest in summer is red spider mite. No special compost is required, but it should be free-draining.

Well known as a pot plant is the lovely *A. podalyriifolia*, the Queensland wattle. This is a valuable foliage plant, with a bonus of flowers. The leaves are covered with a silver-white down, and golden-yellow flowers are borne in winter. It is almost hardy and makes a splendid specimen for a cold conservatory or large porch, or possibly a well-lit entrance hall or a position by a patio door. *A. verticillata*, prickly Moses, is also worth trying as a pot plant because of its neat habit rarely exceeding about 90cm (3ft) in height when grown in pots. It has sharp, needle-like leaves and pale yellow catkins. When the foliage begins to die down in late autumn, reduce watering until the pots are dry. The containers can then be stored dry in a frost-free place during the winter months. Early the following year, turn out the containers and recover the rhizomes ready for replanting. They should have multiplied considerably. At this stage they should not be allowed to become dry, otherwise they will start to shrivel.

Acacia armata.

ACALYPHA HISPIDA
(red hot cat's tail)
*** 16°C/61°F

This is a very striking plant from New Guinea, with long, dangling flower spikes, like catkins, bright crimson in colour when well grown. It has only recently been introduced as a house-plant, but is difficult to grow unless constant warmth and high humidity can be maintained.

At the Royal Botanic Gardens at Kew it is grown in the tropical waterlily house where it reaches almost to the roof, in the warm atmosphere, making a most impressive sight. In the home it will rarely compare; but spraying with a mist of water in summer helps, and the compost – preferably a peat-based type – must also then be kept quite moist. Give a position in good light, but not direct sunshine, as this helps to achieve the best leaf colouring.

The most common pests are red spider mite and mealy bug, and the under-surface of the foliage should be inspected regularly. To deter red spider, spray under the leaves with water during hot dry weather. The plants are soon liable to deteriorate where there is dry heating such as radiators without humidifiers, or electric fires. Standing the plants on a wide tray of moisture-retaining material may help to maintain sufficient humidity. Should the plants become too tall, they can be cut back in spring.

There is a cultivar called 'Alba' with creamy-white catkins. It is sometimes sold by high-class florists.

ACHIMENES *(hot-water plant)*
* 15°C/59°F, during growth

It is unfortunate that this plant has acquired the misleading name hot-water plant, since it leads many people to think that it is tender or difficult. Being of tropical American origin, it was at one time thought to be tender, and there were recommendations to water with warm water, and with time this became exaggerated. In fact, the plant is quite easy and can be grown from small rhizomes started into growth in spring by immersion in moist peat at about 18°C (64°F).

As soon as a sign of growth is seen, the rhizomes can be planted about three to five to a 13cm (5in) pot, only just covering them with potting compost. There are many cultivars and numerous species, all with attractive, velvety foliage and flowers in a wide range of sizes and colours. Some achimenes are trailers and can be planted in hanging-baskets. Most achimenes will need a few twiggy sticks for support to keep them neat when grown in pots. Flowering is usually from about June to late autumn. Keep the compost moist and shade from direct sunshine. A few recommended varieties for window-sills are 'Purple King', 'Paul Arnold' (violet purple), and 'Peach Blossom' (rich pink with a dark eye). Splendid for hanging pots or baskets is 'Cattleya' (blue and white). The 'Michelssen Hybrids' are very popular and have large flowers in various colours. These have a neat habit, but can be used in baskets too.

ADIANTUM
see page 139

AECHMEA
see page 152

Acalypha hispida.

An achimenes hybrid.

AEONIUM
* 7–10°C/45–50°F

Several species make excellent house-plants, thriving on a bright window-sill. They are succulents from N. Africa, Madeira and Canary Islands, with the leaves borne as rosettes on short or long stems. Their size varies considerably, according to species.

Perhaps one of the most frequently seen aeoniums is the attractive A. × domesticum 'Variegatum', which forms a neat, spreading plant with pleasant green and cream foliage.

A. tabulaeforme, the saucer plant, is given its common name because the rosettes take the shape of flattish plates and the leaves are tightly packed. Pale yellow flowers are produced on plants two or three years old, but the plant then dies. It is easy to produce new stock by rooting leaves or sowing seed.

A. arboreum is quite different, with trunk-like stems bearing the rosettes. These can reach a height of 90cm (3ft). A. a. 'Atropurpureum' is a form with purplish foliage, and is particularly de-sirable for collections of these plants. Aeoniums usually give little trouble, growing well in John Innes potting compost No. 2, with a little extra coarse sand or grit, but they need to be watered generously during summer.

AGAVE
* 1°C/34°F

There are many species of agave, but only a few are suitable as houseplants, since most eventually grow too large. They form rosettes of long, sword-shaped leaves with toothed edges and are very attractive. Perhaps the best known is A. americana, the century plant. This common name was applied in the erroneous belief that the plant took a century to flower. In fact, it will flower under suitable conditions in from 20 to 25 years.

This species makes an impressive houseplant in its young stages, but in large specimens the leaves may reach over 90cm (3ft) long. There are a number of forms with variegated foliage, having a yellow stripe down the leaf centre or along the edges. These are especially attractive.

Suitable for most ordinary small rooms are A. filifera, the thread agave, and A. victoriae-reginae. The former has spiky rosettes of leaves somewhat curved upwards and bordered with thread-like filaments, suggesting its common name, and longitudinal pale stripes. The latter has a more clump-like leaf formation and dark green colour. Each leaf, stiffly erect, is topped with a brown to blackish spine, and is marked with fine, whitish lines.

Most agaves produce offsets, and these can be removed carefully and separately potted to produce new plants. They like a sunny position and will enjoy standing out in the open air during summer.

Ordinary potting composts suit agaves well, since most enjoy a fairly rich rooting medium, but make sure the pots or containers are well drained. Large specimens of A. americana have been used with good effect in spacious but well-lit foyers of offices and public buildings.

Aeonium arboreum.

Agave filifera.

AGLAONEMA
** 10°C/50°F

Several aglaonemas have attractively variegated spear-shaped foliage and make neat, compact houseplants for warm rooms. They will survive at the recommended minimum temperature, but grow more vigorously if kept a few degrees higher, and produce arum-like flowers. However, the flowers (spathes) are not particularly showy.

Aglaonemas grow especially well in peat-based potting composts, which should be kept moist. A 13 cm (5 in) pot is adequate, and their general preferences are warmth, shade and good humidity, rather like calathea and maranta, with which they can be grouped to make pleasing foliage combinations.

Most popular is *A. commutatum*, which has yellow-banded foliage. *A. crispum* 'Silver Queen' and *A. commutatum* 'Treubii' have bold, silvery variegation. The spathes of both *A. commutatum* and *A. c.* 'Treubii' are often followed by red berries, which gives them an added attraction.

From Malaya and Borneo comes *A. oblongifolium*, which is notable for its size if given freedom of growth in an ideal environment. In its native habitat it forms a trunk and the leaves exceed 45 cm (1½ft) in length. However, grown in a pot it never reaches such a size.

The plants are best propagated by taking suckers or rooted basal shoots in May and setting them in a similar potting compost. These should be kept covered and warm (a polythene bag can be used to enclose the pot) at a temperature of about 21°C (70°F) until they begin making active growth, which is a sign new roots are forming.

A chill will cause leaf deterioration. Otherwise, the plants have few troubles. If winter temperatures tend to be low, keep the compost only slightly moist.

Aphelandra squarrosa.

56

ALOE
see page 165

ANANAS
see page 152

ANTHURIUM
*** 10–16°C/50–61°F

These plants are usually easily identified by their strange flowers, and are most often sold bearing them. The 'flowers' are eye-catching and consist of a very showy and brightly-coloured heart-shaped fleshy and glossy spathe, from the centre of which arises a cylindrical spadix bearing the tiny true flowers. The entire structure is borne on a long, strong stem arising from a cluster of handsome foliage.

Their essential requirement is warmth, coupled with good humidity, and the lack of this is the reason why they tend to fail after a time in many homes.

This plant was grown extensively in Victorian conservatories, and in the high temperatures they maintained reached a considerable size. Gardening books of those days recommend potting-on into very large pots, and describe really massive plants measuring at least 1.2m (4ft) across.

Probably the easiest species is *A. scherzerianum*, from Costa Rica. This plant is happy with a minimum temperature of 10°C (50°F), although a little higher is preferable. It is a beautiful plant of neat habit, with elongated arrow-shaped leaves. The common name of flamingo flower presumably refers to the brilliant red, waxy-textured spathe, with yellow spadix, usually curled.

A number of cultivars with spathes in white or shades of pink, sometimes flecked or spotted, are also available. The flowers are produced over a long period, from spring to autumn.

A. andreanum, which has several common names, such as painter's palette, wax flower, and oil-cloth flower, is from Colombia and needs a temperature a few degrees higher. It has large, dark green heart-shaped foliage. The flowers are similar in structure, but the waxy-textured spathes can be bright red or white and the spadix is stiff and erect, reaching about 6.5cm (2½in) in length.

A. crystallinum is different, in that the spathes are of no great significance. It is grown for its delightful foliage. It bears large, pointed, heart-shaped leaves of dark green and velvety texture, purplish when young. These are contrastingly veined in cream, the colour being pinkish below, and with a crystalline texture.

This species is the most difficult to keep in good condition. It, too, is from Colombia and should preferably be given a temperature a few degrees higher than the absolute minimum, otherwise the foliage deteriorates and tends to go dry and brown around the edges.

A special potting compost is required for anthuriums. It must be fibrous and open. Use a mixture of fibrous peat, sphagnum moss, crushed charcoal, and a little John Innes potting compost No. 2. When potting, place a generous layer of broken clay pots or clean pebbles at the bottom of the pot to ensure good drainage. Do not set the plants too deep in the compost. Deep planting may lead to basal rot. Usually, 13–18cm (5–7in) pots are suitable. Anthuriums are not suitable for positions that are draughty or for where temperatures change widely or rapidly. They like slight shade, but *A. crystallinum* is suitable for quite dull places. Every attempt must be made to maintain a good humidity level, and the plants like to be in groups, with other houseplants, where the humidity is usually higher. Often, roots may appear around the bases of the plants, and these should be well covered with potting compost.

In summer, spray the plants with clean rainwater, whenever possible, and keep the compost moist at all times. However, water more cautiously in winter.

Propagate by division of the roots in March. Various aphids are the most likely pests, and low temperatures and humidity the usual cause of general deterioration.

APHELANDRA SQUARROSA
(zebra plant)
* 10°C/50°F

The cultivar usually favoured as a houseplant is *A.s.* 'Louisae', which has pointed, glossy green foliage, with strikingly contrasting pale cream veining, which has obviously given rise to the common name of zebra plant. As well as delightful foliage, strange, angular and bold yellow flowers are usually freely formed, lasting for several weeks. They are borne erect and appear from summer to autumn.

This plant is interesting, in that although a native of Brazil it will survive remarkably low temperatures. If the temperature falls to almost freezing during winter for a time it will drop leaves and look most sickly, but with the return of warmer conditions will usually send up new growth and eventually flourish again. However, for best results the recommended minimum winter temperature should be the rule. If you wish to try the plant at lower temperatures, remember to keep the roots dry during winter. In summer, water freely and give only enough shade to protect from direct sunlight.

A 13cm (5in) pot is large enough for most specimens, but repotting or potting-on for well-established plants can be done in early spring. After flowering, the stems that carried the blooms are best cut back to a pair of good quality leaves. This will induce new shoots to appear from below and these can be used as cuttings for propagation. Cuttings need a congenial warmth of at least 24°C (75°F) to root quickly.

In warm moist conditions aphelandras can grow to about 60cm (2ft) in height and branch out vigorously. This often happens where there is continuous central heating, such as in offices and public buildings.

Aphids can sometimes attack, but are easily wiped off the foliage with damp cotton-wool.

Aglaonema crispum 'Silver Queen' (left) and *Anthurium scherzerianum* (right).

57

ARAUCARIA HETEROPHYLLA
(syn. A. excelsa)
(Norfolk Island pine)
* 5°C/41°F

When young, this is a popular plant, but be warned that it can eventually reach about 2.1m (7ft) in height. It has a very easily recognized pine-tree appearance, and large specimens can be placed outdoors for the summer if the space indoors is required for other plants. Because it does not demand much winter warmth, it is useful for cool rooms, and in particular hallways or porches, especially in the case of larger plants which can look impressive.

Young plants can be potted in 15cm (6in) pots initially, but will need moving to at least 25cm (10in) pots if they are to be kept when large plants. Growth is quite slow, and potting-on will not need to be done frequently. It is best to retain the pots as long as possible, top-dressing or giving liquid feeds rather than disturbing the roots unnecessarily.

Slight shade or good light, but not direct sunlight behind glass, is tolerated. When standing plants outdoors during summer, choose a slightly shaded spot, protected from wind.

The most common trouble is needles falling. This is usually due to the air being too dry, and most often occurs in centrally-heated homes and where arrangements for adequate humidity are unsatisfactory.

ARECA
see page 137

ASPARAGUS
* 5°C/41°F

Several species and forms of this genus, frequently wrongly described as ferns, are extremely popular houseplants prized for their dainty and graceful needle-like foliage. However, they are in no way related to true ferns. The trailing kinds are very useful for hanging-baskets, where they can be mixed with flowers to create a beautiful effect.

The foliage is excellent for cutting and putting with flower arrangements and table decorations utilizing flowers like carnations and sweet peas.

The plants like a position in good light, but not direct sunlight. They can be watered freely in summer, but should be kept only slightly moist in winter.

A great favourite is A. densiflorus 'Sprengeri' (syn. A. sprengeri), reaching at least 90cm (3ft). It is especially employed in hanging containers. A dwarf cultivar, 'Compactus', is more erect and less trailing and better as a pot plant.

Very erect and bushy, and only suited to pots, is A. densiflorus 'Meyeri' (syn. A. meyeri). The seeds have recently been introduced by most seed firms and it is easy to grow from a spring sowing. It is slow growing and it takes about two years for plants to reach a useful size. Both these species may produce red berries after small whitish flowers that

have no special decorative merit. *A. setaceus* (syn. *A. plumosus*) is rather different in appearance, having much smaller needles and a habit very like the growth shape of the cedar of Lebanon tree. This species also has a cultivar named 'Compactus' that is the best for pots. The original form may be neat and erect in the early stages, but shoots out to give long trailing stems when mature. It is then suitable for baskets and hanging containers. This species may have black berries.

In the dry air of the home, check that red spider mites are not present – they cause yellowing. Scale insects may cause a black, sticky fungus to appear on the stems and needles.

ASPIDISTRA ELATIOR
(cast iron plant, parlour palm)
* 5°C/41°F

The aspidistra has been the most publicized of all houseplants, being the subject of a popular song. Unfortunately, it is also often regarded as an old-fashioned plant, since it was a favourite of the Victorian era and subsequently was commonly seen covered with dust and cobwebs in fusty boarding houses.

The plant is remarkable for its ability to withstand neglect and air contaminated with smoke, paraffin or gas fire fumes.

Extreme left: A grouping of three *Araucaria heterophylla* seedlings. Older plants have branches in tiers.
Below: *Asparagus setaceus.*

This does, of course, encourage people to forget to give it the attention it requires. However, properly looked after the aspidistra is quite handsome and can rival the beauty of many more modern houseplant introductions, and certainly outlive them. Its bold, broad spear-shaped foliage also looks well in houseplant groups. The leaves respond well to treatment with a proprietary leafshine preparation. They then acquire a brilliant gloss which is retained for a long time.

There is a particularly attractive cultivar, *A.e.* 'Variegata', which has cream to whitish banding or striping on the leaves, but unfortunately this plant is not so resistant to neglect.

To develop fine foliage, a good potting compost must be given and the plants well watered and fed in summer. A position of slight shade is best. In winter,

keep on the dry side, but continue to wipe the foliage with wet cotton-wool from time to time to keep it free from dust. Repotting or division of the roots for propagation can be done in spring. Star-shaped dark purple flowers are formed almost at compost level, but are of no decorative merit.

In the dry air of the home, red spider mite can cause yellowing of the foliage. The undersurfaces of the leaves should be sprayed or wiped frequently with wet cotton-wool in summer, when this pest will be most active.

Aspidistra scale is another possible pest, which can be seen as small brownish scales on stems and foliage. These can usually be wiped off by hand. Neglected plants may show browning of the leaf edges and tips, and this may also occur where the plants are frequently brushed against in passing.

Aspidistra elatior.

ASPLENIUM
see page 139

AZALEA
** see text for temperature

Azaleas are very popular gift plants sold by florists, just as they are coming into flower. It is wise to buy them just as the buds are beginning to show colour. However, there are two types, needing quite different treatment. The one usually seen at Christmas is the Indian azalea, *Rhododendron simsii*, which is tender and forced into bloom for the Christmas trade. From late winter to spring, the hardy Japanese azaleas – the Kurume hybrids which are rhododendron hybrids – are sold. These may also have been gently forced. Both of these azaleas form neat, low-growing shrubby plants and bear masses of glorious flower in rich colours, forming very impressive displays in the home.

Indian azaleas are difficult to cultivate in normal home conditions. After purchase, place the plant where it is cool and there are no draughts, but not cold. About 10°C (50°F) is ideal. Keep the roots nicely moist. Wide changes of any kind can cause the flowers to drop. In summer, put the plant outdoors where it's shady, and continue to keep the roots moist. In autumn, the plant can be brought into a cool room with a minimum of 7°C (45°F). It is not easy to provide the warmth and humidity achieved by nurseries when forcing these plants, so flowering may be much later than Christmas.

The Japanese azalea is much easier to grow, but they really need to spend most of their life outdoors in the garden, or on a patio or balcony. The plants are best brought into the home when just coming into bud, and put into a cool, airy room out of direct sunlight. At all times, shade should be provided, or an outside position chosen on the north side of the house.

When potting or repotting, remember to use an acid potting compost. The plants dislike alkaline or limy composts, and also hard tap-water. This invariably leads to yellowing of the foliage, poor growth, and eventually failure.

Use clean rainwater for watering. Often, erratic watering can result in leaf and bud drop. This may not occur until some time after the period of maltreatment. Whitefly is the most common insect pest.

BEGONIA
/ 5–10°C/41–50°F

This is an important family for house-plants; there are numerous very beautiful species for flowers and foliage. They have widespread origins throughout the sub-tropics and tropics.

The tuberous begonias make splendid pot plants for the summer and autumn months, bearing large, showy flowers and handsome foliage. There are also types with smaller and more pendent or tassel-like flowers, which are excellent for hanging pots or baskets. All these tuberous kinds have been derived from several species and were introduced by James Veitch and Sons from 1865 to 1868, but have now been greatly developed.

Named cultivars of giant double-flowered begonias can be bought from specialists, but are expensive and better suited for exhibitions or for growing in greenhouses or conservatories. For the home, it is better to buy tubers offered by well-known nurserymen. Start the tubers into growth from February onwards, by immersing them in a pan of moist peat placed on a warm window-sill. As soon as the shoots appear, pot them into any good potting compost,

Left to right: Azaleas ('Rosa Bella', pink; 'Ambrosius', pinkish-red; 'Euratom', brick red). *Begonia* 'Anita' and *Begonia rex*.

setting one tuber to each pot.

Large-flowered begonias need at least 13cm (5in) pots. The same applies to multi-flowered sorts that produce a large number of smaller blooms. The pendulous kinds are best grouped three or more in larger pots or baskets and planted near the edge, so that the stems can hang over. Set them so that the top of the tuber is level with the compost's surface. If there is any doubt, the concave side of the tuber should face upwards.

The large-flowered begonias will need a cane for support as they grow, and it is best to remove the female flower buds – which have winged seed capsules attached – as soon as they can be picked off without damage. This allows the large, showy male flowers to develop fully. Keep the plants in good light, but not in a window receiving direct sunlight, which will scorch the foliage and bleach the blooms. At the end of the year, reduce the amount of water given and let the soil become dry. Place the dry pots in a frost-free place or remove the tubers and store them in clean, dry sand during winter. The tubers can then be repotted when it is time to start them into growth. The evergreen begonias, which have fibrous or rhizome-like roots, are prized for their very beautiful foliage which has attractive flowers too, but these generally take second place. A species that deserves to be grown more extensively is *B. corallina*, together with its hybrids such as 'Lucerna'. This has impressive silver-spotted foliage, purple-red below, and bears enormous clusters of glorious pink flowers from summer to autumn. If allowed, the plant will reach more than 90cm (3ft) in height, but small plants also flower well. It will survive very cool rooms in winter, but may then deteriorate. New growth quickly resumes in spring.

A great favourite is *B. rex* with arrow-shaped foliage of various tints marked with silver. It makes a neat pot plant. There are numerous named hybrids with different colouring. Similar in habit and very striking is *B. masoniana*, popularly called the iron-cross begonia because of a very bold chocolate-brown marking on each leaf. Also popular are *B. metallica*, so-called because of the metallic sheen of its leaves, which have purplish veins too, and *B. boweri*. The latter has the common name eyelash begonia, since its leaves have a border of long lash-like hairs and are prettily coloured with brownish streaks. It bears pinkish flowers in spring. *B. manicata* shows its pink flowers during winter and again has charming foliage having red hairs below and a reddish border. *B. coccinea* is similar to *B. corallina* and is

usually seen as the hybrid 'President Carnot'. *B. scharffii* (syn. *B. laageana*), elephant's ear, has dark green hairy leaves tinted red below, and attractive pale pink flowers.

Fibrous-rooted cultivars of *B. semperflorens* and various hybrids, extensively used for garden bedding, make splendid houseplants. Sometimes, they can be lifted and potted in autumn, but it is better to start from seed sown in early summer. Given a bright window-sill, the plants will often flower during winter. Their foliage is pleasing, being glossy and often having dark, bronzy or reddish tints, against which the flowers show up particularly well. The habit is very neat and compact, and 10cm (4in) pots are adequate. Some recommended cultivars are 'Muse Rose' (large-flowered), 'Colour Queen' (with cream-variegated foliage), and 'Devon Gems' (mixed coloured foliage), easy vigorous growth, and very free-flowering.

The Elatior hybrids produce small clusters of long-lasting flowers, and these make very good houseplants. 'Elfe' is a delicate pink with deeper shading, 'Nixie' a deep red. 'Ballerina' has slightly larger flowers of a lovely orange, while 'Balalaika' is an attractive yellow.

Quite new is 'Emerald Isle', a houseplant to grow from seed on a window-sill. It forms a neat group of shiny, oval leaves with pointed tips borne on short, strong stems, and has pale pink flowers.

All the foliage begonias do best in winter if the temperature is not allowed to fall below about 10°C (50°F), as then they are liable to lose their foliage, or it may turn brownish. In summer, watering can be generous and spraying the foliage with a mist of water from time to time will encourage new growth. Any repotting or division of roots for propagation should be done in spring.

Many of the foliage begonias can be propagated from leaf cuttings. Although most of the types used as houseplants will tolerate fair shade, they usually only develop the best leaf colours in good light. However, this does not mean exposure to direct sunlight, which could scorch and bleach the leaves.

Fibrous begonias of the *B. semperflorens* type are exceptions in that they will often withstand even direct sunlight on a window-sill. These certainly need all the winter sun they can get to encourage winter flowers and good foliage colour.

Generally, begonias are remarkably free from pest or disease troubles. Yellowing of foliage is generally due to overwatering or letting the plants go dry. Low temperatures will cause this too, as well as leaf drop.

BELOPERONE GUTTATA
(shrimp plant)
* 7°C/45°F

This plant has suffered from several name changes and is occasionally known as *Drejerea* or *Justicia brandegeana*. The common name is derived from the appearance of the pinkish bracts surrounding the inconspicuous flowers. These form pendent spikes of shrimp-like appearance, usually borne freely from spring to mid-winter. A well-grown plant, which may reach about 60cm (2ft) in height, bearing a profusion of bracts, is most eye-catching. However, it is not unusual for plants kept in the home to deteriorate in winter, especially if they have been grown for some years and are getting old. Such plants are best cut back in late winter to early spring. They will send up new growth to form handsome specimens. Most plants bought from florists are young and recently raised from cuttings.

In winter and up until spring, only sufficient water should be given to prevent the roots drying out completely, then water can be applied freely. There is some difference of opinion about the light requirements of beloperone, most horticulturists suggesting shade. In fact, it is a good idea to stand the plants outdoors in full sunshine during summer, making sure, of course, that watering is not neglected.

In general, February to March is the best time to do any pruning or trimming to keep plants shapely and neat. Any straggly weak shoots should be removed entirely.

Beloperone has no special problems, but neglect of pruning and trimming may lead to spindly, untidy growth.

Beloperone guttata.

Browallia speciosa.

BILLBERGIA
see page 153

BOUGAINVILLEA
see page 176

BRASSIA
see page 175

BROWALLIA
* 13°C/55°F, see text

B. speciosa, from Colombia, is a valuable winter-flowering pot plant. Plants are usually available from florists, but it is easy to grow your own from seed sown in a pot and placed near an ordinary window-sill. The older hybrids are usually tall, reaching about 60–90cm (2–3ft) by winter. The flowers, rather campanula-shaped but more starry, are various shades of beautiful blue. Flowering can be expected to continue all winter.

Recently, an excellent new dwarf form has been introduced called 'Blue Troll'. This is very compact and bushy, growing only 15cm (6in) or less in height. It is best if several seedlings are planted in each pot as these will then form clumps smothered with flowers. The colour is a rich, vivid purple-blue, with a small, central black-and-white eye effect. It is a great improvement on the older forms and should prove extremely popular.

Seed can be sown in spring and the seedlings potted, using any of the usual branded potting composts. Keep the plants free from chill, if the sowing is early, and protect from direct sunlight. Although this species is perennial, old plants usually become straggly and, in the old forms, too tall.

Seedlings of the non-dwarf types are best stopped at an early stage to promote bushiness. If plants are saved, these should be cut back in spring to encourage new growth from the base.

A little-known charming easy species you can also grow from seed on a window-sill is *B. viscosa*. This is a summer-flowering annual with white-eyed pretty blue flowers. It is quite neat in habit, reaching about 30cm (1ft) in height. Discard after flowering. Browallias rarely have pest or disease troubles. In fact, these are very resilient plants and thrive exceedingly well in the home as well as a conservatory.

BRYOPHYLLUM
see Kalanchoe

CALADIUM *(angel's wings)*
*** 15°C/59°F

The huge, beautifully-veined and coloured arrow-shaped foliage of caladiums means that they are often displayed in the windows of florists, but they are not easy houseplants to save from year to year. They may make delightful plants for late spring or early summer to early or late autumn, depending on the temperature.

Caladiums are native to tropical South America, and need warmth and good humidity to retain their good looks. They mostly take the form of named cultivars of *C. bicolor*, which is extremely variable, and there are consequently very many. Some may be natural varieties, and from seed it is possible to obtain a selection of colours often better than the parents.

Plants sold by florists are usually quite expensive, but it is not difficult to start far more cheaply from the tuberous rhizomes supplied by bulb merchants. These can be immersed in moist peat on a warm window-sill in spring and potted into 15cm (6in) pots as soon as they sprout. If kept in a warm room and moist, the arrow-shaped leaves will soon form. These may be a plain, uninteresting green at first, the later foliage should show the true veining and delightful colouring.

Often, small arum-like flowers are formed in summer, but these are of no decorative merit. Give only slight shading, but avoid direct sunlight which may scorch the leaves. High humidity is essential, and a misting with water will greatly accelerate growth.

In late autumn, when the foliage begins to deteriorate, gradually reduce watering. Eventually, remove faded foliage and keep the pots where they can be prevented from drying out completely during winter. The temperature should not be allowed to fall below 13°C (55°F). This is perhaps the most difficult aspect in saving the plants, and most people may prefer to regard them merely as summer to early autumn houseplants. However, caladiums are among the most impressive and beautiful of all foliage subjects and are well worth trying. They are most successful in centrally heated homes, where there is humidification to prevent the air becoming dry. Restart saved tubers in spring. Draughts, erratic temperatures, chills, and dryness or direct sunlight, can all cause leaves to turn brown and shrivel. Aphids may sometimes attack, otherwise caladiums have few pest or disease problems.

CALATHEA
** 10–13°C/50–55°F

Several species of calathea are very lovely foliage plants, and particularly good for shady places, but they do need moderate humidity and congenial warmth to retain their beautiful foliage and prevent deterioration. They are native to the West Indies and Tropical America, and closely related to marantas, some having been classified under this genus. However, calatheas are usually less tolerant of a cooler, drier environment, and the leaves, although of similar oval shape, are usually larger. The most delightful species is probably *C. makoyana* from Brazil, the peacock plant. It has a feathered pattern with a silvery background on the upper surface of the leaf and a suffusion of red below. Seen against the light, the effect is extremely colourful – hence the common name. This species needs a minimum temperature of 13°C (55°F).

Another favourite species for the home is *C. ornata*. The dark green leaves have pinkish veining which changes to cream as they mature.

C. lancifolia (syn. *C. insignis*), the rattlesnake plant, has more elongated and wavy leaves, maroon below and with light and dark green snakelike patterning above. *C. zebrina* also has longer narrower leaves, with purplish colour below. Its contrasting light and dark green banding gives rise to the common name zebra plant.

Calatheas grow well in any of the usual potting composts, in 10–18cm (4–7in) pots, provided they are never allowed to dry out and are fed when making active growth, as they tend to be greedy plants. Careful attention to humidity is essential. They do well in centrally-heated homes, provided this aspect of culture is not neglected. Too much strong light is liable to cause the foliage to bleach and lose good contrast in variegation.

They do particularly well in groups of houseplants, which helps to maintain a humid micro-climate. Chills and draughts soon causes leaf browning. Aphids may attack and in dry conditions so may red spider mites.

Caladium bicolor cultivars.

Calathea lancifolia.

CALCEOLARIA *(slipper flower)*
* 2–5°C/36–41°F

These very showy plants, mostly of Mexican or South American origin, bear masses of pouch-like flowers chiefly in shades of yellow and red, and are often exotically spotted and blotched in contrasting colour. They come into florists' shops from just before Christmas until spring, and are popular gifts.

They are biennials, mostly grown from F$_1$ hybrid seed, and should be discarded after flowering. Those sold by florists are usually dwarf and compact forms, but there are very impressive taller giant-flowered hybrids of *C. × herbeohybrida* which are not so transportable without damage. They are easily grown from seed in a frost-free greenhouse or frame.

It is, of course, best to buy plants when they are just in bud and showing colour. They will then last in bloom for several weeks if kept cool, moist and shaded. Warmth and direct sunshine rapidly causes wilting. If this happens, do not apply more water unless the compost is dry. Saturating with water may instigate root or basal stem-rot. Wilted plants should be put in the shade and kept cool. They should then recover by morning.

Aphids are fond of calceolarias and plants should be carefully inspected for their presence before buying. Spraying as a preventive measure is best done early, when the plants are in bud. Spraying the flowers, even with water, is liable to cause brown spots or patches.

CAMPANULA ISOPHYLLA
(Italian bellflower, star of Italy)
* 2°C/36°F

There are about 300 campanula species, but this is the only one popular as a houseplant, although it is certainly a very old favourite. In mild areas, it may be hardy outdoors, so is a good choice for cold rooms, hallways and porches.

It is a trailing plant, and suitable for hanging-pots or baskets, or pots raised to give room for the stems to cascade over. The foliage is small and dainty and the plants become smothered with lovely starry flowers from summer to autumn. There is a blue form, which is most favoured, and a white one. The form named 'Mayii' with variegated foliage is rather more hairy than normal. Very

often, plants will sport to form shoots with cream-variegated foliage. These can be cut off and rooted to form new plants with an entirely variegated appearance. However, these sports are sometimes less vigorous, slower growing, and have smaller flowers.

Campanula isophylla should be given an airy, bright position, watered freely in summer but sparingly in winter. The stems are brittle and care should be taken in moving plants, since large pieces can easily be broken off. To extend the flowering time to the maximum, try to remove flowers as they pass over so that the buds still to open do not become covered with decaying remains.

Plants are easily propagated by division when new growth begins, or from cuttings.

Campanula isophylla 'Alba'.

Campanula isophylla.

Calceolarias

CAPSICUM ANNUUM
(winter pepper)
* 7°C/45°F

This is a neat, bushy pot plant notable for its bright red berries. In modern cultivars, these are often formed as early as late July, so that the old name winter pepper now hardly applies. However, it is possible for plants to retain their fruits all through Christmas and well into the New Year.

The species is notoriously variable and there are forms with fruits of many different sizes and shapes. The berry is usually more elongated and chilli-like than in solanum, and although it may often be hot and peppery to the taste, it is not poisonous as in the case of solanum. The berries of ornamental peppers are not as well flavoured as the culinary type. There are numerous named cultivars from which to choose, but plants bought from florists are rarely named. When buying it is wise to choose plants with berries only just forming or in a green to cream stage. In most cases, there is a transition of colour, from green through cream to orange and finally red, as the berries mature and ripen. This is one of their attractive qualities.

A cultivar called 'Red Fangs' has elongated berries, often slightly curled, which are borne in great profusion. There is 'Variegated Flash' and similar cultivars with variegated foliage blotched with cream and purple. This cultivar is unusual in having very dark purple berries.

The plants like a bright, airy position where it is cool but not chilly. In excessive warmth and where temperatures change rapidly, the foliage may turn yellow and fall. The same occurs if they are overwatered, and therefore the compost should be kept just moist. Eventually, there will be deterioration and shrivelling of both leaves and berries. The plant should then be discarded since, unlike solanum, they are annuals and cannot be grown for another year. Capsicums are easier to grow from seed than solanums, and set berries much more readily. Good plants can often be obtained from window-sill sowings, but do not attempt to save seed. Buy seed of named cultivars or hybrids from seedsmen. Saved seed will rarely give plants true to type, although there may be some in a batch. Usually, it is best to start with fresh seed.

Capsicums generally are easy and relatively trouble-free, and they deserve greater popularity. The most likely pest is aphids.

CARYOTA
see page 136

CATHARANTHUS ROSEUS
(syn. Vinca rosea)
* 13°C/55°F

This tropical periwinkle is very easy to grow as an annual from seed sown in late winter to early spring under window-sill conditions. A temperature of about 18°C (65°F) is needed for germination. If the seedlings are potted into 13cm (5in) pots, neat and bushy plants giving a profusion of typical periwinkle flowers can be obtained by summer, and they will continue well into winter if the recommended minimum temperature is maintained. The foliage is glossy and dark green, and the flowers may be pink, carmine or white, usually with a contrasting eye.

Young plants are sold from late spring to early summer. Provided the minimum winter temperature is maintained, the plants are evergreen and can be saved. In spring, they can be pruned back to keep them neat.

A recently introduced new strain is 'Little Gem'. This has a variety of flower colours and is exceptionally vigorous. It grows to 30cm (1ft) in height. This species likes moderate humidity, moist conditions, and slight shade in summer. It grows especially well in peat-based potting composts.

Plants with particularly good flower colours can be propagated from cuttings taken in spring. Chill, neglect in watering, and an excessively dry atmosphere, may cause leaves to turn brown at the edges or curl. Troubles from pests or diseases are very rare indeed, and the plant should present few problems.

CATTLEYA
see page 174

Capsicum annuum.

Catharanthus roseus.

CEPHALOCEREUS SENILIS
(old man cactus)
** 7°C/45°F

There is some difference of opinion about the ease with which this very unusual-looking cactus can be grown. In some homes it will flourish and in others it tends to deteriorate. It is certainly unlikely to flower well in room conditions, if at all, but the dense covering of long, whitish, silky hairs means that it is always attractive.

Specimens that have reached a fair height are striking. In their native habitat of Mexico they can reach a very great height, but in the home they are slow-growing. This species does need rather more warmth than most houseplant cacti, and the minimum temperature that is recommended should be maintained.

It prefers a slightly alkaline compost, and some powdered chalk or limestone can be incorporated. Centrally-heated homes usually give good growing conditions, provided rooms are airy and a bright position is selected for the plants. In winter, water very sparingly and at no time allow moisture to fall on the silky hairs. Repotting or potting-on should be done in spring, when the plants are growing strongly.

A problem with this plant is that the hairs may trap dust and this is extremely difficult to remove. It should not be positioned in rooms such as bedrooms where the air tends to become contaminated with fibres.

Some people can successfully obtain excellent plants from window-sill sowings of the seed in spring. Plants started in the environment in which they are to remain often do better than bought specimens that have to undergo a drastic change.

CEROPEGIA WOODII
* 10°C/50°F

A number of descriptive common names have been inspired by the charming appearance of this delightful succulent. For example, string of hearts, heart vine, and rosary vine suggest the shape and the way the leaves are spaced on the stems. It is also called Chinese lantern plant because of the form of the small but quaint flowers.

The dainty leaves are heart-shaped and unusually well spaced on the thread-like stems. They are prettily marbled with silvery markings and purplish below, and the small pitcher-shaped flowers are reddish-brown. This species is nearly always grown as a trailer in hanging

pots or baskets, but it can also be grown trained up a plastic trellis of the type now sold for insertion into flower pots.

The plant forms a large tuber, and the stems often form tiny tubers at their ends. These can be detached and planted for propagation if a segment of stem is removed with them. This species will be happy with less light than most succulents, but too much continuous gloom should be avoided.

The compost must be well drained and the pots need free drainage. In winter, watering must be cautious, as the tubers are liable to rot. In summer, water can be given freely, but constantly saturated compost must not be allowed. The plant is a native of Natal, and the recommended minimum temperature should be observed.

Troubles are rare. Yellowing of the leaves may indicate rotting of the tuber due to overwatering or low temperatures maintained for too long. In such cases, there is little hope of recovery.

CHAMAECEREUS SILVESTRII
(peanut cactus)
* 2°C/36°F

As a houseplant, this cactus almost ranks with the aspidistra in its resistance to ill-treatment and neglect, and even survives temperatures down to near freezing – if not below – for brief periods. It can exist for a long time without water, to the stage of becoming sick-looking and shrivelled, and then make a remarkable recovery when moisture is available. It is best grown in fair-sized shallow pots where, with reasonable care, it will quickly spread to give complete coverage and form a clump of prickly, cylindrical branches.

This Argentinian species, the only one of the genus, is outstanding for its lovely showy flowers, borne for at least two weeks. They are starry in shape and bright red, and well-grown plants become smothered with them. It is certainly a cactus to show those people who seem to think cacti are dull and uninteresting, or rarely flower. Give the plant a bright position such as a sunny window-sill and water reasonably freely while growing during summer.

In winter, hardly any water should be given. If the compost is kept too moist, flowering may not be so generous. The same may apply in shady conditions.

Left: *Cephalocereus senilis.*
Left, below: *Ceropegia woodii.*
Right, above: *Chamaecereus silvestrii.*
Below: *Chlorophytum capense.*

Propagation can be easily carried out by carefully pulling away one of the young branches and potting during summer. Roots soon form.

CHAMAEDOREA
see page 134

CHAMAEROPS
see page 137

CHIONODOXA
see page 145

CHLOROPHYTUM CAPENSE
(spider plant, St Bernard's lily)
* 7°C/45°F

There is considerable botanical disagreement about the naming in this genus – the South African species described here is also called *C. elatum* and *C. comosum*. There are forms with different leaf variegation, and there is some argument as to whether these are natural varieties or distinct species. However, this need not be a cause for concern, for all these forms are popular and make decorative houseplants.

The foliage is long, narrow, arching and rush-like. There are mainly two different types of variegation. There may be a creamy-white band down the leaf centre, or the leaf may be margined, the centre being green. There are also forms with irregular stripings, and all are attractive.

During summer, long stems arise from the leafy clumps and bear small, white, starry flowers. These stems can reach 75cm (2½ft) long, and among the flowers small plantlets – exact miniatures of the mother plant – are formed. These ultimately weigh down the stems to give a spidery effect, hence the common name. In nature, these plantlets root when they touch the soil. For propagation, they can be pegged into the surface of compost in separate pots – using wire loops – until they have rooted.

The little plants can be severed from the main stem. In conditions of good humidity, the plantlets may form roots while still on the stems. They can then be removed and potted, without the necessity of pegging down.

Because of the ease of propagation, this plant is frequently passed from friend to friend. The plants can be effectively displayed in hanging pots or baskets, or in pots raised on pedestals. These plants are also useful on shelves of room dividers – anywhere, in fact, where the plant's stems can hang freely.

A position in good light and out of direct sunlight should be chosen. In winter, only water to prevent complete drying out of the roots, the minimum temperature should, preferably, be maintained to keep the foliage in first-class condition. Chills and draughts may cause yellowing or browning of the leaf tips. Browning may also occur through inadequate feeding.

Pot or repot in spring. Usually, 13–18cm (5–7in) containers are suitable. Pest or disease troubles are uncommon. If the plants become too large, it is possible to divide them by cutting through the clump with a very sharp knife. This is best done in spring when the plants make new growth.

CHRYSALIDOCARPUS
see page 137

CHRYSANTHEMUM
* 2°C/36°F

Chrysanthemums are usually received as gifts. The glorious blooms last for a number of weeks, especially if the plants are in the early stages of bud development when bought. However, they are quite impossible to keep as houseplants from year to year. It is far better to throw away a plant that has stopped flowering, and to buy another – they are still excellent value.

The plants have been specially treated with dwarfing chemicals and given artificial light or darkness to control daylength, to encourage out-of-season flowering. If the plants are saved and grown on they will usually grow to a height quite unsuitable for a houseplant, and flower at a different time – usually after a long period of readjustment to natural daylength.

CINERARIA
see Senecio

CISSUS
*/** see text for temperature

There are two species of cissus sold as houseplants. They are quite different in appearance and requirement. The very easy and popular species is *C. antarctica*, an Australian climber commonly called kangaroo vine. Its foliage is oval and pointed, with toothed margins. It grows vigorously, requiring a minimum winter temperature of 7°C (45°F). It is very useful for decorating the sides of picture-windows, patio doors and stair-wells, where a plant providing pleasant greenery to a fair height is required.

It can grow to over 2m (7ft) if potted in 20cm (8in) pots, but kept shorter and compact by pruning and cutting back as necessary. For large specimens, the plant is usually best trained up canes. Water the plant freely in summer, but only sufficiently to keep the roots slightly moist in winter. Possible pests include aphids, whitefly, and red spider mite.

The other species of importance as a houseplant is *C. discolor*, the begonia vine. However, it demands a minimum temperature of 16°C (61°F) if it is to retain its outstandingly beautiful foliage in winter. The leaves are remarkably like those of the foliage begonias, and have shades of green with silvery markings and a variety of colours such as red, purple, pink, cream and white, depending on the age of the leaf and intensity of light. It is classed as a climber, although nearly always it is better grown as a trailer in a hanging-basket.

Given enough warmth, coupled with humidity, it will trail down for a considerable distance.

It is native to the East Indies, and if conditions are too cool it will lose its foliage in winter. If then kept dry, it may recover with the return of warmer, spring conditions. In summer, it can be watered freely.

Both the cissus species described here will shed their leaves if the air becomes too dry, but in the case of *C. discolor* it is usually quite difficult to avoid losing foliage during the winter. Even in centrally-heated homes, with humidification, there may well be deterioration. However, it is such a beautiful subject that it is well worth growing.

A position in good light, but out of direct sunshine, develops the best leaf colours. The chief problem is inability to maintain adequate warmth and humidity, when deterioration and leaf shedding are inevitable.

CITRUS (orange, lemon, grapefruit)
** 7°C/45°F

It is a great temptation to grow citrus plants from pips obtained from commercial fruit. Pips usually germinate well in window-sill conditions, and it is possible to grow attractive young plants. However, these plants become far too large and it is a matter of chance whether they produce flowers or fruit.

Most of the fruit that comes on to the market is from grafted trees, or plants specially treated, and seed may not give identical results. Oranges are particularly unreliable, but lemon and grapefruit sometimes flower and bear fruit. For conservatories it is best to buy known species, such as *C. sinensis*, from a specialist nursery.

Undoubtedly, the finest species for the home is *C. microcarpa* (syn. *C. mitis*) from the Philippines. It is dwarf and neat, and bears flowers and fruit, often together and on the same plant, over a long period – usually when the plant is young. In good conditions, the plant may exceed 90cm (3ft) but it is easy to keep it small by pruning.

As with most citrus fruits, the starry waxy-white flowers are delightfully fragrant. These are followed by miniature fruits about the size of a walnut, green at first but soon turning to a rich orange colour. The fruit is edible, but sour. If there is a good crop, they can be preserved in syrup and used for desserts or cocktails.

Little success will be attained in centrally-heated homes. The plants like a cool atmosphere, not too dry. Hence, conservatory conditions are ideal. A cool and airy room, or sometimes a hallway or porch, provided the minimum temperature can be maintained, may be suitable places. Select a position with good light, but not direct sunshine as the foliage may be damaged.

When repotting or potting make sure an acid potting compost is used. This ensures a fine, healthy green leaf colour and vigorous growth. In alkaline conditions, yellowing is common. For the same reason, avoid watering with hard tapwater. If there is difficulty in this respect, collect clean rainwater.

If a plant shows a tendency to yellowing, water with a solution made by dissolving a saltspoonful (1ml) of aluminium sulphate (obtainable from a chemist or supplier of horticultural chemicals) in 500ml (1 pint) of water. This can be done from time to time during summer, when watering should be generous.

Keep the plants only slightly moist in winter. Treatment with one of the special sequestrinated trace-element preparations sold by garden shops may also be beneficial from time to time where the water tends to be limy.

Pruning or cutting back can be done during March, and all weak, straggly growth removed each year. The plant likes a spray with a mist of water, especially during the hottest time of the year. If there is too much chill in winter, the foliage may fall, but provided the temperature does not fall to near freezing for long, the plants usually make fresh growth in spring.

The most probable pests are aphids, mealy bugs and scale insects, which may cause the foliage to become covered with a sticky secretion on which a black fungus grows.

CLEISTOCACTUS STRAUSII
(silver torch cactus)
* 7°C/45°F

Of the several species in this genus, this is the favourite for window-sills. It is native to Bolivia and the common name originates from its appearance. It forms groups of long, slender stems, pale green in colour and covered with a greyish-white wool, and the red flowers are about 7.5cm (3in) long, tubular and flame-like.

This cactus is attractive at all times because of its white, woolly covering and neat habit. In well-grown specimens the stems can reach a considerable height. Provide a very bright position and keep almost dry in winter.

Cuttings of the stem tips will root if taken during late summer, but the cut surfaces should be allowed to dry before insertion in the rooting compost. It is rare for this cactus to have troubles.

Left to right: All-year-round chrysanthemums; *Cissus antarctica; Citrus microcarpa.*

Cleistocactus strausii.

69

CLIVIA MINIATA (Kaffir lily)
*** 2°C/36°F

For some unaccountable reason this plant is sometimes described as a bulb. In fact, it has very fleshy roots. Although native to Natal, it is almost hardy, but if exposed to frost will be caused immediate disaster. The leaves become soft and glassy, eventually rotting.

With only brief exposure to temperatures below freezing, the roots may survive, and new leaves will form during the following summer. It is, therefore, a good plant for quite chilly but frost-proof places around the home. In cold places in winter the roots should be kept almost dry – but not bone dry.

Well-grown plants produce handsome, arching strap-shaped foliage, but it is the extremely showy flowers that really catch the eye. These take the form of large umbels of bright orange-red, large trumpet-shaped blooms, borne on stout stems above the foliage. They appear in late spring under normal conditions, but will flower earlier with extra warmth.

For the plant to be at its best it is necessary to have large pots – a final 25cm (10in) pot, if possible. However, quite good flowers can be obtained with 18cm (7in) pots. The plants are best left with their roots undisturbed for as long as possible, potting being carried out early in the year for young plants.

Old plants will eventually have to be divided, as the roots will cram the pot. It is usually best to cut through the roots with a very sharp knife if it is difficult to separate them without causing bruising and damage. Divide the roots so that each segment has a clump of foliage, and repot in a pot that comfortably takes the roots. Water cautiously immediately after potting – wet conditions may cause roots to rot. The best time to divide the plants is in early summer, when they begin to make new foliage.

After flowering, cut away the flowers low down the stem. If left, large seed-capsules will form which turn red when ripe. This puts an unnecessary strain on the plant's resources.

The plants rarely have pest troubles, but red spider mites are a possibility, and so are mealy bugs. If exposed to excessive sunlight, the foliage may become scorched and developed brown patches.

COCOS
see page 137

CODIAEUM VARIEGATUM PICTUM
(croton, Joseph's coat)
**** 15°C/59°F

This species has a vast number of cultivars – many named – and is extremely varied in form. The leaves may be laurel-like in shape, spoon-shaped, branched, or thin and ribbon-like. In all cases, there is glorious colouring and, usually, contrasting veining. However, they are plants to select only for places which have constant, congenial warmth and reasonable humidity. Where it is cool and draughty – or the air is dry where there is central-heating without humidification – the leaves are most likely to fall. The plants are so lovely that this usually causes much disappointment.

The finest leaf colours develop in plants positioned in maximum light, but avoid direct sunlight. In such conditions, the foliage becomes suffused golden-yellow,

Left: Codiaeums; right, clivia; front, coleus.

with shades of red and salmon, and purplish tints, depending on the cultivar. The plants are highly sensitive to temperature and environmental changes, and are best bought during the warmer months of the year to avoid the chill of travelling.

The plants are best bought from a reliable source where they have been properly looked after. The reason for this is that ill-treatment may not show until some time afterwards. It may be a few weeks before the leaves start to fall. The minimum recommended temperature should be maintained but a few degrees higher is desirable. Changes in temperature must be avoided. The situation should be bright and draught-free.

Codiaeums often do well in centrally-heated buildings, where the heat is on all the time, and they like to be grouped with other warmth-loving plants to create a humid micro-climate.

In summer, spray the leaves with a mist of tepid water. In winter, water sparingly and never use extremely cold water. Leave a jug of water in the room to reach the minimum air temperature. Codiaeums rarely need pots larger than 18cm (7in), and in the home they seldom need pruning. However, if through accident the leaves do fall, the top stems can be cut back in spring to encourage new shoots to arise from the base. If this is not done, a straggly plant results.

Plants that have been cut back should be given as much warmth and humidity as possible, to promote rapid growth. If the cut stems exude a sticky, whitish latex, dust the surfaces with charcoal powder. A popular cultivar with boldly-veined multi-coloured laurel-like leaves is 'Reidii', and 'Carrierei' is also very colourful. 'Disraeli' has slender foliage, and 'Holuffiana' bears leaves with a 'forked' shape and striking cream veining. Two other cultivars likely to be encountered are 'Norma' and 'Bravo'. With 'Norma' the top and bottom leaves are deep green with red veins, while those in the centre are a more intense green and also have yellow blotches. 'Bravo' has markedly green leaves with yellow blotches, those at the base being edged with red.

Coffea arabica.

COELOGYNE
see page 175

COFFEA ARABICA *(coffee plant)*
** 13°C/55°F

Seed of this species is now commonly sold by seedsmen for home growing, but it needs a temperature of 26°C/79°F for germination. However, this can usually be done on a window-sill during summer. *Coffea arabica* is interesting because it is the plant from which coffee is obtained. It is native to the Ethiopian highlands and the name *arabica* probably arose because it was first extensively used as a beverage in Arabia.

As a houseplant it is mainly a curiosity. Its foliage is not outstanding, although attractively dark green and glossy, and in average room conditions it is hardly likely to produce its clusters of white, fragrant flowers which open for only 12 hours. The red berries contain the coffee beans of commerce.

Seedlings and young plants that come on to the market should be potted in small pots holding an acid compost, and the same compost can be used for subsequent potting. In a warm, humid greenhouse the plant may grow more vigorously.

It is often successful in centrally-heated homes, provided the air is not too dry. Give a position in good light, with slight shade during summer. Spraying the leaves with water from time to time during the summer will keep them shiny and encourage growth. The best cultivar for use as a houseplant is 'Nana', the dwarf coffee plant.

Given congenial warmth, the coffee plant rarely has any problems. Chill causes leaf yellowing and fall, and gradual general deterioration.

COLCHICUM
see page 145

COLEUS *(flame nettle)*
* 13°C/55°F

Coleus are remarkable in providing a treasure of exciting and multi-coloured varied leaf shapes very cheaply indeed. Although often named *C. blumei*, the history of this plant is so long and complicated – and has involved many natural varieties, cultivars and species – that few present-day coleus plants resemble the original.

A misnomer about this plant is the description 'nettle', as coleus belongs to the *Labiatae* and not to the family of nettles, which is *Urticaceae*.

Each year, seedsmen introduce new seed strains, and the plants are quite easy to grow from this source, although a greenhouse gives better results than a window-sill. Most of the plants bought are raised from seed, as this is more economical than starting from cuttings, which demand congenial winter warmth. However, if any special type or colour is required, only cuttings can be relied on to give an exact replica.

Most houseplant enthusiasts regard coleus as a spring to late-autumn plant. Sub-tropical and tropical species have been involved, and the plants need moderate warmth. Growing plants to form large specimens needs greenhouse conditions. As temporary houseplants, the various forms of coleus are easy to grow and only need to be given a position in good light and to be kept well watered and fed during their growing period. With good treatment, they often last well into winter in warm homes.

A final 13cm (5in) pot is usually adequate, but for conservatories, where forms such as 'Red Velvet' and 'Rainbow' reach 1.2m (4ft), larger pots will be necessary.

The colours of coleus are enormously varied and just about every shade imaginable can be seen. Leaf shape is varied and some forms have waved or frilled leaf-edges to enhance their beauty still further – such as the new cultivar 'Salmon Lace'.

During autumn, coleus form thin spikes of flowers which have no merit and spoil the appearance of the plant. Recently, there has been an attempt to produce cultivars with shorter spikes. In all cases, the spikes are best removed at an early stage.

The new cultivar 'Sabre' has an unusually dwarf and compact bushy habit, and the flowers are very much shorter and less freely produced. The leaves are narrow and sabre-like, and there are many lovely colour combinations.

Seed of selected strains exhibiting particular colour or leaf shapes can be purchased. Alternatively, colourful mixtures can be bought. When growing coleus from seed on window-sills, remember that the tiny seedlings look uninteresting at that stage and do not have their true colours. These develop later.

Coleus may be attacked by aphids and whitefly, but are not especially subject to pests. Erratic watering may cause the leaves to become limp and brown, or even to fall. Generally, they are easy plants to manage from spring to late autumn, and well worth growing afresh each year from seed.

COLUMNEA (goldfish plant)
** 13°C/55°F

Because of their showy winter flowers, two columneas are valuable plants for hanging containers in warm homes. In both cases, the flowers are 6.5cm (2½in) long, bright orange to red in colour with a yellow or orange throat. The tips are hooded and lobed, suggesting the fins of a goldfish and giving rise to the common name. The flowers are borne from October to April.

C. gloriosa, from Costa Rica, has trailing stems of pale green spear-shaped hairy leaves, borne in pairs, and tinted purple in the form 'Purpurea'. The flowers are very bright red with yellow throat markings. C. × banksii, a cross between C. oerstediana and C. schiedeana, is quite different in that the leaves are dark green and glossy – not hairy. The flowers have a reddish-orange colour, with pure orange throat markings. The flowers are often followed by pale violet berries. In favourable conditions, both these columneas trail to a length of 90cm (3ft) or more. There are other species that can at least double this, but they tend to be better suited to greenhouses and conservatories.

Columneas like a moisture-retentive compost that is well aerated. A wire or teak slatted basket is the best container. Use a peat-based compost mixed with about a third of its volume of sphagnum moss and a little crushed charcoal. Year-round humidity and a high temperature are required. Even in winter, the compost must be kept moist. Overhead spraying with clean rainwater is most beneficial, and encourages healthy growth. During summer slight shade should be given. Young plants can have the ends of the shoots removed to induce branching and to provide plenty of stems to trail over the edge of the container. A well-grown plant is beautiful when a cascade of flowers is produced.

The plants can be propagated from cuttings taken in spring, but they are not usually easy to root without greenhouse facilities. Established plants should have all straggly, weak shoots or decayed growth removed in spring.

Columneas are rarely successful in centrally-heated homes with dry air, but may do well if there is some form of humidification. If the atmosphere is dry, care has to be taken to spray the plants and keep the air moist. Lack of humidity and adequate temperature leads to sickness, otherwise the plants are remarkably free from pests and disease problems.

CONOPHYTUM
see page 160

CORDYLINE
** 7–13°C/45–55°F

Three species of cordyline are grown as houseplants, and are often called palms by the layman. In fact, cordylines belong to the lily family and have no relation to true palms – but they do have handsome palm-like foliage.

C. australis, the cabbage palm, is often seen outdoors in milder parts of the country where it will grow to form a small palm-like tree, and even bear large panicles of scented creamy flowers in summer. If grown in pots, it can be kept until it reaches about 90cm (3ft). It is very slow-growing. As a pot plant it forms a cluster of long, narrow, sword-shaped leaves, the lower ones arching gracefully. Similar remarks regarding culture and habit also apply to C. indivisa, which is easy to raise from seed. The leaves have a reddish or yellowish raised rib down the entire length. There are reddish to purplish cultivars of C. australis, which look especially attractive as pot plants.

Different, because it demands a minimum temperature of 13°C (55°F), is Cordyline fruticosa (syn. C. terminalis), the ti plant, and sometimes called flaming dragon because of the lovely green foliage variegated with cream and flashed with a flame-like red flushing. It is from tropical Asia and the minimum

Columnea

Cordyline 'Prince Albert'.

recommended temperature must be maintained if it is to thrive. It is suitable for centrally-heated homes where humidity is reasonable. The leaves are broad and can reach 60cm (2ft) in length in ideal conditions. This plant is often sold in the form of the ti log to tourists in warm countries, and the logs are often brought back from holidays. They are now sold by florists, nurserymen and some bulb firms. The logs are cuttings, and should be planted in any sterilized potting compost, preferably with the addition of a little washed grit. In a warm, shaded position, if kept nicely moist, they soon root and the leaves sprout from the top. The cutting should then be potted into a sterilized potting compost. A warm, reasonably humid position, slightly shaded in summer, should be found. It will fail in chilly, draughty homes and where the temperature fluctuates widely.

There are numerous cultivars of the species, and the colour and striping may vary. Often, it is the younger foliage that has the finest colours. Older leaves tend to become plain green, and may lose their variegation. However, they are still quite handsome and decorative.

Cordylines rarely suffer from pests or diseases. The most common problem with C. fruticosa (syn. C. terminalis) is the inability to maintain adequate warmth and humidity.

CRASSULA
see page 163

CROCUS
see page 145

CRYPTANTHUS
see page 153

CROSSANDRA INFUNDIBULIFORMIS
(firecracker flower)
** 55°F/13°C

This species is often given the incorrect name *C. undulifolia*. It comes from the East Indies and is notable for long-lasting flowers produced from spring to autumn. In its natural habit it forms a large shrub, but retains a neat, compact shape when grown as a pot plant.

The foliage is spear-shaped, shiny, deep green and slightly waved along the edges. The flowers, formed generously even on small and young plants, are an attractive salmon-orange. The lobed flowers, 2.5cm (1in) or more in diameter, are borne on spikes 10cm (4in) long.

Excellent plants can be grown in 13cm (5in) pots, but they like a rich compost such as John Innes potting compost No 3. This species is not successful in chilly homes or where temperatures fluctuate

widely, and the winter minimum must be rigidly observed.

In winter, water must be applied cautiously, and the compost only just prevented from drying out completely. In summer – and all the time active growth is being made – water can be given freely, particularly during the period of flowering. In summer, the plants should be given a shaded position and moved to full light during winter. Propagation can be effected from cuttings taken in spring, and also from seed sown at the same time. If the seed is reasonably fresh it is not difficult to germinate it on a window-sill. A temperature of 17°C (63°F) is required. Crossandras have few pest or disease troubles. Low temperature and an excessively dry atmosphere are the commonest cause of deterioration.

CTENANTHE
** 16°C/61°F

Ctenanthes are beautiful plants, similar to calatheas, and their culture is also much the same. They originate from Brazil and must be given congenial warmth – if possible, a little higher than the recommended minimum – and good humidity. Although there are several species, only one is frequently seen as a houseplant, and this is C. oppenheimiana tricolor. Why the strange common name never never plant has been given to this species is in some doubt. However, it has the curious habit of curling its foliage if exposed to too much light.

The leaves are boldly banded in contrasting light and dark green and often cream or tinted with other colours. The undersides of the leaves are purple. Like all plants in this family, it likes shade. It also seems to thrive in groups of plants.

It is an excellent plant for case-gardens and where there is artificial lighting for plants.

Ctenanthes are not much troubled by pests and diseases when grown under good conditions. Chills and wide temperature changes will soon cause leaf deterioration.

Crossandra 'Mona Wallhed'.

Ctenanthe oppenheimiana tricolor.

Cuphea ignea.

CUPHEA IGNEA
(Mexican cigar plant)
* 7°C/45°F

This is a very easy and delightful species sometimes used for outdoor bedding. Recently, it has been sold as a house-plant, the plants usually being in the form of seedlings coming into flower during spring.

This is remarkable for its long flowering period. Seeds sown early in the year start flowering at a very early stage, and continue well into autumn.

It is an extremely neat and compact little plant, forming a dainty, miniature shrub with a branching habit. The leaves are small and in keeping with its size, and the black-and-white tipped brilliant-scarlet flowers are borne in profusion. The flowers are tubular and 2.5cm (1in) long.

Seedlings should be potted into 13cm (5in) pots, using any of the modern potting composts. It is very easy to raise plants from seed on a window-sill. Germinate at about 18°C (65°F).

No stopping or support is needed and the plants can be left to grow naturally. They will do well in a bright position or slight shade, but good light produces the best flowers.

This Mexican species is evergreen and can be kept during the winter at the minimum recommended temperature. However, better specimens which are free-flowering can be obtained by raising young plants from seed each year. In autumn, the flowers often scatter their seed and this can be collected by placing a sheet of white paper under the plant.

CYCLAMEN (alpine violet)
* 7–10°C/45–50°F

This is one of the most popular pot plants, and sold from early autumn to spring, the time of flowering depending on seed strain and sowing time. There are a number of species, some hardy and others suited to rock gardens, but those used as pot plants for the home are nearly always hybrids or cultivars of *C. persicum.*

The beautiful butterfly-like flowers of cyclamen are well known, and some varieties also have exceptionally delightful foliage with pretty silvery banding and edging.

Some people associate the cyclamen with scent, but not all the modern cultivars have retained this desirable characteristic. However, for those houseplant enthusiasts fortunate to have facilities to raise their own plants from seed, there are some special fragrant strains. Modern cultivars also offer strains with extra-fine leaf patterning, miniatures, and fancy flowers which may be frilled.

The 'Triumph' cyclamen are very popular with florists and are beautiful, with a wide range of colours, attractive foliage and large flowers. The 'Rex' strain is notable for leaf patterns, and makes neat foliage plants. 'Puppet' is a dainty miniature, having the distinction of sweetly-scented flowers. 'Decora' has an unusual flower colouring and very pleasing foliage.

Cyclamen are usually bought in bud or when coming into flower. They are not easy to raise from seed in the home, but can be grown more easily from corms started into growth from mid to late summer. To do this, immerse the corms in moist peat until they are seen to be sprouting, and then place one to a 13cm (5in) pot, so that the top of the corm is just above the surface of the compost.

C. persicum is of East Mediterranean origin and does not tolerate chills. The minimum recommended temperature should be maintained, although when flowering a few degrees lower will prolong the decorative period.

It is important to avoid hot, stuffy rooms. Too much cold, too much warmth, widely fluctuating temperatures, and overwatering, will result in wilting and sickly plants. Shade is also essential, and this means reasonable light but out of direct sunshine. The plants do very well under artificial light.

There seems to be some difference of opinion about the best treatment of the plants after flowering. Some growers dry the corms, storing them quite dry from about June until the next starting time. However, better results may be obtained if the corms are merely rested. This is done by putting the plants in a cool, shaded place outside during summer, giving only just enough water to maintain the foliage. A few leaves may deteriorate, and if so they should be removed cleanly. New leaves will arise when growth begins again. In autumn, bring the plants into a cool but not chilly room and water them. In all cases, it is wise to avoid wetting the tops of the corms too much, since this may encourage the lower parts of the stems to rot. This is liable to occur in places where the air is stagnant and ventilation poor. Some people manage to save cyclamen for a number of years with excellent flowering, although this should not be expected as the general rule. With age, the corms usually become large and covered with corky tissue and their flowering potential decreases.

Cyclamen are not usually much troubled by pests, but grey mould (*Botrytis cinerea*) is a fungus that often attacks the lower parts of the plants if conditions are too cool and excessively damp, or the plants are overwatered and wetted too much. In such circumstances, even the flowers and buds may be affected.

Cyclamen persicum.

CYMBIDIUM
see page 174

CYPERUS (*umbrella plant*)
* 10°C/50°F

The common name of these plants is an apt one, as the leaves are borne like the spokes of an umbrella at the top of a stout, long stem. They are also aquatic plants, making them ideal for anyone too generous with the watering-can – a frequent cause of houseplant failure.

Two species are common as houseplants, both native to warm countries – *C. alternifolius* and *C. diffusus*; the latter is usually taller. They are best grown with their pots standing in a shallow pan of water, something that must never be done with the majority of houseplants. To keep the water fresh it should be changed daily.

When potting them, it is a good idea to include some small pieces of charcoal with the compost, to keep it fresh. This lessens the risk of unpleasant smells which may arise when wet compost becomes sour. However, these plants are adapted to thrive in rather mucky bogs. Like most aquatic plants, they can become rampant and invasive. If this happens, they can be reduced in size by division of the roots. They can also be grown from seed.

These plants are especially useful for placing in groups needing higher humidity. The flowers are brownish spikelets borne at the tops of the umbrella formation.

The impressive *C. papyrus*, the famous Egyptian paper-rush, is sometimes seen as a houseplant where there is space to display its grandeur. It is extremely easy to grow from seed, and from a spring sowing plants at least 90cm (3ft) in height can be obtained by the end of summer. The tall stems have, at the top, a dense cluster of thin foliage, and the plants can be placed by patio doors or near picture-windows where there is plenty of light. Because of their size it is not usually practical to grow them during winter.

Cyperus plants are not often attacked by pests, but red spider mites should be watched for. They should be suspected if there is any sign of yellowing of the upper foliage and it is very important to take prompt action. During summer, spray the foliage with water in an upward direction.

CYRTOMIUM
see page 138

CYTISUS (*broom*)
* 7°C/45°F

Of the many brooms grown in gardens and conservatories, only one is sufficiently compact to make a neat pot plant for the home. This is the hybrid *C. × racemosus*, a tender evergreen with rich golden-yellow flowers borne freely from winter to early summer. Even this species will grow to over 1.5m (5ft) if given a large pot or planted in a conservatory, but it can be kept compact by pinching back the shoots after flowering.

Cytisus × racemosus

The greyish-green foliage is very attractive. The sweetly-fragrant flowers are borne as racemes, arching gracefully on well-grown plants. It should be bought when the buds are just beginning to show colour. Give this species a position in as much light as possible, but shade slightly from direct sun in summer.

Large plants can stand outdoors in a sheltered spot during the summer if the space is wanted indoors, but watering must not be neglected and the foliage can be sprayed when the weather is warm. The best time for potting is during May and June. The flowers often form seeds, but it is unwise to try growing plants from these, as they may not produce identical specimens. As with most plants of the pea family, feeding should be moderate – otherwise they may become lush and too leafy, and flower poorly.

DAVALLIA
see page 138

DENDROBIUM
see page 175

Cyperus alternifolius (left) and *Dieffenbachia* 'Exotica' (right).

DICKSONIA
see page 138

DIEFFENBACHIA MACULATA
(syn. D. picta)
(dumb cane, leopard lily)
*** 15°C/59°F

The handsome foliage of this plant – beautifully variegated and coloured to give bold contrasts – makes it a much admired houseplant. Unfortunately, it is rather fussy about its environment, and unless there is adequate warmth the year-round, together with good humidity, it invariably deteriorates. Where it is too cool it will drop its lower leaves, but with the return of warmth it may recover.

There is some doubt as to whether this plant is a true species or a natural variety of some other plant, since it is very variable. Its various cultivars have been given fancy names such as 'Roehrsii', which has markedly contrasting cream veins on the leaves, and 'Exotica' with pale yellow leaf colouring and a vivid-green mid-rib. 'Exotica Perfecta' has ivory markings and green margins and veins. Very similar, but with an overall white tinge, is 'Marianne'. 'Bausei' is pretty with silvery leaf spotting. In all cases, the leaves can exceed 30cm (1ft) in length in well-grown specimens, and they are broadly spear-shaped. Some cultivars have been selected for compact, bushy growth with sideshoots more readily produced from the base: 'Compacta', which resembles 'Exotica Perfecta', is one of these, while 'Camilla' has an overall whiter tinge.

All parts of this plant are poisonous, the sap especially so. If it gets into the mouth it is said that speech will be impeded for some time. Hence the common name dumb cane.

Give it a very bright position, especially during the winter months, but shade slightly in summer. The plant likes excellent humidity, although it should always be watered carefully and the compost should not be allowed to stay wet for long periods.

In ideal conditions, where there is central-heating with humidification, or the plants are grown in with groups of others to achieve a humid micro-climate, the plant will grow vigorously and look delightful the year-round.

It is a waste of time to try growing this plant where the temperature falls below the recommended minimum, or where there are wide temperature fluctuations. The plants are native to the West Indies and Tropical America. In good conditions they may require potting-on each year and a final 20cm (8in) pot.

Chills and inadequate humidity are the main causes of deterioration, yellowing and leaf drop.

DIPLADENIA SPLENDENS
** 13°C/55°F

It is only possible to keep this plant in homes with central-heating, moderate humidity, and a constant temperature. It is a vigorous climber from Brazil, and in the right conditions will exceed 3m (10ft) in height. However, as a pot plant it can be kept within bounds by cutting it back drastically after flowering. Its special merit is that it bears showy rose-pink trumpet-shaped flowers very freely, and when still quite young. The flowers are produced over a long period, from summer to autumn.

Good plants can be grown in the home by training them up bamboo canes, the height allowed depending on the space available. The leaves are spear-shaped, glossy and evergreen.

From summer to autumn the plants can be watered generously. After flowering, reduce the amount of water considerably, and keep only slightly moist to maintain the foliage during winter.

Splendid specimens can be grown as houseplants in 18cm (7in) pots. The best time to pot them is in spring. During summer, spray the foliage with water from time to time, and protect from direct sunshine. Chills and wide temperature changes will cause the foliage to turn yellow and fall. Otherwise, dipladenias are little trouble. This species is often labelled and listed in catalogues as *Mandevilla splendens*.

Dipladenia splendens.

DIPTERACANTHUS
** 15°C/59°F

The Brazilian *Dipteracanthus makoyanus* (syn. *Ruellia makoyana*), the monkey plant, is a low-growing plant with a tendency to ramble, and is best grown in the half-pots sometimes used for alpine plants. It does well when trailing over the edges of pots.

The leaves are spear-shaped, purple below and olive-green above, with the veins in contrasting creamy-green. It has solitary deep rose-pink flowers.

Rather similar is *Dipteracanthus portellae*, (syn. *Ruellia portellae*), but only the central leaf vein shows much contrast. The flowers are of a similar colour. It can be grown as an annual from seed, and although it may sometimes continue to grow it seems to be short-lived.

D. portellae can be propagated from cuttings taken in spring. The young plants should be stopped to promote a branching habit, but established plants are best left alone as much as possible. To get good winter flowering, a temperature slightly higher than the recommended minimum must be maintained. These plants are unsuitable for chilly homes, or where central-heating is used without humidification. In chilly conditions they soon deteriorate, and the leaves turn yellow and fall.

Above: *Dipteracanthus portellae.*
Right: *Dizygotheca elegantissima* (near) and *Dracaena marginata* (far).

DIZYGOTHECA ELEGANTISSIMA
(false aralia, spider plant)
** 13°C/55°F

This is an elegant and graceful foliage plant, originating in Australia. It has a limited useful life of a few years. It is usually seen as a single stem, but it may also branch. The stems carry regularly-spaced slender stalks, terminating in a group of thin foliage, giving a spider-leg effect and inspiring one of the common names.

The young foliage is reddish, but as it matures turns a deep olive-green. When the plant reaches about 1.5m (5ft) in height, the foliage loses its graceful form and becomes coarser and broader. If growing conditions are good, it can be cut back to induce new shoots.

For satisfactory vigorous growth the recommended winter minimum temperature should be strictly kept, and in summer the plants will enjoy quite high temperatures provided a high humidity is also maintained. The foliage should be sprayed with water and slight shading provided in summer. In winter, the plants need as much light as possible, and preferably to be put in a window facing south. In winter, water just enough to keep the compost slightly moist.

A well-grown plant makes a very beautiful sight and the foliage is quite distinctive. It forms an excellent feature plant for groups. However, in some homes it can be troublesome, and sheds its lower leaf stalks so that a plant looking like a palm with a leafless trunk results. This is most likely to occur where it is chilly or draughty, or if kept too wet.

DRACAENA
** 7–13°C/45–55°F, see text

This is an important genus for house-plants, since several species and cultivars have attractively marked and coloured foliage. They are not infrequently incorrectly described as palms by the layman, but this is understandable because of the shape and arrangement of the foliage in some of the species.

A common name sometimes used is ribbon plant, since the leaves are frequently striped or bordered.

Of special interest is *D. draco*, the dragon tree. It is one source of dragon's blood, which is the name of a reddish resin used in the colouring of varnishes. This species can grow into an enormous tree, such as the famous one at Icod in Tenerife, but it can be easily grown from

seed and makes a useful pot plant for some years. It can also be used outdoors as a feature plant for sub-tropical bedding effects.

When small, it is happy as a houseplant in a position of good light, and needs only about 7°C (45°F) winter minimum. It can make an impressive foliage plant for a porch, foyer or entrance hall, where it can be left to reach an imposing size. The other dracaenas are less tolerant of cool conditions.

Palm-like in habit, and bearing its sword-shaped foliage as a cluster at the top of its stem, is *D. marginata*, the Madagascar dragon tree. This too can grow very tall, but is extremely slow in developing and therefore a useful pot plant. There are forms with cream-striped foliage or reddish-edged leaves. *D. deremensis* has broad, strap-shaped

foliage with banded colours, varying according to the cultivar. 'Warneckei' has a dark green border, with a striking white stripe centred with a fainter green and very attractive stripe.

'Bausei' is similar, but without the central stripe. 'Janet Craig' has fine white striping, and 'Rhoersii' has a pale green central stripe bordered with a pair of fine white bands.

D. fragrans bears many similarities to *D. deremensis*, but the foliage is considerably longer and wider, and is usually much less pointed. The striping is a deep cream to gold in colour. The most frequently seen cultivar is 'Massangeana', the corn plant, so called because of its cream-striped foliage, like variegated maize.

D. sanderiana is distinct, since it tends to branch readily at its base and bear foliage evenly up the stems to give a bushy appearance. It is often called the ribbon plant. The long leaves are slightly waved and are usually pale green, with cream to silver contrasting margins. When well grown, it is very attractive and in the home can reach 1m (3½ft) in height in good conditions, but can be kept much smaller by restricting the size of its pot. This species is also easier to keep in centrally-heated homes, where the humidity may be low. The others need reasonable humidity coupled with congenial warmth, and during summer can be watered freely and sprayed from time to time. In winter, keep them slightly dry. At all times, choose a position of maximum light, avoiding direct sunshine in summer. In dim places, the leaves will not develop their best colour and contrast.

Plants will need potting-on, the frequency depending on the species and the environment. Young plants can usually be kept in 13cm (5in) pots, but a final size of 18cm (7in) or larger may be needed for vigorous species. The best potting time is April.

Scale insects are the most frequent invaders of these plants, but are easily removed by wiping the leaves. Root aphids are a less common pest.

The more tender species described here will deteriorate in cold or draughty homes, and the plants will become sickly and the foliage turn yellow. These beautiful plants are worth a little care.

DYCKIA
see page 153

ECHEVERIA
see page 163

EPIDENDRUM
see page 170

EPIPHYLLUM
see page 162

ERICA (heath, heather)
* 5°C/41°F

Two species – which also have a number of named hybrids – make favourite florists' plants for the Christmas period, but they are usually forced to flower earlier for this purpose.

E. gracilis is of South African origin, and has both white and pink forms. It grows like a clump of heather, with stems 45cm (1½ft) high. The flowers are heather-shaped, and borne similarly, making a very pretty and neat pot plant that will enhance any home.

E. hiemalis is rather a mystery, since the identity of its origin is not really certain and it may well not be a true species. However, it is popularly called the Cape heath. It bears flowers more tubular than *E. gracilis* and they are pink with white tips. The normal flowering time is from October to January.

Commercial nurseries manipulate temperatures to bring about timed flowering for Christmas, but high temperatures must be avoided at all times. The plants should be given an airy, cool room and a bright position, and not allowed to dry out at any time, winter included. It is wise to water them with clean rainwater where the mains tap-water is hard.

The plants must be given an acid compost when being potted. These heaths will be happy in an atmosphere drier than most other houseplants and even in summer the temperature should be kept down. It may be more convenient to stand the plants outside in a cool sheltered place, but don't forget to water them, especially during dry weather.

The best time to pot them is March, Pests and diseases are uncommon, but lime in the water or an alkaline compost will soon cause yellowing and sickly growth. It is common for ericas that have been forced to deteriorate. They are difficult to save from one year to another.

EUCALYPTUS (gum tree)
* 2–7°C/36–45°F, see text

There are a number of eucalypts that make very attractive foliage plants in their young state. Unfortunately, all of them will eventually become too large, and they usually form adult foliage which is quite different from the more decorative juvenile types.

Many species can be grown from imported seed, so it is usually not much trouble to raise fresh, young plants to replace old ones which have outlived their usefulness.

Two species are of particular interest as houseplants. *E. globulus*, the blue gum, is almost hardy and useful for chilly places, provided there is plenty of light. If allowed to grow to an appreciable size it can be put in hallways, foyers and porches, where it will make an impressive sight. The leaves on young plants are greyish-blue-green. When crushed they emit the familiar pungent smell of eucalyptus oil used in the treatment of nasal colds.

Quite different is the species *E. citriodora*,

Erica gracilis.

Eucalyptus globulus.

native to Queensland. This is popularly called the lemon-scented eucalyptus, because in this case the leaves have a pronounced sharp lemon scent. In warm conditions, the plant will scent the air of the room and is very pleasant. The leaves are pointed and elongated, pale green and covered with short, bristly hairs. It is a very desirable houseplant and can be kept bushy and compact by pinching out the growing tips of young shoots. If this is not done, the plant will become tall and spreading and there may not be space to keep it for more than two years or so. This species is also less cold resistant and needs a minimum of about 7°C (45°F) in winter. It also prefers a more humid atmosphere, and will wilt rapidly if the compost is allowed to become too dry.

Both species are quick growers and the pot size should be restricted to discourage rampant development.

It is most unusual for eucalypts grown as houseplants to be troubled by pests or diseases. The lower leaves of *E. citriodora* may sometimes turn reddish in colour if watering is erratic.

EUPHORBIA
*/**/*** see text for temperatures

This is an enormous genus, of at least 1,000 species, and they vary greatly and include trees, shrubs, succulents, annuals and perennials. Their appearance also varies, but many have a succulent nature, and all exude a whitish latex if cut. In spite of the size of the genus, only a few are important houseplants, two in particular.

Some of the lesser-known succulent species sometimes make an appearance as window-sill plants. The best known for the home are *E. pulcherrima* (poinsettia) and *E. milii* (crown of thorns). They are totally different in appearance and in their requirements. The poinsettia, native to Mexico, is an extremely popular Christmas gift plant. The true flowers are insignificant, but the extremely showy leaf-like bracts, particularly when coloured bright red, make a dazzling display for the festive period. There are also pink and cream cultivars. These plants are specially produced by nurseries, being given treatment with artificial light to extend the normal day length and delay their development – which would otherwise be earlier – and dwarfed with chemicals to make them compact. For this reason, it is usually a waste of time to try saving the plants. Moreover, they need congenial warmth, and for most of the year will look far from decorative, even if saved.

To keep bought plants in good condition for as long as possible, place them in a room of moderate temperature where there are no extreme changes, and preferably with other houseplants so that they benefit from a humid microclimate. Shade them from direct winter sun, and keep them moist. In good conditions, the plants should remain attractive for several weeks. They then turn yellow and the leaves fall.

The crown of thorns is a long-lived and permanent houseplant, and is sometimes listed as *E. splendens*, now thought to be a form with bright red flowers. Another form, *E. milii tananarevae*, has yellow flowers. These make neat, shrubby plants with roundish succulent leaves and long spines growing from the stems, forming a handsome plant that will enhance any home.

The showy part of the flower is a pair of bracts, and these may appear erratically throughout the year, but mostly in winter. Minimum temperature for this species from Madagascar is about 13°C (55°F). It enjoys an atmosphere drier than most houseplants prefer, but should be given good light and an airy position.

It can be watered freely from spring to late summer, but kept only slightly moist the rest of the time. Too much water will often cause the leaves to fall, usually after turning yellow. If this happens allow the plant to become almost dry and remain so for about two months. After this rest, new buds and leaves may begin to form, and watering can then be resumed, though cautiously at first.

The milky juice from this plant is poisonous. The plant is rarely affected by pests or diseases.

Euphorbia pulcherrima.

81

EUTERPE
see page 137

EXACUM AFFINE (Persian violet)
* 10°C/50°F

This charming little plant might be more appropriately called Arabian violet, since it originates from the island of Socotra in the Arabian Sea. It is an annual or biennial, and sold in autumn or in spring. Several plants are grown in small pots to give a more bushy and compact effect, and the height should be about 23cm (9in).

The flowers are small, but freely produced. They are mauve with yellow centres, and violet-like in shape. The most notable feature – which makes them readily saleable – is their exquisite spicy scent. However, in attempts to breed more compact and larger-flowered plants, this scent has, in some seed strains, been lost. Fortunately, a well-known seed firm has recently introduced a specially-raised strain called 'Starlight Fragrance' which has all the desirable characteristics as well as an excellent and distinctive scent.

This is a temporary houseplant, and should be bought when just coming into flower. Keep the pots nicely moist, in a congenially warm room out of draughts, and shaded. The flowers should then give pleasure for several weeks, after which the plants can be discarded.

This is an easy plant to raise as an annual on your window-sill, making the sowings in spring. Choose the seed strain mentioned, and place about five seedlings to each 13cm (5in) pot. Pinch out the tips of each seedling to encourage branching growth.

FASCICULARIA
see page 150

× FATSHEDERA LIZEI
(tree ivy, climbing figleaf)
* 4°C/37°F

A bigeneric hybrid, × *Fatshedera lizei* was obtained by crossing an ivy, *Hedera helix* 'Hibernica', with *Fatsia japonica* 'Moseri'. The resultant plant has both characteristics, and it can be trained as a climber or, if the shoots are cut back, given a more bushy habit. The leaves are shiny and palmate with five lobes.

The plant is of quite exotic appearance, yet is excellent for cool, even cold, rooms. There is a variegated form, 'Variegata', with cream markings which is especially attractive.

The plants are also useful for fairly shaded positions, and bright places exposed to direct sunlight must be strictly avoided since the plants readily wilt in such circumstances. Greenish panicles of flowers may appear during late autumn on well-grown specimens, and when they are a few years old.

Fatshederas have few problems, but the variegated form will enjoy a few degrees higher temperature than the recommended minimum.

FATSIA JAPONICA
(false castor oil plant)
* hardy

This is not the true castor oil plant, but its leaves are certainly a similar shape to *Ricinus communis*, although they are smoother and more glossy. Despite its ability to withstand frost, the palmate foliage is suggestive of the tropics, and it makes a fine and impressive plant for a porch, hallway or chilly entrance hall, provided there is reasonable light. It is slow-growing, fortunately, but can eventually reach a considerable size. Outdoors it exceeds 3m (10ft) in height and spread. There is a variegated form with cream blotched or edged leaves, and this develops very much more slowly. It is also far less cold resistant, and the temperature should not be allowed to fall below freezing, otherwise the leaves could fall in winter. This variegated form is an especially desirable houseplant, with paler green leaf colour and more suited to limited space.

Both forms look splendid if treated with one of the leaf-shine products sold by garden shops.

Exacum affine.

82

The plants can be kept in relatively small pots for some years, but eventually will need 20cm (8in) pots, and finally small tubs if retained for hallways and the like. Mature specimens produce creamy-white globular flower clusters in October. Water just sufficiently to prevent the compost drying out during winter. Pests and diseases are extremely rare.

FAUCARIA
see page 160

In small pots: × *Fatshedera lizei.*
In large pots: *Fatsia japonica.*

FICUS
/ see text for temperatures

To this large genus belong some of the most well-known of the impressive foliage plants for the home and for public buildings. It includes figs and so-called rubber plants, although commercial rubber is mostly obtained from *Hevea brasiliensis*, belonging to an entirely different family.

Undoubtedly, the greatest favourite is *F. elastica* 'Decora', the India rubber plant. This plant usually grows as a single stem, bearing large, shiny, oval leaves. The top leaf, as it is developing, is surrounded by a reddish sheath. The young leaves, especially the mid-ribs, are also tinted red. Mature plants may branch naturally from the base, and in ideal conditions can reach 2.4m (8ft).

F. lyrata, the fiddle-back fig, also grows as a single stem, but is usually much shorter, and rarely branches. The leaves are very large and shiny and, of course, fiddle-shaped, as the common name suggests. The leaf edges are wavy and the leaf veining may be tinted yellow or gold to give a marked contrast to the dark green background. Both these species need a minimum winter temperature of 15°C (59°F), or a few degrees higher, although they will survive much lower if scarcely watered during the cool period.

There are some variegated forms of *F. elastica*, such as 'Doescheri'. This has leaves blotched with cream, and sometimes flushed pink. 'Tricolor' is similar, but 'Black Prince' has plain, very dark green shiny foliage. All of these are said to need a higher minimum winter temperature.

Ficus benjamina, the weeping fig, is more tree-like in shape, and has rather drooping spear-shaped foliage, changing from pale green when young to dark green when mature. It can exceed 1.8m (6ft) in height, being quite vigorous.

F. radicans, trailing fig, in contrast, grows only to about 10cm (4in). It is a trailer for hanging pots or baskets and is best seen in the form 'Variegata', which has a creamy coloured edging to the small, sharply-pointed spear-shaped leaves. Both these species can have about 13°C (55°F) winter minimum.

F. deltoidea, the mistletoe fig, is of bushy habit, with oval leaves tinted brownish yellow, and bearing small greenish berries most of the year.

F. pumila, the creeping fig, can be grown as a climber or trailer, and has heart-shaped foliage with prominent veins in the juvenile form. These two species can be given a winter minimum of 7°C (45°F). They will come to no harm even at this low temperature.

Different – in that it is extremely easy to raise from seed from a window-sill sowing – is *F. benghalensis*, the Bengal fig. It is similar in habit to the India rubber plant, but not so attractive. All the large-leaved species will be enhanced by treatment with a leaf-shine preparation from time to time – or the leaves can also be washed.

Most ficus prefer a position in good light, but direct sunshine may cause leaf scorch. The trailing species will tolerate more shade. Those species preferring warmer conditions may drop their leaves if chilled for any length of time, and especially if temperatures fluctuate widely. Every attempt must be made to prevent this happening, since the plants can be spoilt, although not usually killed. Plants that have become leggy will have to be propagated by air layering (see pages 34–35).

Leggy plants may also be induced to sprout new shoots from the bare stem if the stem is sprayed frequently with one of the special foliar feeds containing a growth stimulant. The spraying should be done during the warm summer months. *Ficus elastica* often responds particularly well to this treatment.

All species can be watered freely in summer, but sparingly in winter. The lower the temperature the more careful must be the watering. Potting, when necessary, is best done in May. Most of the taller species will be happy in pots that may appear too small, provided feeding is not neglected.

Given large pots and good growing conditions, they can grow too fast and become large too quickly. In all cases, moderate humidity is preferred. *F. pumila* likes more moisture in winter than the others, and it will also do well in quite shaded positions. All the taller ficus make excellent feature plants for groups of houseplants.

Generally, there are few troubles to be expected from pests or diseases, mealy bugs and scale insects being the most frequent invaders. These are easily wiped off the shiny leaves or brushed from between the leaves with an artist's brush dipped in an insecticide solution. The most usual trouble with large ficus plants is the shedding of leaves encountered in chilly homes or where temperatures fluctuate and there are draughts. The warmth-loving species are best bought in summer, since they are less liable to suffer shock from chill during their journey home.

It is important to buy plants from a reputable florist or nursery where the proper temperatures are maintained. A plant may drop its leaves some time after being subjected to ill-treatment, and after you have paid for it.

Three forms of *Ficus elastica*. **Left to right:** 'Abidjan', 'Belga', and 'Robusta'.

FITTONIA
*** 13–16°C/55–61°F

Two species from Peru are grown as houseplants, but they are quite unsuitable for cold homes where humidity is low and temperatures fluctuate. Both are more suited to case or bottle gardens. *F. verschaffeltii* 'Argyroneura', aptly called lace leaf or snakeskin plant, is exceedingly beautiful. It is a trailer with oval leaves, delicately and contrastingly veined in creamy-white, giving the effect of intricately fine lace. It requires the higher of the two recommended minimum temperatures.

F. verschaffeltii itself is happy with the lower minimum temperature, and is the easier of the two. The foliage is bigger and the veining not so fine, and is coloured carmine-red. Both these plants should not be allowed to dry out completely at any time, but watering in winter should be less. Shade and a high humidity are essential. Both are usually best grown in half-pots.

Plants in pots should be frequently sprayed with a fine mist of water in summer to attain a high humidity. In low temperatures and where the atmosphere is dry, both species soon become sickly. Otherwise there are few troubles, although an attack of aphids is a possibility.

Although often difficult to grow, these two species soon reward the enthusiast attempting to grow them. They are often best bought early in summer so that they will be well established by the time winter arrives. By then you will be attuned to their needs.

FUCHSIA *(lady's ear drops)*
** 2–5°C/36–41°F

Although one of the most popular pot plants, and extremely beautiful, the fuchsia is often a failure if an attempt is made to keep it in a room for a long period. It is a plant which is more suited to a conservatory, garden room or porch, or any other place that is reasonably humid and has good light and air circulation.

There are innumerable types from which to choose, mostly named cultivars. It is best to visit a specialist grower – or to obtain a catalogue for description – if you wish to make purchases. There are hardy types which should be chosen for cold places. Where it is frost-free, the more exotic greenhouse cultivars can be selected. Some are especially suited to hanging pots or baskets and have a trailing habit, others are more erect and best when trained as a bush. Standard fuchsias are not usually suited to room conditions at all and are best avoided, although they are splendid for a conservatory.

A few fuchsias have coloured or ornamental foliage. These must have a position in good light to develop their finest tints. Other fuchsias also need plenty of light to produce generous flowers and strong growth, but direct sunlight should not be allowed. It is best to buy either rooted cuttings in spring or adult plants just as the buds are opening. The cuttings should have the growing tip removed to encourage bushy growth. For hanging-baskets it is usually necessary to have about three plants set evenly around the edge. If hung in a window, the baskets should be turned daily to even out the light distribution, and prevent one-sided growth. Choose a cool place where the temperature does not fluctuate, and keep the plants nicely moist. In some cases, the shoots can be stopped to obtain a more dense and bushy plant and increase the number of flowers. The plants need plenty of feeding as the buds are just beginning to form if they are to be strong.

Flowering will normally continue from summer to autumn. After flowering, reduce the amount of water and trim back to strong stems. Keep the plants in a frost-free place during winter, giving just sufficient water to maintain any foliage remaining on the plants.

In spring, when new shoots appear, cut back further if necessary – the aim being to begin with a strong basal stem system to support the new growth. If this is not done, the plants may become too large and very straggly, and untidy later on. Erratic watering may cause both leaves and flowers to fall. Aphids, whitefly, and red spider mites are frequent pests, but are easily controlled.

Anyone with a conservatory or large porch of glass could make an exciting collection of fuchsias and include the graceful singles and modern large-flowered doubles. Some of the latter have very unusual marbled colourings. The hybrids and cultivars of *F. triphylla*, with elongated blooms are sometimes not readily recognized as fuchsias, but often make better houseplants than others and are worth trying, particularly in a bay or bow window where light is more even.

Fittonia verschaffeltii 'Argyroneura'.

Fuchsias ('Dollar Princess' at front).

GLOTIPHYLLUM
see page 160

GLOXINIA
see Sinningia

GREVILLEA ROBUSTA
(Australian silky oak)
* 7°C/45°F

This beautiful foliage plant is very easy to grow from seed sown in spring and reaches a useful size during the first year. It is generally sold when about 45cm (1¼ft) high, and is then in the form of a single stem bearing large, finely-divided fern-like leaves. However, after a few years it may become too large to keep in the average home. If cut back, it will send out new shoots from the base and then acquire a more branching habit. It is a great favourite for conservatory decoration.

The plant should be given an acid potting compost – as used for ericaceous plants – and preferably watered with clean rainwater in hard-water areas. Otherwise, the foliage may tend to become yellow and there will be less vigorous growth. If allowed to become too cold in winter, the foliage may be shed. Recovery takes place with the warmer conditions of spring.

During summer water well and stand the plants outdoors occasionally in a sheltered place, especially when there is fine rain. In winter, give only sufficient water to prevent the compost drying out. The plant likes a position in good light, but not the warm, dry atmosphere of a stuffy room. Red spider mite is a possible pest to watch out for.

Grevillea robusta.

GUZMANIA
see page 152

GYMNOCALYCIUM
see page 162

GYNURA
** 13°C/55°F

Two of these plants, with beautiful foliage, are usually seen as houseplants. The favourite is *G. procumbens* (syn. *G. sarmentosa*) from India, the velvet plant or purple passion vine. In its natural habitat, it is a vigorous climber or trailer, but in the home is usually best regarded as a trailer. The leaves are dark green, spear-shaped and pointed and toothed along the edges, and covered with purplish fine hair.

G. aurantiaca is similar, but with larger leaves. Both may flower, the former in March and April and the latter in January and February. The flowers in both cases are orange, the latter having larger flowers which are about 2.5cm (1in) long.

Below: From left to right are *Gynura aurantiaca, Hedera helix* 'Sagittaefolia', *Hedera helix canariensis* 'Variegata', and *Hedera helix* 'Eva'.

Unfortunately, both plants can become straggly and untidy with age and are best propagated from cuttings taken in spring and old plants discarded after two or three years. These cuttings can also be used in hanging pots or baskets, and if there is adequate warmth will grow quickly to cascade over the edge.

Other flowering or foliage plants can be mixed to give contrasting colour effects. Some people prefer to train the plants up canes, and when grown this way are useful to give height to a group. Although requiring slight shade in summer, winter light should be good, and the minimum winter temperature maintained as far as possible. Plants may survive much lower temperatures, but are liable to drop their foliage or become sickly. In summer, every attempt should be made to provide adequate atmospheric humidity, but the velvety leaves should not be sprayed with water since there is the possibility of marking them and causing the formation of brown spots or patches. Trimming and cutting back is best done in March. Pests and diseases are rare and seldom present a problem.

HEDERA *(ivy)*
* 2°C/36°F

The ivies constitute a group of the most useful of all foliage plants. They are generally easy to grow, able to adapt to a wide range of temperatures, can be grown as climbers or trailers, and in some cases as bushes, and have many pleasing leaf shapes and variegations.

By far the greatest number of houseplant ivies are cultivars of the common ivy, *H. helix*. They are quite hardy and excellent for chilly places in the home, as well as situations where light may be poor. This makes them especially valuable, because it is often difficult to find plants suited to such situations. The ivies are useful for beginners, as they are robust and not very demanding.

A selection of named cultivars can be made from the following: 'Cristata' (wavy-edged leaves), 'Sagittaefolia' (star-shaped with narrow segments). 'Conglomerata' (wavy leaves and neat, compact habit, more bushy than climbing), 'Chrysophylla' (yellow variegated leaves), 'Russell's Gold' (a beautiful golden ivy), 'Jubilee' (boldly blotched golden-yellow), 'Lutzii' (light and dark green mottling), 'Glacier' (light and dark green with creamy-yellow patches mostly around leaf edges, sometimes paler with greyish and whitish colouring), 'Silver Queen' (grey-green and blue-green with cream border, sometimes pink-tinted in cold positions), 'Discolor', popularly called marble ivy (small mottled leaves tinted pink), 'Pittsburgh' (dark green with lighter veins), 'Chicago' (similar to 'Pittsburgh' but larger leaves and brighter green), 'Harald' (ivory edge to the leaf, mottled grey and dark green in centre), 'Tricolor' (a very pretty ivy with white-bordered light green leaves changing to carmine in autumn). The last-mentioned cultivar is very slow-growing, but in general these plants are not fast and rampant growers like the original species.

Rather different and a very popular houseplant is *H. helix canariensis*, the Canary Island ivy. This is nearly always seen in the form 'Variegata'. The leaves are irregularly marked with contrasting light and dark green, grey-green and cream. In cold or cool situations there are often reddish tints and flushing, greatly enhancing its beauty. Although from a warm climate, this ivy is almost hardy and often survives outdoors in milder parts of the country. However, it may lose most, if not all, of its foliage. Given a warm room it grows vigorously, perhaps too rampantly, and may soon reach the ceiling. Even so, it seems to have a strange quality of only filling the space provided and then slowing down. It can make a handsome specimen for a stair-well, hallway, foyer or porch.

All the ivies can be kept in check by cutting back or removing unwanted growth at almost any time, but is best done in spring. Propagation is usually easy if small cuttings are taken in July. Often, aerial roots form, especially when humidity is good. Stems bearing these can be pegged down into small pots until rooted sufficiently to be severed very carefully from the parent plant.

A careful watch must be kept for scale insects. Their presence may not be realized until a black covering is seen on the foliage; this is due to a mould that grows on their sticky secretion. It is a difficult pest to eradicate once an infestation has become severe. It is hardly practical to wipe them off all the leaves borne by a large specimen, and they are remarkably resistant to most pesticides.

HELXINE
see Soleirolia

HELIOTROPIUM *(cherry pie)*
* 7°C/45°F

This plant usually appears in florists' shops from early summer onwards, and remains in bloom until autumn. It has large, flattish corymbs of usually deep blue flowers, although there are pale blue and purplish forms. A popular cultivar grown from seed is 'Marine', which has a violet-blue colour. The plant is a result of hybridization between *H. peruviana* and *P. corymbosum*, and its important feature is its delightful powerful and penetrating scent, of a quality characteristic of the plant. The new forms make neat, compact pot plants and they are invaluable for filling the air of a room with scent.

The plants should be kept where it is cool and shady during summer. In winter, it is not unusual for plants to deteriorate, and they can be cut back and kept slightly moist. New growth will appear in early spring and the plants can be potted-on. Where there are facilities for raising plants from seed, it is doubtful whether it is worth trying to over-winter the plants. They are easy to grow from spring sowings.

Aphids and whitefly are possible pests. Erratic watering and letting the plants flag and go dry may cause the edges of the leaves to turn dry and brown.

HEPTAPLEURUM ARBORICOLA
see Schefflera arboricola

Heliotropium 'Lord Roberts'.

88

HIBISCUS ROSA-SINENSIS
(Chinese rose)
** 7–15°C/45–51°F, see text

Although a Chinese species, this lovely plant is grown extensively in most tropical countries, where warmth – coupled with high humidity – produces a growth to over 1.8m (6ft). It is frequently sold as a houseplant, but is best for centrally-heated homes with good humidification. In cool homes it will survive at temperatures down to 7°C (45°F) if kept on the dry side in winter. It may well lose its leaves, but usually makes new growth in spring with the return of warmer conditions. It makes a fairly neat, bushy plant when grown in pots and its glossy dark green foliage is always attractive.

From summer to autumn the plants have large and showy flowers, usually with a projecting cluster of stamens of golden-yellow colour. These last only one to two days, but are freely formed in succession.

There are numerous named cultivars with double or single flowers in yellow, salmon, pink and shades of red. 'Cooperi' is distinct for its dwarf habit and foliage variegated cream flushed red. The flowers are also red, and it makes an attractive houseplant suitable for small pots. The continued success of this hibiscus in the home depends on the maintenance of adequate humidity and warmth in winter. During summer, the plant can be frequently sprayed with water, but this should be done between flowering, so as not to risk damaging or marking the delicate flower petals. The plant should also be given a shaded place out of direct sunlight. If warmth can be maintained in winter, the plants should be kept slightly moist – cultivars with variegated foliage particularly so – to prevent leaf drop or deterioration. Otherwise, drier conditions are essential until spring, when new growth is made.

Potting can be done in the spring, and it may be necessary to trim the plants to a neat shape and convenient size. If growth has been vigorous it will do no harm to cut the plant back severely. All weak and straggly shoots should be removed completely.

The most likely pests are aphids and mealy bugs. Usually these can be wiped off the very glossy leaves.

Hibiscus rosa-sinensis.

HIPPEASTRUM
see page 145

HOWEIA
see page 137

HOYA *(wax plants)*
* 5–10°C/41–50°F, see text

These are valuable houseplants, having a number of notable features. They are easy to grow and tolerate quite low temperatures. They have attractive evergreen foliage and very pretty flowers over a long period, which usually have a pronounced scent. These plants are suitable for a shaded place.

H. bella has a rather shrubby habit, but with pendulous stems, and rarely exceeds 30cm (1ft) in height. It is best displayed on a pedestal or in a hanging-basket, so that the branches and flowers dangle down. The leaves are spear-shaped, rather fleshy and glossy, and in some forms spotted with silvery markings. The waxy-textured flowers are starry, white and borne in clusters. The centres of the flowers are contrastingly coloured in shades of red or purple.

Blooming usually continues sporadically from spring to autumn. The formation and texture of the flowers are suggested by the common names – shower of stars and miniature wax flower. The latter has been applied to distinguish it from the other popular species *H. carnosa*, usually called wax plant or porcelain flower. This is quite different in being a climber that can, if allowed, exceed 4.5m (15ft). However, it is easy to restrict growth by keeping the plant well cut back and the roots confined to small pots.

The leaves and flowers are similar to *H. bella*, but the florets and clusters are larger. There are also two attractive forms with variegated foliage. In one, the leaf is margined pinkish-cream, and in the other the leaf is yellowish to cream, with a green margin. Both make splendid foliage plants apart from the bonus of dainty flowers.

H. bella is of Indian origin and prefers a winter minimum of 10°C (50°F), or a few degrees higher. *H. carnosa*, from Queensland, is almost hardy and will survive temperatures down to freezing if kept slightly dry during winter. It is a useful plant for cool conservatories, porches or rooms, and if there is height and space it is best allowed to grow as tall as possible. It is then seen in its full beauty and is exceptionally lovely if it can be trained into the roof of a garden room or conservatory, where the flower clusters can be viewed and admired from below.

In a room it can be trained up canes or sometimes around a wire loop. The plants need about two years of growing before they flower and are strange in that they form very long stems which remain quite bare for a time before the leaves form.

The flower colour in *H. carnosa* can vary slightly from white to rose-pink, the darker colour usually being seen in the variegated forms. The scent intensity also seems to vary and the variegated forms tend to have a rather less pronounced fragrance. During summer, water can be given freely and the foliage should be sprayed with water from time to time to create a buoyant atmosphere. In winter, plants in cold places should be watered sparingly. When cold, leaves may curl or turn yellow in winter, but growth usually begins again with the return of warmer conditions. If possible, keep pruning to the minimum, but when necessary this can be done in spring.

Propagation is easy from cuttings taken in summer. Pest and disease troubles are extremely rare, but too much water soon causes leaf yellowing.

HUERNIA
see page 161

HYACINTHUS
see page 143

Hoya carnosa.

HYDRANGEA
** 7°C/45°F

Most hydrangeas sold as pot plants are forms of *H. macrophylla*, many of which are named and have cream, pink or blue flowers borne in large globular heads. The plants are specially grown and forced by nurseries, and appear in shops from mid-winter to summer. They will last in flower for a very long time, often well into autumn, if kept shaded, moist and cool, but they are not easy plants to save for the following year. After flowering, it is a good idea to plant it in the garden or in a large patio pot. It will then usually continue to grow and to flower, reaching an appreciable size.

If you wish to try saving a plant for further pot culture, cut off the dead flowers and weak stems after flowering. Stand the plant outdoors in a shady position – preferably with the pots plunged in moist peat – and keep moist during summer. Shoots that have flowered should then be cut back to a point just above a sideshoot. New shoots will produce flowers the next season, but to keep the plant neat and compact some may be removed cleanly. During active growth, give liquid feeds and treat blue-flowered forms with a special blueing compound available from garden shops. In autumn, when the foliage is shed, bring the plant into a cool room where the temperature does not exceed 10°C (50°F). Higher temperatures may inhibit flowering. Keep only slightly moist until early February. The temperature can then be allowed to rise gently to encourage early flowering and watering can be increased gradually. Saved plants will eventually become too large to keep indoors. If potting becomes necessary, use an acid compost, with some added peat if necessary.

When watering, use clean rainwater if the tap-water is hard and limy. Under alkaline conditions, blue varieties may turn pinkish or lose their rich hue. Do not attempt to turn normally pink forms into blue ones by using a blueing compound.

The most common pest is aphids. If the compost is too alkaline, the foliage may turn yellow, as well as producing poor flower colours.

HYPOCYRTA GLABRA
(clog plant, pouch flower)
* 15°C/59°F

The common names of this plant are derived from the appearance of the orange-red tubular flowers borne in summer. It is a comparatively recent introduction as a houseplant and has attractive glossy-green, dainty, although somewhat fleshy, evergreen foliage. The plant is of South American origin and only suitable for moderately warm conditions maintained in winter, but an occasional fall below the minimum temperature seems to do little harm.

The plant is useful for slightly shaded positions, more especially during summer. It grows well in peat-based compost, but a little extra grit can be added to ensure good drainage, and the pot must be well crocked to avoid any chance of waterlogging. Water freely in summer and sparingly in winter.

Potting can be done in spring, and established plants propagated by dividing the roots. Cuttings also usually root

A grouping of *Hydrangea macrophylla* Hortensia group cultivars.

readily if taken after flowering. To encourage bushy, branching plants, the shoots of rooted cuttings and repotted plants can be pinched out. This will keep the plants compact and give a neat shape.

Chills and overwatering may cause yellowing and deterioration of the foliage, but otherwise the plant has very few troubles.

HYPOESTES PHYLLOSTACHYA
(syn. H. sanguinolenta)
(polka dot plant)
* 10°C/50°F

Lately, this has become an extremely popular houseplant, probably because it can be easily raised from seed on window-sills. Seed sown in spring will give nicely shaped plants by summer, and indeed this is really the best way to acquire plants other than to buy them. Old plants may become untidy and straggly and look anything but attractive. Moreover, to keep the plants in good condition during winter requires the maintenance of moderate warmth. They will survive a considerable chill, but then deteriorate miserably. They then have to be cut back severely in spring for the production of new growth. The leaves are oval, olive-green and smothered with small, white to pinkish spots. The quality of colouring varies in a batch of seedlings, pink being the most desirable. Good colours can be propagated from cuttings taken in spring, but both saved plants and those from cuttings should have their growing tips removed

several times to produce branching growth. If left to grow normally, they can reach 60cm (2ft).

In favourable conditions, this plant – which is from Madagascar – will flower. However, the purple and white blooms are not particularly interesting. This species is useful for a shaded position, but in summer likes moderate humidity. To keep the leaves in good condition, spray them with water from time to time. For short-term plants, 13cm (5in) pots can be used as the final size for seedlings or rooted cuttings.

Aphids and whitefly may attack, but the plants are not especially susceptible to pests or diseases. Chill causes leaf yellowing and fall.

Hypocyrta glabra.

Hypoestes phyllostachya.

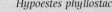

IMPATIENS *(busy Lizzie)*
* 13°C/55°F, see text

Busy Lizzie is probably the most ubiquitous of all houseplants. Unfortunately, it is so often seen as one of the least decorative of plants, with straggly leafless stems, an ungainly shape and few flowers.

A good specimen of this plant should be neat, spreading and dwarf in habit. It should have fine leaf colour, and be covered in beautiful blooms. This perfection is not easy to achieve in old plants. Moreover, since the plants are derived from species native to Zanzibar (now part of Tanzania) and other parts of East Africa, a congenial winter warmth is needed to keep them in healthy condition.

The best results in growing these plants are achieved by making frequent starts with seed or cuttings during early spring. Seed is the most practical method, since it can be difficult to save plants over winter if conditions are not suitable. Plants which have experienced a temperature as low as 7°C (45°F) can be saved, but they inevitably lose their foliage and become tatty-looking. Nearly all the best impatiens are hybrids or cultivars, mostly derived from *I. walleriana* (syn. *I. holstii*) and *I. sultanii*.

There are numerous excellent seed strains available, and as well as making fine pot plants they are splendid for outdoor summer bedding.

'Futura' is an F_1 hybrid with a wide range of uses. It is not so compact as many others, but is strong and vigorous and very free-flowering, with a mixture of beautiful colours and large blooms. It can be used in hanging-baskets as well as ordinary pots. It does well in slight shade and positions of good light.

'Minette' (F_1 hybrid) is particularly good for pots and has a very dwarf and flattish habit of growth. It is very quick to flower, giving a mixture of bright colours. 'Imp' is similar, but not quite so dwarf. Both are useful for outdoor bedding or for window-boxes and patio pots, as well as for indoor plants.

'Zig-zag' is a recently introduced F_1 hybrid, notable for its white flowers, all with contrasting gay stripes in rose-red, orange or salmon. This hybrid can be used outdoors or indoors. The proportion of white to other colours varies somewhat between batches, and in some the effect may be of a white star or cross on each bloom. The flowers are large and the habit neat and compact.

'Miss Swiss' is a new hybrid, remarkable for the brilliance of its very freely-produced salmon to scarlet flowers. Exceptional for its huge flowers, which can exceed 5cm (2in) in diameter, is 'Grand Prix'. This is very compact and spreading. It has a mixture of good colours and can be used outdoors.

If it is possible to save plants there are some specially fine cultivars having attractive foliage. 'Fanfair' has golden-yellow green-edged foliage and rose-pink flowers. 'Aflame' is rather similar, but with more marked reddish veining and darker green borders and pinkish flowers. 'Red Magic' and 'Cotton Candy' have dark, bronzy foliage with vivid red flowers in the former and pinkish flowers in the latter. These cultivars may not flower so generously as the hybrids raised from seed – particularly those with variegated foliage – but they are very beautiful. They are not so easy to keep, since they are more insistent on winter warmth and humidity and come from species native to Papua New Guinea.

Generally, busy Lizzie plants like plenty of moisture, although this does not mean waterlogging, and a high humidity.

Although they grow well in partial shade, they also enjoy plenty of light, avoiding direct sunshine behind glass. There is a tendency for these plants to be excessively overwatered, and this leads to yellowing and shedding of foliage. Most plants for the home can be given 13cm (5in) pots, and any of the modern potting composts will produce splendid growth. The plants sometimes benefit from a feed of magnesium sulphate (Epsom salts), at $2\frac{1}{2}$ml (1 teaspoon) to 500ml (1 pint) of water. This helps maintain a good leaf colour.

The recommended method of propagation of the hybrids is from seed, with cultivars raised from cuttings. Impatiens are liable to most of the common pest infestations, such as aphids, whitefly, and red spider mites.

IPOMOEA *(morning glory)*
* 13°C/55°F, see text

There is considerable difference of opinion about the naming of this genus. The popular name morning glory is usually applied to *I. tricolor*, which is also called *I. rubrocaerulea* and *Pharbitis tricolor*.

It is raised from seed quite easily on a warm window-sill in early spring. For germination, a temperature of 20°C (68°F) should be maintained. The seedlings can be expected to appear within two to three weeks. It hastens germination if the large seeds can be soaked in tepid water for about 48 hours before being sown.

There are now a number of fancy forms, but still the most beautiful is the old favourite 'Heavenly Blue', with large convolvulus-like flowers in a glorious vivid-blue, and very freely produced. 'Flying Saucers' is striped blue and

Impatiens 'Fantastic Rose'.

Ipomoea tricolor 'Sapphire Cross'.

white, and 'Wedding Bells' is mauve. 'Scarlet O'Hara' is probably derived from *Pharbitis purpurea* (syn. *I. purpurea*), and there is a form 'Sapphire Cross' with very large vivid-blue and white flowers, which is probably a hybrid.

All of these plants are vigorous climbers and are best regarded as annuals, being discarded after flowering. The more height they can be given the better, and in the home they are usually trained up bamboo canes. A position in a tall, sunny window or by patio doors will give the most impressive display, but they can be kept low by snipping off the tops of the growing stems to induce plenty of base growth. They are self-twining and support themselves.

The flowers open only during the morning and fade by early afternoon, but there are usually abundant buds ready for opening every morning over a long period.

The seedlings do not like chilly conditions, and as a result may grow slowly and poorly and turn yellow. The final pot size depends on the space available, and can go up to 20cm (8in) for tall windows or porches, when 1.5m (5ft) canes can be provided for the plants to climb up.

Where there is plenty of room, three seedlings can be put in a 25cm (10in) pot. A position in good light is essential, and the compost should be kept nicely moist all the time. The most likely pests are greenfly, blackfly, whitefly and red spider mites.

IRIS
see page 145

JASMINUM
* 7°C/45°F

Two species are sold as houseplants, although they are more suited to a conservatory or garden room where they can be allowed to adorn a wall or be trained to a considerable height. When bought, they are often trained around a wire loop, but it is not long before their rampant nature leads them to search elsewhere for support.

The favourite plant is undoubtedly *J. polyanthum*, pink jasmine, because of its exquisite and powerful scent, The white, tubular flowers, pinkish in bud, are freely produced and a mature plant will become smothered with bloom during winter if the minimum temperature is maintained. The plants will survive at considerably lower temperatures, but are liable to lose their foliage. Unfortunately too much warmth is likely to encourage very quick growth, and plants should be confined in relatively small pots if space is limited.

J. mesnyi (syn. *J. primulinum*), the primrose jasmine, has no scent, but the pretty, bright yellow flowers make a gay show from March to May. This is not a twiner like the other species and has less tendency to become invasive, and therefore may be more suitable for the home. Because of the rampant nature of *J. polyanthum*, it is a good idea to take cuttings in March and to grow these in a sunny place during summer, training around a wire loop or up a cane. The plants can be taken into the home in autumn and should give a presentable display of flowers from winter onwards. Old and inconveniently large plants can then be discarded or given to friends with conservatories or greenhouses.

If possible, take the cuttings with a heel, since these usually root easily at 16°C (61°F). Cutting back and pruning can be done after flowering.

J. mesnyi is best thinned rather than cut back too much. In all cases, weak and straggly stems should be removed entirely. Both species seem to do well in either slight shade or good light. In winter, keep the roots nicely moist but not waterlogged. Aphids are the most likely problem.

Jasminum polyanthum

KALANCHOE
* 7°C/45°F

There are several kalanchoes of considerable importance as houseplants. They are succulents, generally of a very easy nature, yet most rewarding. Some types are grown primarily for their flowers, while others are cultivated for their interesting leaves.

K. pumila makes an excellent hanging-basket plant with small, toothed and elongated leaves borne on trailing stems, the whole being covered with a pinky-white farina. Pink flowers are produced freely in January and February.

Far more popular, and the more frequently seen, is *K. blossfeldiana*. This is now rarely grown as the original species, except in conservatories and greenhouses where it can reach 90cm (3ft) in height and bear very large and flattish heads of brilliant scarlet flowers from late winter to spring, the seed having been sown the previous spring. Much more useful as houseplants are the more recent hybrids – particularly the F_1 hybrids – which are much more compact and lower-growing, and have a wide range of very attractive colours. The foliage is thick, succulent, oval in shape, and slightly toothed around the edges, and generally smaller, so that the plants rarely need supporting like *K. blossfeldiana*. For some years, 'Vulcan', a sturdy dwarf bushy hybrid, has been very popular. It reaches 15cm (6in) in height and bears a profusion of scarlet flowers as bright as, but much smaller than, the original species.

More recently, an F_1 hybrid strain of seed has been introduced called 'Melody'. This gives taller plants, reaching 30–45cm (1–1½ft) in height but still sturdy and self-supporting. The unusual feature is the range of flower colours, which include rose red, dark red, orange and yellow shades, as well as scarlet. The flower-heads are also large and showy. Two attractive hybrids are 'Annette' (red) and 'Christina' (orange).

It is very easy to raise the flowering kalanchoes from seed on a window-sill. Pot the seedlings into 13cm (5in) pots, keeping the plants steadily growing during winter at the recommended minimum temperature. The compost should be slightly moist. A position in good light produces sturdy plants. Flowering time can be erratic and depends on lighting conditions.

Commercially, kalanchoes are often induced to flower at unnatural times of the year by adjusting the amount of light the plants receive. Plants from a January sowing are given restricted day length for about ten weeks, beginning in June.

This is done by blacking-out frames to reduce daylight to nine hours each day. By the end of that time, flower buds should have normally begun to form.

Old plants sometimes tend to get straggly, but good colours can be propagated from cuttings, taken any time from late spring to summer. They usually root easily.

Seed, which is very fine, is best germinated at 21°C (70°F). At first the seedlings are slow to grow, but leave them in the original seed-tray to attain a manageable size before attempting to prick them out. F_1 hybrid seed must be purchased each time from a reputable seedsman.

Many plants which at one time were known as bryophyllums are now called kalanchoes.

A species of special interest is *K. daigremontiana* (syn. *Bryophyllum daigremontianum*), for some unknown reason called good luck plant. The succulent leaves are often packed in polythene and sold to tourists and holiday visitors of warm resorts, such as Hawaii, to take home. The leaves, if placed flat on any potting compost and kept warm and humid, soon form plantlets around the edges. When rooted, these can be separated and individually potted. It is an easy species to grow on most window-sills in a bright position, and may reach 90cm (3ft) in height.

The leaves are irregularly edged and little plantlets readily form along them. The tubular flowers vary in colour from yellowish, through pink to purplish.

Similarly packed for tourists are the leaves of *K. fedtschenkoi, K. pinnata* (syn. *Bryophyllum pinnatum*) and other species that freely form plantlets along their leaf edges. These have pendent orange-red, reddish, or cream to greenish tubular flowers.

Rather different in appearance is *K. tubiflora* (syn. *Bryophyllum tubiflorum*) which has cylindrical leaves spotted reddish-brown and bearing the little plantlets at the tips. The flowers are very pretty and usually coloured rich-salmon to scarlet.

Kalanchoes rarely have problems. Erratic watering may cause browning of the leaf edges, and mealy bugs are a possibility on the leaves. Should it become necessary to treat the plants with an insecticide, check with the label that kalanchoes are not likely to be damaged.

LILIUM
see page 145

LITHOPS
see page 160

LYGODIUM
see page 139

MAMMILLARIA
see page 162

MANDEVILLA
see Dipladenia

MARANTA *(prayer plant)*
** see text for temperatures

An important genus of beautiful foliage plants, the marantas are closely related to calatheas. However, the marantas tend to be easier to manage in the home, being more tolerant to lower temperatures and humidity. Ideally, a winter minimum temperature of 13°C (55°F) should be maintained, but they often survive down to near freezing if kept dry. They will then deteriorate severely, the foliage turning brown and shrivelling, but even though damaged new leaves may appear with the return of warmer conditions. Their survival is probably due to their rhizome-like roots; one species not grown for ornament, *M. arundinacea*, is the source of arrowroot starch used for making easily digested foods for invalids.

The most important maranta grown as a houseplant is *M. leuconeura* and its cultivars. Their curious behaviour in closing their leaves together and holding them erect during the evening has led to the popular name prayer plant. *M. leuconeura* is also called domino plant or rabbit track plant, owing to the bold contrasting chocolate-brown spots arranged symmetrically along each side of the central leaf vein. The leaves are oval, pale green, and slightly ribbed. *M. l.* 'Kerchoveana' is a name often given to this form, the original species being variable in leaf markings. *M. l.* 'Massangeana' has similar leaf shape, but is slightly smaller and more spreading in habit. The leaves also tend to be rather blunt at the end. They are pale green, with a contrasting herring-bone pattern and dark green blotches between the 'bones'. The undersurface is a lovely rose-purple. *M. l. erythrophylla* (also called *M. tricolor*) is a real beauty, but is far less easy to grow and is most intolerant of chills. It also needs higher humidity. A minimum winter temperature of 13°C (55°F) should be maintained to avoid the risk of deterioration from which the plant may not recover. The oval leaves, usually held more erect than in the other forms, are richly coloured dark green with reddish veins and yellowish mid-rib. Often the whole can be suffused with reddish tints.

All the marantas grow well in any good potting compost, and can be potted into 13cm (5in) pots. They will benefit from high humidity and should be well watered and fed in summer and autumn. Keep them on the dry side in winter, but regulate watering according to the temperature maintained. If it is rather cool, water very sparingly, and if conditions get very cold keep the plants almost dry. In spring, carefully snip off any dead or shrivelled foliage to make room for the new leaves. Old plants can be multiplied by root division in spring.

Marantas are particularly useful for shady places and if exposed to too much light the best leaf variegation and colours may not develop, or the leaves may become bleached and pale. In summer, they will appreciate a spray with water from time to time. Aphids and red spider mites are the only possible pests.

MICROCOELUM
see page 136

MICROLEPIA
see page 138

MILTONIA
see page 174

Far left: *Kalanchoe blossfeldiana.*
Below: *Maranta leuconeura erythrophylla.*

MIMOSA PUDICA
(sensitive plant, humble plant)
* 13°C/55°F

This species may not be one of the most decorative houseplants, but it is certainly the most fascinating. Children are particularly intrigued by the remarkable phenomenon of plant movement that it so dramatically demonstrates. Both the foliage and the flowers have a resemblance to mimosa (*Acacia dealbata*). However, in *M. pudica* the flowers are of little consequence, only a few being produced. They are purplish to pinkish in colour – they will appear on young plants the first year from spring sowings, usually in July and August.

The striking feature of the plant is its sensitive foliage. The leaves are composed of a number of small leaflets. At the base of each leaflet is a tiny, pale, raised spot. This is the touch-sensitive organism, and is called a pulvinus. If it is touched with a needle point, the leaflet will instantly fold upwards. Usually, the leaflet opposite will also fold and the movement may continue along the entire leaf, each pair folding. A sharper vibration will, of course, cause the whole plant to collapse dramatically, the leaf stalks also folding downwards so that it appears wilted and dead. If left alone, the plants slowly regain normality. The time taken for this is variable and may be half an hour or more. The performance can then be repeated.

The movement is believed to be caused by a hydraulic effect due to cells in the pulvinus taking in or discharging sap from the surrounding tissues, but the exact mechanism is still a mystery.

The plant may fold its foliage in the evening. This is called sleep movement and it is common in plants of the pea family.

The sensitive plant is a native of tropical America although it grows widely in a number of warm climates. It is perennial, but needs a congenial warmth to survive the winter. Moreover, old plants are less sensitive and do not react so spectacularly to touch. It is, therefore, more convenient to buy seedlings in spring, or grow your own from seed. The seed germinates easily under windowsill conditions, and is sown from April to May. Prick out the seedlings into 7.5cm (3in) pots, later transferring them to 13cm (5in) pots. The height reached by autumn is only about 30cm (1ft) or so. Keep the plants moist and give a slightly shaded position.

There are usually no problems associated with this plant, but red spider mites are a possibility. If difficulty is experienced in germinating the seed, it may be because it is not reasonably fresh. Try soaking it overnight before sowing, using tepid water.

MONSTERA DELICIOSA
(Swiss cheese plant)
** 13°C/55°F

Despite its need for moderate warmth the whole year, this species has become a popular houseplant in recent years. It does best in centrally-heated homes with reasonable humidity, but it is probably seen at its best in public buildings and offices where it can be allowed to grow to its full size. Its botanical name can be interpreted as delicious monster.

The leaves are very large and roundish, even on young plants. On fully-grown plants, they can become enormous, tending to elongate to 1m (3½ft). The plant itself can grow to at least 3m (10ft) in a conservatory and much taller in its natural environment which is Mexico and tropical America.

These plants make excellent large features in the home, growing to form a shape that easily fits a corner. They often require good strong stakes for support, and large pots.

The leaves are curiously slashed and in mature plants, tend to display elongated holes rather than wide slits. Their colour is a pleasing medium green, and there is a glossy sheen. The description 'delicious' refers to the fruit. Mature plants produce large arum-like flowers, usually in groups of two or three, at any time of the year. The spathe of the flower is creamy-yellow and the interior surface has an extraordinary fine diamond-like pattern impressed over the entire area. The large, central spadix develops into a fruit looking like an elongated pale green pineapple. When ripe, it has a fruity taste, like a mixture of pineapple and banana. Unfortunately, it has a very fibrous texture, and these numerous sharp fibres can stick in the tongue and throat.

The plant sends out long aerial roots. When growing in its native habitat, these roots penetrate moss growing on tree trunks, but on a pot-grown plant they may turn downwards and enter the pot's compost, travelling a long distance. The best way to grow this plant is up a moss-covered stake. The support must be a stout one, with at least 5cm (2in) thickness of sphagnum moss, mixed with a little bonemeal, wound around it and secured with wire. Monstera is a greedy feeder and the bonemeal will provide extra nourishment for the aerial roots when they penetrate the moss. The plant grows tall, but can be kept within bounds by cutting off the top. This encourages the formation of sideshoots. The tops should be removed when they have formed aerial roots, and they can then be potted and will grow away quite

Mimosa pudica.

quickly, provided there is adequate warmth and humidity. The operation is best done in early summer.

This species will survive at temperatures as low as 7°C (45°F), but it is risky – especially in the case of a large well-grown specimen which may then deteriorate. Ideally, a minimum of 18°C (65°F) should be maintained, although this will encourage more rapid growth which may be inconvenient if there is limited space.

The plant must have plenty of moisture at all times, unless the absolute minimum temperature has to be maintained in winter. Watering should then be cautious and the roots kept slightly dry. At other times, spraying with water is most beneficial and the moss used on supports must be kept moist. The plant will tolerate shade or a bright position. In shade, the leaves tend to remain relatively small and oval in shape and the plant seems to stay more compact. However, direct sunlight should be avoided, since the leaves can easily become scorched, especially after being sprayed with water. The foliage responds very well to treatment with a leaf-shine preparation, and takes on a brilliant gloss.

When potting, use peat-based compost. Eventually, large pots or even small tubs may be needed if it is proposed to grow the plants to maximum size. Potting is best done in spring, and plants not so treated should be fed with a liquid feed during the summer growing period.

Monstera deliciosa is very rarely troubled by pests, but low temperatures, low humidity, or erratic watering, causes leaf yellowing and brownish patches on the foliage.

Monstera deliciosa.

NERTERA *(bead plant)*
* 1°C/34°F

This is a small genus of creeping evergreens with tiny oval leaves, sometimes forming mounds or hummocks. The flowers are minute and greenish in colour, but the berries that follow are just like brilliant orange or red beads. These berries – or drupes as they are correctly called – are often borne in profusion, almost covering the plant. They are also retained for up to about two months, making the plant decorative for a long period. The most common pot species is N. *granadensis*, a native of Mexico, which has very bright orange berries. It is often confused with N. *depressa* and wrongly labelled. The latter species is of New Zealand origin, usually faster growing and more vigorous, and has smaller, bright-red berries. It is often hardy in sheltered places outdoors, especially in the south.

N. *balfouriana* is also from New Zealand, but the berries are yellow to pale orange. The plants are best grown in pans or half-pots, since they are not deep rooting. A fairly wide container is needed so that there is plenty of room for the plants to spread and form an attractive and pleasing cushion.

The plants like to be kept moist at all times, but not waterlogged. A good humidity is also appreciated, although it is unwise to spray the plants. If the matted growth is kept wet for too long it is liable to rot or encourage the mould botrytis (*Botrytis cinerea*), which forms brown to greyish furry growth, ultimately leading to rotting. In summer, a shaded place should be found, but plenty of light can be given in winter. Dividing the plants in spring is a simple form of propagation or sow seeds.

NOTOCACTUS
see page 163

ODONTOGLOSSUM
see page 174

OLEANDER
see page 178

ONCIDIUM
see page 174

OPUNTIA
see page 161

PACHYSTACHYS
** 10°C/50°F

Pachystachys is very similar to jacobinia, and the culture and requirements are also alike. The plants are evergreen and mostly from tropical America. The most frequently seen species is *P. lutea*, popularly called lollipop plant and gold hops. These names allude to the flowers, which consist mainly of yellow bracts covering small, white flowers. They somewhat resemble those of the aphelandra.

The leaves are spear-shaped, crinkled, and of a glossy texture. The flowering period is a long one and may begin in spring and end in autumn.

This Peruvian species will reach about 1m (3½ft) in height, and can make an impressive houseplant. The species *P. coccinea*, from the West Indies and North and South America, grows considerably taller, but can be kept compact by pruning. The foliage is similar, but the flowers are very like those of the jacobinia. In this case, the plumes are bright scarlet, very showy, and borne in winter. It is not quite so amenable to room culture as the former species and demands a little more warmth and humidity. It has been sold by florists under the common name cardinal's guard. Both plants are ideal for a conservatory or garden room where they can be given large pots and allowed to display their full glory in the space available.

PAPHIOPEDILUM
see page 174

Nertera depressa.

Pachystachys lutea.

PASSIFLORA (passion flower)
* see text for temperatures

There are about 300 species of passion flowers, and they have earned fame for several reasons. Many have extremely beautiful and unusual flowers. The structure of the flowers has been given religious significance, for which the early South American missionaries are said to be responsible. They identified the long structure at the centre of the flower (the gynandrophore) as the scourging post, the filament-like corona as the crown of thorns, the stamens as the five wounds, and the flat-headed stigmas as the three nails, all concerned with Christ's passion.

A number of the species have delicious fruits which come on to the market from time to time, but generally do not keep or travel well. They are usually of more importance in the countries where the plants grow naturally, and this means mostly warm climates. They are mostly vigorous climbers, but there are a few shrubby, tree-like, and annual species. Some, such as *P. quadrangularis*, which gives the fruit called granadilla, and is of exceptional beauty, make fine climbers for a warm conservatory or greenhouse. Others can be used for a frost-free place, a few flowering in the first year from a spring sowing – but they need plenty of space and tend to be rampant and invasive.

The most popular species is undoubtedly *P. caerulea*. This is hardy outdoors in many parts of the country and will cover a south-facing wall with masses of its striking blooms when established. It also produces large, decorative, golden-yellow inedible fruits. It is this species that so often appears in florists and is sold as a houseplant. It vividly shows the structure of the flower that has given rise to religious interpretations. As presented for growing in the home it is usually trained around a wire loop. The plants are usually grown in nurseries from cuttings taken from mature flowering plants. Plants grown from seed often take several years to mature and flower, especially in the case of this particular species. The flowers, which are about 7.5cm (3in) in diameter, continue from early summer to autumn. This species is from Brazil and needs a position in maximum light to flower well. In shaded places it may merely produce a rampant tangle of its vine-like leaves. During the summer months the plants can stand outside for a time. However, there usually comes a time when the plants will become a problem owing to their demand for space. It helps to keep the pots as small as possible, and to be very cautious over feeding.

Balanced plant feeds should be given to maintain health and good leaf colour, but excessive feeding will only encourage the plant's rampant nature. Plants will soon outgrow their wire loop. They can be potted-on into larger pots and given bamboo canes to climb up. They are useful for placing in picture-windows or by patio doors and will give pleasure for some time. Later, the plants can either be planted outdoors, preferably on a south-facing wall, or transferred to the wall of a sunny lean-to greenhouse or conservatory.

The plant is relatively hardy, but the leaves are liable to deteriorate or fall during a winter chill. In cold positions it should be given little water, if any, during winter if planted in a conservatory border. Pot plants should be kept just slightly moist.

In summer – and for the growing period – plenty of water becomes necessary. During late winter or early spring the plants will usually need drastic pruning to keep them within bounds, more especially if they are house or conservatory grown.

Lateral shoots can be cut back to the main stem and the plant thinned. Usually, the true species of *P. caerulea* is preferred as a houseplant. This is blue and white. There is also a pure white form called 'Constance Elliott', and a few hybrids, but these are not so satisfactory grown in pots.

Passifloras have few pest troubles, but cucumber mosaic, a virus disease, can cause yellowing and mottling of the foliage during summer. Unfortunately, as yet there is no cure for this.

Passiflora caerulea.

PELARGONIUM
* see text for temperatures

Along with fuchsias, pelargoniums are among the most popular pot plants. However, from the houseplant point of view they are far more important and useful, since they generally enjoy far less humidity and drier conditions. As well as being very free-flowering, and bearing magnificent blooms with many lovely colours and markings, they often have delightful foliage.

Pelargoniums include the well-loved 'geranium', the flamboyant show or regal pelargoniums, some charming trailers, miniatures, and a number of species and cultivars with fragrant and decorative foliage. Generally, these all grow quite easily under ordinary home conditions, as well as making excellent conservatory, greenhouse or garden room plants. However, they are unsuitable for hot, stuffy rooms and they must have a position in good light.

Most of these plants can be kept for many years if given frost-free winter conditions, and some will even give a good show of bloom in winter if the temperature can be kept higher. With a winter minimum of about 7–10°C (45–50°F), most forms will remain evergreen and may, within a couple of years, reach a considerable size if not drastically pruned back. Such large plants, if moderately pruned to maintain a neat shape, can make magnificent specimens, bearing masses of blooms. They need at least 25cm (10in) pots at this stage and may have to be transferred to a position of greater space, such as a garden room or conservatory, or perhaps a porch. The plants can also be used on a patio for the summer and autumn.

Sometimes, old plants can also be trained as climbers and grown against the wall of a conservatory. Zonal pelargoniums are sometimes trained as standards, but these are not usually very convenient as room plants.

Zonal pelargoniums are the plants popularly called geraniums, an incorrect name leading to confusion with the true geraniums, which are mainly hardy border plants. Zonal pelargoniums are distinguished by their more rounded foliage, often with bold and contrasting zones or bands of chocolate-brown colours.

The flowers may be single or double, and come in all shades with the exception of blue and yellow. In some cases, the foliage is so excitingly coloured and

patterned that the plants can be grown for that interest alone.

The miniatures are also of the zonal group. Generally, the zonals are of mixed parentage, the most important being *P. zonale*. There are many named cultivars, and to get some idea of the full range it is wise to obtain a catalogue from a specialist grower.

A cultivar famous for many years was 'Paul Crampel', a bright vermilion, but there are now many superior cultivars, the vigour having been improved. Their colours are also often outstanding. For example, 'Orangesonne', of more recent introduction, has astonishingly vivid, salmon-orange blooms that seem to fluoresce. The semi-double 'Irene' geraniums also have lovely colours, large blooms and a strong and compact habit. The recent introduction of F_1 hybrid seed marks an important progress. This is very easy to germinate under window-sill conditions if sown at a temperature of 18°C (65°F) in early spring. If the seedlings are potted into 13cm (5in) pots they will flower well from summer to autumn and, with congenial warmth, well into the New Year. There are also numerous strains becoming available, and most grow 30–45cm (1–1½ft) during the first year from seed, the more compact strains remaining at about 30cm (1ft).

Miniature zonals usually grow from 15–30cm (6–12in) in height, remaining neat and compact for a number of years. These can be grown in 10cm (4in) pots.

Regal or show pelargoniums have more triangular, pale green leaves with serrated edges. The flower heads usually have fewer blossoms than the zonals, but the individual flowers are much larger and often colourfully marked or patterned in contrasting colours. Flowering is not quite so continuous, the main period being summer, with perhaps more blooms in late autumn. They mostly comprise hybrids involving *P. cucullatum*, *P. fulgidum*, and *P. grandiflorum*. These can be grown in 13cm (5in) pots initially, but can be grown on in much larger pots to form quite shrubby specimens.

Variegated-leaved geraniums originate from the same sources as the zonal types.

Ivy-leaved geraniums are mostly derived from *P. peltatum*, and have plain or zoned ivy-shaped leaves. Their trailing habit makes them ideal for hanging-baskets, for which purpose they are highly prized. They flower freely and have large, showy, single to double blooms in a wide range of colours, from summer to autumn. If it is difficult to have a hanging-basket situated in a bright position, the plants can be put in wall pots, on pedestal stands, or placed on any improvized support designed to allow the stems room to hang down.

Scented-leaved geraniums are a mixed group, also including some species. Although some have a good show of flowers, they are really grown for their delightfully scented foliage. The flowers are usually of no great consequence. The leaves are of great value for making potpourri and may be quite decorative. The following cultivars are all splendid foliage plants. 'Crispum Minor' (finger bowl geranium, neat habit, citron scented), 'Crispum Variegatum' (silvery variegated foliage, lemon scent), 'Mabel Grey' (serrated foliage, powerful citronella scent), 'Attar of Roses' (pale mauve flowers, rose scent), 'Clorinda' (large

cerise flowers, eucalyptus-like scent), 'Fragrans' (silvery-green foliage, white flowers, pine scent), 'Variegated Fragrans' (as previous, but extra compact and with white and green variegated foliage), 'Citriodorum' (vivid green orange-lemon scented foliage, mauve flowers), 'Odoratissimum' (powerful apple scent), 'Tomentosum' (peppermint scent), 'Prince of Orange' (orange scent), 'Endsleigh' (pepper scent).

Cactus-flowered pelargoniums are a small group of the zonal type, with curiously quilled narrow, pointed petals. They are very attractive and deserve to be better known. They are grown as for zonal pelargoniums.

General culture. All the pelargoniums described here will grow well in a good potting compost. Generally, 13cm (5in) pots are a convenient size, but plants saved over several years may need potting-on into larger pots in spring. Watering can be moderate during the period of growth, from late spring to September, but the rest of the time must be judged according to the temperature. Where it is very cold, little if any water should be given. In warmer conditions, where the plants may be flowering in winter to some extent, enough water should be given to keep the compost just slightly moist.

Zonal geraniums can be flowered in winter. For this purpose, take cuttings early in the year from established specimens that have been saved from the previous year. Root the cuttings at about 16°C (61°F) and pot on to final 13cm (5in) pots. During summer put the pots outdoors in a sunny place, preferably plunging the pots in moist peat, and don't forget to keep the plants watered. When the stem is about 10cm (4in) high, snip off the top and also remove any premature flower buds. In autumn transfer the plants to a sunny window-sill. If a temperature of from 7–10°C (45–50°F) can be maintained there should be plenty of winter blooms.

To save plants over winter the temperature should be kept above zero. About 5°C (40°F) is quite adequate. Never be afraid to cut back the plants. Indeed, this is essential to produce neat sturdy plants with plenty of side growth, and must be done in the case of saved plants. If not, they become tall and straggly, anything but decorative. Cutting back is best done in spring when new growth begins. Plants to be saved in cool conditions over winter can also be cut back in late autumn.

A small collection of pelargoniums, showing their wide range of form and colour.

PELLAEA
see page 139

PELLIONIA
** 13°C/55°F

This is a genus of small, creeping or trailing plants, with prettily marked and variegated foliage, all liking warmth and humidity. They are excellent for small hanging containers or wall pots in a relatively shaded situation.

Only two species usually appear as houseplants. The best known is *P. repens*, often called *P. daveauana*. The common name water-melon pellionia probably refers to the leaf marking. The undersurface of the foliage is pinkish. The upper surface is light green patterned dark green and with a purplish tint, particularly around the margins.

P. pulchra is of similar appearance, but the colouring is given contrast by very dark purplish veining. Both of these plants come from Vietnam, and grow especially well in peat-based potting composts to which crushed charcoal has been added. They like to be kept moist the whole year, but rather less so in winter. In summer, spray the foliage with tepid water.

The plants are easily propagated by division in spring, and are not too difficult to grow provided adequate warmth and humidity can be maintained. They are quite unsuitable for chilly homes, but do well in bottle gardens (see page 167). Cold soon causes deterioration and leaf yellowing, but the plants are rarely troubled by pests and diseases. If possible grow pellionias with other warmth-loving houseplants, to create a humid micro-climate. The plants are especially useful for the edges of troughs and containers, where the stems can trail over.

Pellionia daveauava.

PEPEROMIA
*/** 10–13°C/50–55°F

There are about 1,000 species in this genus and a number are important house and greenhouse plants. The individual species often vary considerably in appearance and habit, but they have very attractive foliage shapes and colours. They are usually neat or reasonably compact, and can be grown in relatively small pots or containers.

With a few exceptions, they are moderately easy to grow. Some produce peculiar catkin-like creamy-white flowers, which may be quite decorative, but the foliage is usually of the most importance. Of the several species grown as houseplants, the one likely to prove difficult is *P. argyreia* (syn. *P. sandersii*), from Brazil. It is popularly called the water-melon plant, but should not be confused with *Pellionia repens*, which is also given this name.

P. argyreia is a charming little plant, excellent for bottle gardens. It forms a clump of stout, reddish stems carrying broadly spear-shaped leaves, beautifully banded in green and silvery-green. It rarely exceeds 20cm (8in) in height. This species should be given about 13°C (55°F) minimum, or a little higher. It must be carefully watered in winter. It has a marked tendency to rot at the base of its stems, much more so that the other species, and many plants seem to be lost this way.

P. caperata is of a similarly neat, dwarf habit. The leaves are quite different, being smaller and very corrugated. They are deep green, but there are some variegated forms with cream markings. From spring to winter, quaint creamy-white flowers, looking like erect mouse-tails, and borne on pinkish stems, are sent up in great profusion. These add greatly to the attraction of the plant. It originates from tropical America, and is liable to rot at the base if a minimum temperature of 10°C (50°F) is not maintained.

P. griseoargentea (syn. *P. hederifolia*), the ivy peperomia, is very similar in appearance, but the leaves are not nearly so corrugated and they are greyish-green, often with a metallic sheen. This is another Brazilian species and needs similar care.

P. magnoliifolia, desert privet, from Panama and the West Indies, forms a bushy and shrubby plant about 25cm (10in) in height. The leaves are much larger and about 5cm (2in) in diameter. They are fleshy and glossy and variegated in cream and green.

The true species has plain leaves and is rarely grown as a houseplant. The form

'Variegata' is mostly creamy-green, particularly in young plants, the colour changing to pale green as the plant ages. The cultivar 'Green Gold' has larger, cream-bordered foliage and changes much less as it ages.

P. obtusifolia, popularly called baby rubber plant, is of similar habit. In this case, the leaves are rather smaller, fleshy, oval and dark green, sometimes with a reddish tinge at the edge. There is also a cream bordered form. It originates from Tropical America and southern Florida, but in fact seems to be one of the easiest species, surviving lower temperatures. The whitish flower spikes contrast nicely against the dark foliage and are borne from summer to autumn.

P. serpens variegata (syn. *P. scandens variegata*), the cupid peperomia, from Peru, is a trailer, but it can be encouraged to climb erect as well as being useful for hanging containers. The stems

Peperomia magnoliifolia 'Variegata'.

can exceed 60cm (2ft) long and in ideal conditions reach a considerable length. The stems are green and the leaf stalks pink. The foliage is heart-shaped and green with a cream border, but mostly an overall creamy colour when immature. The leaves of young plants have a tendency to fall easily, but this annoying characteristic is fortunately lost as the plant matures.

P. glabella, wax privet, from Tropical America, is of similar habit but with smaller leaves. The stems are reddish and again there is a plain green true species which is rarely grown.

P. marmorata resembles both *P. argyreia*, in leaf shape and marking and *P. caperata* in its corrugated surface, which however is only slight in comparison. The colouring is brownish and a metallic shiny green, giving the common name silver heart. It has a similar clump-forming habit, but is easier to grow.

Most peperomias can be grown in any good potting compost, but the pots should be well crocked and if a few pieces of charcoal can be added it is an advantage. In nature, the plants often grow like epiphytic bromeliads. They also rarely need large pots. Most of the small, clump-forming species do well in 10–13cm (4–5in) pots. Give a position in good light, but avoid direct sunlight. In summer, water can be freely given, but in winter watering needs great care. Try to maintain very slightly moist conditions and keep water away from the base, where there is a cluster of stems. Although it is also important to keep the minimum temperature suggested, the air should preferably have some movement and in winter it should not be too humid. This does not imply dry air, since the plants dislike centrally heated homes with a dry non-humidified atmosphere. If the air is too stagnant, there is some-

times a problem with the fungus grey mould (*Botrytis cinerea*), and again it is among the clump of stems where this furry mould will usually begin rotting the tissues. In the case of *P. argyreia* and *P. serpens* (syn. *P. scandens*), extra care is needed. Excessive watering and constant wet conditions at the roots should never be permitted. It is very unusual for insect pests to prove troublesome. Potting should be done in late spring, so that generally warmer conditions can give a good start. The clump-forming species can be propagated by simple division, and the trailers from stem cuttings rooted in the normal way for cuttings of that type. Little trouble should be experienced given adequate warmth.

PHALAENOPSIS
see page 175

PHILODENDRON
** 13–16°C/55–61°F, see text

There are at least 270 species in this genus, and many of these have found their way on to the houseplant market. It is only possible to describe some of the more popular ones here. Some botanists used to put the well-known *Monstera deliciosa* in this genus, naming it *P. pertusum*. This plant is described under monstera in this book. The philodendrons are, however, similar in habit, being vigorous climbers, and they usually produce aerial roots.

In their natural environment, they grow up mossy tree trunks or ramble over rocks or hummocks of leafy plant debris in forests, mostly in South America. In nature, they often reach a considerable size. When grown in pots in greenhouses and homes, they usually show only their smaller juvenile foliage, which may also be of different structure to the mature form on older plants.

Undoubtedly, the most popular species is *P. scandens*, from Panama, and called sweetheart vine. It can be grown as a climber or a trailer when it is best to pinch out the growing tips frequently to encourage plenty of stems. It is moderately tolerant of neglect. It will also survive a certain amount of chill.

The normal species is plain green with somewhat pointed heart-shaped leaves, but there is a variegated cream-blotched form, believed to be caused by the presence of a virus. The foliage of this form sometimes distorts.

P. bipinnatifidum, the tree philodendron, from Brazil, is a non-climbing species, and will also withstand cooler conditions. It has handsome, large, incised foliage, rather like the monstera, the Swiss cheese plant, but it remains relatively compact, reaching only 1m (3½ft) in height. However, the leaf incisions are more numerous, more particularly as the plant matures. A fully-grown leaf may measure about 45cm (1½ft) in diameter. Similar is *P. selloum*, and when young it may be difficult to distinguish the two. As the plant develops, it forms a thickish trunk-like stem, and the edges of the leaf segments become ruffled, creating a charming effect, and inspiring the common name of lacy tree. It is a notable species for living to a very great age producing a stately plant.

The fiddle-leaf philodendron is the common name given to *P. panduriforme*, although this name is an extreme exaggeration of the leaf shape. The foliage is dark green, leathery, and has four upper lobes with an elongated central one. It is a climber from Brazil.

Elephant's ear is another inexplicable common name, this one being given to *P. domesticum* (syn. *P. hastatum*). It is a climber with very glossy leaves.

A very beautiful philodendron has been given the dramatic name black gold. This is sold as *P. melanochrysum*. The spear-shaped foliage has a velvety texture, dark green above and pinkish-purple below. The foliage, therefore, appears a very dark green, with golden iridescence. It originates from Columbia and needs a little extra care to make it happy as a houseplant. It certainly should not be subjected to temperatures below 13°C (55°F). *P. erubescens* is especially beautiful too, but easier. It is a fairly vigorous climber, with rather arrow-shaped foliage, often elongating to a considerable length, perhaps exceeding 20cm (8in).

The young leaves are rose-pink and the leaf stalks and stems purplish. Mature leaves acquire a bronzy-green colour. There is a form called 'Burgundy' which has a delightful coppery-red colour, and this is a hybrid probably involving several other species. Other named hybrids come on to the market from time to time. Philodendrons grow well in peat-based composts, and the climbers are best grown up moss-covered supports, as described under monstera. This helps the aerial roots to give support and to obtain extra nourishment and moisture. Give a position in good light, but not in direct sunlight. They all like a humid

atmosphere and can be sprayed with a mist of water now and then during summer, and kept nicely moist, but never waterlogged.

In winter, water cautiously, since over-watering can soon instigate rotting of the roots. Potting is best done in late spring when the plants are about to begin active growth.

The climbing species are easily propagated from pieces of the stems carrying roots. The non-climbers can usually only be propagated from seed, for example *P. bipinnatifidum*. This is not practical without greenhouse conditions. Pest and disease problems are unusual, but erratic watering, overwatering and chill will soon cause leaf yellowing.

A grouping of foliage houseplants.
Back: *Philodendron bipinnatifidum* (left) and *Philodendron* 'Red Emerald' (right). **Front:** *Pilea mollis* (left) and *Pilea cadierei* (right).

PHOENIX
see page 136

see page 136

PHYLLITIS
see page 139

see page 139

PILEA
* 10–13°C/50–55°F

There are about 400 species, but only a few are grown as houseplants. However, these are of considerable merit, and very attractive as foliage plants. A great favourite is *P. cadierei*, the aluminium plant. It is extremely neat in the form *P. c. nana*, which is usually sold as a houseplant, and grows only 30cm (1ft) high. It makes a compact, bushy little plant with very pretty silver-blotched rich-green spear-shaped foliage. It is native to Vietnam. In cultivation it tends to suffer from magnesium deficiency, to which it appears extra sensitive. If this happens the leaves may become distorted and pale, losing their contrasting colours. It is a wise precaution to water from time to time with a solution of Epsom salts – 5ml (1 teaspoon) to 500ml (1pt) of water.

P. microphylla (syn. *P. muscosa*), the artillery plant or gunpowder plant, is absolutely different in appearance, forming a neat, bushy plant with delicate ferny foliage. From May to September, inconspicuous greenish-yellow flowers are produced. These, on the slightest disturbance, issue clouds of pollen from their anthers, looking like puffs of yellow smoke and suggesting the common name.

It comes from tropical America, and is easy and seems happy with quite cool conditions.

P. involucrata, the friendship plant, is from Peru and Venezuela, and is a low and slow-growing plant with leaves of similar shape to *P. cadierei*. The oval leaves are slightly hairy, and much corrugated, purplish below and bronzy-green above. There is some confusion with this plant, often being mistaken for *P. spruceana*.

P. nummulariifolia, creeping Charlie, is a dainty creeper, useful for hanging pots or baskets. It has wiry, reddish stems, bearing small, corrugated heart-shaped leaves. It comes from South America.

P. mollis, the moon valley plant, is easy to grow from seed. It has spear-shaped yellowish-green crinkled foliage, with contrasting darker green veining. It can be raised from spring sowings on a window-sill.

The pileas grow easily in most potting composts, and generally 13cm (5in) pots are suitable. In winter, a position in good light should be found, but slight shade is necessary at other times.

At all times, maintain a moist compost, giving more water in summer when active growth is being made. If grown for too long, the plants become leggy or deteriorate. They are best propagated from cuttings every three or four years. The best time for potting is spring, and at this time any trimming or pruning should be done. In cold, damp conditions, where the air is stagnant, grey mould fungus may attack, particularly affecting *P. cadierei*, the central stems at the base of the clump being most affected. The most likely pest is aphids, but these are easy to control.

105

PIPER ORNATUM
(ornamental pepper)
*** 16°C/61°F

The name pepper is given to a number of ornamental plants, although this is the only one strictly deserving that title. It is the related species *P. nigrum* that is the source of most culinary pepper. The genus is large, with about 600 species, and all are natives of warm, moist climates, mostly tropical America. It is this that makes them difficult to grow as houseplants. However, given the right conditions the plants can become rampant.

P. ornatum is attractive and worth trying in a centrally-heated home. Without steady heat, it is a waste of time to attempt growing it. This species is a climber best grown up a mossy support. The leaves are broadly spear-shaped with bronzy-green colouring, the veins being flecked pink with a reddish tint below. Older leaves tend to become paler, with whitish variegation. The leaf colour and contrast varies with light conditions, the best contrast being developed where the light is good. However, direct sunlight should be avoided. This species comes from Celebes and warmth coupled with a good humidity is essential.

Spray with a mist of water from time to time, and grow them with other warmth and moisture-loving plants, so as to maintain a humid micro-climate. Better local humidity, as well as moisture for the aerial roots, will be obtained if a mossy support is used. Moreover, this method will help the plant, as it does not have an extensive normal root system. Chills will quickly cause drastic leaf fall.

PLATYCERIUM
see page 139

PLECTRANTHUS
* 10°C/50°F

This is a large genus of shrubby plants and perennials related to coleus. The best known is *P. oertendahlii*, which although popularly called Brazilian coleus is from South Africa. It is a low-growing rambling plant suitable for hanging containers, wall pots or baskets.

The leaves are very attractive. They are almost circular in shape, bronzy-green in colour, and with the veins boldly marked silvery-white. From June to October, erect bunches of tubular. purplish-white flowers are freely produced. In greenhouses, this is a useful plant for growing under the staging and for ground cover, as it likes subdued light.

P. coleoides, candle plant, from India, has a bushy habit, and as a houseplant will reach 30cm (1ft) in height. It is usually grown in the form *P. c.* 'Marginatus', which has roundish leaves, slightly triangular, and with irregular edges. The main colour is green and there is a wide border of cream, often with a greyish sheen. The flowers are white or purplish.

These species seem to prefer a loam-based compost, such as John Innes potting compost No. 2. They prefer shade in summer, although they should be given a place in good light in winter. They can be watered freely from spring to autumn, but sparingly during winter months. *P. oertendahlii* is the easier and

hardier of the two, and will endure temperatures down to 4°C (39°F) for short periods if kept dry. When grown in pots, the stems often send roots into the compost. When repotting in spring, these rooted sections can be cut off and potted individually to provide further plants. Pests and diseases are rarely troublesome.

PLUMBAGO AURICULATA
(syn. P. capensis) (Cape leadwort)
* 7°C/45°F

This South African shrub is notable for its beautiful clusters of phlox-like flowers borne over a long period, from spring to autumn. The most commonly seen one is a beautiful pale blue form, but there is also a white one. A delightful effect is obtained by growing the two together, so that the colours intermingle.

It is a favourite plant for cool conservatories or garden rooms, where it is best trained against a wall. If allowed to

Plectranthus oertendahlii.

Piper ornatum.

Plumbago auriculata.

106

reach an appreciable size, the somewhat straggly stems need support. However, young plants – and properly pruned specimens – can be kept as reasonably neat pot plants for some years.

In the home, this species is especially useful for glassed-in porches. It is also ideal in bright foyers and entrance halls, and particularly for glass-roofed corridors. It is nearly always recommended that this plant should be grown from cuttings, although it can be raised from seed sown in March. This will produce plants to bloom from summer onwards, making conveniently sized pot plants. Seed is quite easy to germinate under window-sill conditions, and the seedlings grow quickly, needing potting into their final 18cm (7in) pots the first year. To keep this species compact, prune by reducing all shoots by at least two-thirds after flowering. If space allows, the plants will reach over 3m (10ft) in height. For large specimens, a 25cm (10in) pot, or small tub, will be needed. If the minimum winter temperature is maintained, the plants should remain evergreen. In cooler conditions, they may lose foliage in winter, but they should easily survive if kept on the dry side. In summer, water can be given freely. A position in good light helps to keep the plants sturdy, but in summer protection from direct sunlight is necessary.

Plants grown against a wall can be given a trellis or wires for support. Free-standing plants can be given bamboo canes and kept tied to these.

Potting is best done in early spring. Cuttings for propagation should be taken with a heel during early summer. They usually root easily in plastic bags designed for window-sill propagation. Another species, *Plumbago indica* (syn. *P. rosea*), is occasionally sold as a houseplant. It is from the East Indies and needs considerable warmth and humidity, and at least 15°C (59°F) in winter. It has the advantage of being a compact, shrubby plant, suited to pot culture. The flowers are a lovely rose-red colour. Unfortunately, it seems very temperamental as a houseplant and grows best in a warm greenhouse. The most likely pest of plumbago is aphids.

POLYPODIUM
* see text for temperature

There are about 75 species of these attractive ferns. The best known is *P. vulgare*, of which there are a number of cultivars. The common names are wall fern and common polypody, and this species and its cultivars are frequently used to provide decorative foliage for the outdoor garden. *P. v.* 'Pulcherrimum' makes a useful plant for cold places in the home, and it can be grown either in pots or in wall containers and hanging-baskets. The fronds are very graceful and delicately structured, making a very distinctive plant.

It is an excellent plant for shady, chilly porches, corridors or entrance halls. Once potted, it is best left undisturbed as long as possible. It prefers a peaty but well-drained compost. Any good potting compost will do if some coarse grit or small pebbles and some charcoal granules are added.

Keep the roots, which are rhizome-like and creeping, moist at all times, but water more freely during the summer. The plants can be propagated easily by dividing the rhizomes in spring. *P. aureum*, now more correctly known as *Phlebodium aureum*, is entirely different and, coming from tropical America, needs about 10°C (50°F) in winter. It also has creeping rhizomes and is sometimes called hare's foot fern, because of the appearance of these.

The fronds are deep green, with the veins delicately contrasting in cream or paler green, and their structure is much simpler, being more palm-like. They usually have a slightly glossy sheen and grow 90cm (3ft). It can be given a compost similar to *P. vulgare*. Troubles are rare.

POLYSTICHUM
see page 139

Polypodium aureum.

PRIMULA
* see text for temperatures

A large genus of about 500 species, embracing the well-loved primrose and polyanthus. These plants in their modern forms make excellent pot plants for the home, even if only of a temporary nature. Several other species and cultivars or hybrids are also firm favourites, and are especially favoured for conservatory and greenhouse decoration as well as for window-sills. Very many species are used for alpine greenhouses, and some of these can also be grown on window-sills in cool, airy rooms.

P. vulgaris is the common primrose, but this has been developed by plant breeders in recent years to produce plants of immense beauty and in an exciting range of wonderful colours. These plants are quite hardy and excellent for the chilliest places in the home. They have now become popular pot plants, some strains tolerating gentle forcing so that they are in the shops just after Chirstmas.

The plants have the neat habit of the wild primrose, but the flowers are very much bigger and borne usually in large, roundish heads. The colours include just about everything possible. There are rich reds, yellows, oranges, rose-pinks and creams and whites, and often there is a contrasting bright yellow eye.

There are several seed strains of the F$_1$ hybrid type, such as 'Formula' (actually of Japanese origin), 'Ernest Benary', especially suited to forcing, and 'Mirella', which is extra-dwarf.

After flowering, the plants can be put in an outdoor garden or given to a friend with a garden.These coloured primroses also make fine window-box plants.

Polyanthus are hybrids also derived from P. vulgaris, but are sometimes called P. v. elatior. Again there are numerous strains, the great heads of large flowers being borne well above the foliage on strong stems. The F$_1$ hybrids have great vigour and strength and the colour range is wide. Most primulas have a scent, the intensity of which may vary according to type and growing conditions. The F$_1$ hybrid 'Jumbo' has an especially strong fragrance and the largest flowers of all. Most polyanthus can also be put in a garden after flowering, and may continue to flower and multiply each year.

The following primulas are tender and need a winter minimum of 5–7°C (41–45°F). They usually come on to the market from February onwards, and are sown by nurseries from May to June. The earliest to flower is P. praenitens (syn. P. sinensis), the Chinese primula, usually from February to March, but sometimes earlier. An old favourite is 'Dazzler', with brilliant vivid orange-scarlet blooms, but there is now an assortment of colours and variation in flower shape. This species is a short-lived perennial, and is best discarded after flowering. P. obconica, also of Chinese origin, is a longer-lived perennial and can be kept for a number of years. It is remarkable for producing flowers nearly all the year round, and is an excellent houseplant. It is a species that is widely grown, and often offered for sale.

A modern strain of *Primula vulgaris*.

However, young plants flower more freely, and many people only grow it for a year or so, since it is easy to produce from seed. There are a number of named F₁ hybrids and other strains in a variety of splendid colours. The large flower heads are borne on strong stems well above the foliage. A word of warning: both P. praenitens (syn. P. sinensis) and P. obconica are liable to cause a painful, itchy, reddish skin rash on people allergic to them. The other primulas are very unlikely to cause skin irritation.

P. malacoides, again from China, has earned the common name fairy primrose, because of its extremely dainty appearance. However, the flowers are borne in whorls, one above the other, on long stems rising above a rosette of dainty foliage, and the plant does not really have much resemblance to the common primrose.

It is a fine spring-flowering pot plant, and there are a number of named strains with delicate colours. Although a perennial, it is rarely worthy saving and should be discarded after flowering.

P. ×kewensis can be saved and is a perennial hybrid, originating at the Royal Botanic Gardens, Kew. It has whorls of golden-yellow flowers, often sweetly fragrant, on long stems from winter to late spring. The leaves and often the stems and buds are covered with a whitish farina.

All the primulas should be given a cool, shaded position in the home, and kept moist. Plants rarely need potting-on unless they happen to be seedling plants. P. malacoides grows well in 10cm (4in) pots. Peat-based composts are suitable, but if the plants are to be saved and grown on for more than a year – for example P. obconica and P. × kewensis – it is wise to water with clean rainwater. The plants do not like the alkaline conditions that may arise with the use of hard limy tap-water. The use of this may cause leaf yellowing. Aphids and red spider mites can attack primulas, the latter should be especially checked for on polyanthus if they are being grown on from plants bought during the summer. If exposed to excessively low temperatures the tender species may have their leaves damaged, and this is usually shown by blackening around the edges or sometimes by rotting brown patches on the leaves. This is most likely to occur if the plants are left on cold window-sills overnight where they may become frosted during winter or early spring.

PTERIS
see page 139

PUNICA GRANATUM 'NANA'
(dwarf pomegranate)
* 7°C/45°F

The miniature pomegranate is a charming little pot plant for a bright window-sill, and is very easy to grow from seed sown in early March. Flowering and fruiting should take place the same year. It forms a neat, shrubby little bush and, in pots, usually grows to only 45cm (1½ft) in height. The foliage is tiny and slightly glossy, but the flowers are large and brilliantly showy in bright scarlet. The petals are thin and papery and often slightly crinkled, and the blooms are followed by tiny fruits, just like miniature pomegranates.

The type species from South-eastern Europe is deciduous, but the dwarf form seems to be semi-deciduous; with congenial winter warmth the leaves may be largely retained. In cooler conditions, they may be entirely shed, but this does not matter much since they grow quickly again in spring. When new leaves are forming it is a good time to prune the plants to any shape you want. Good specimens can be kept in 13–15cm (5–6in) pots for several years. Any good potting compost can be used, but a bright position must be found for best results and to ensure the development of the little fruits. The fruit of this houseplant is not edible.

During summer, water well, but be careful not to saturate the compost. In winter, regulate watering according to the prevailing temperature. If it is cool enough to cause leaf fall, keep the plants on the dry side. Otherwise, maintain only very slightly moist conditions. Pest and disease problems are usually uncommon.

PUYA
see page 150

Punica granatum.

REBUTIA
see page 163

REINWARDTIA TRIGYNA
(syn. R. indica) (yellow flax plant)
** 13°C/55°F

This species is sometimes named *R. indica*, and at other times *Linum trigynum*. It is from Northern India and is notable for its lovely bright-yellow flowers, freely produced during winter. To do this it requires the recommended minimum temperature. The foliage is spear-shaped and when grown to full size the plants may reach about 60cm (2ft), forming an impressive plant.

As young plants, they can be grown in 13cm (5in) pots for at least a year, and potted as required. To encourage good winter flowering, it is wise to stand the plants outdoors in a sunny position during the summer. During this time it is imperative not to neglect watering, and it is best to plunge the pots, so that the soil is well covered with moist peat.

This plant is quite happy with any good potting compost. During winter, a good circulation of air around the plants is beneficial, but not draughts that may be chilly. Watering should be free from spring to autumn, but sparing the rest of the year.

During summer, the foliage can be sprayed with water from time to time, but not during periods of sunshine when the plants are standing outside. After flowering, the plants can be cut back and potted as soon as new shoots appear. However, old plants tend to deteriorate, and if possible new stock should be raised each year from cuttings taken in spring. These root easily on a window-sill, especially in a light position.

Red spider mite is the most troublesome pest likely to attack during summer, more especially if conditions are too hot and dry.

Reinwardtia trigyna.

RHIPSALIDOPSIS
see page 162

RHOEO SPATHACEA
(boat lily, Moses in the cradle)
* 10°C/50°F

This is is the only species of the genus, and is usually sold under its other name of *R. discolor*. It is of Mexican and West Indian origin, and in its young stage grows as a rosette of pointed, broad, sword-shaped leaves, later developing a short thick basal stem.

In the species the leaves are dark green and purplish below, but there is a form 'Vittatum' or 'Variegata' with the foliage finely striped in cream along its entire length. Normally, the leaves reach 20cm (8in) long or more, but there are dwarf cultivars with foliage very much shorter. The common name is derived from the flowers. These are white and formed at irregular intervals throughout the year. They are small and inconspicuous, each one being surrounded by a boat-shaped purple bract about 5cm (2in) in length. The plants are useful for relatively shaded positions in the home, and can be grown in 13cm (5in) pots for some time.

Any good potting compost will suit and potting is best done in spring. After a few years, the plants tend to deteriorate but the plants are easily air layered. Alternatively cuttings can be taken from old plants that have branched out; these should be from basal shoots 7.5cm (3in) long, and can be rooted easily on a window-sill in spring if given a temperature of 15°C (59°F).

Maintain high humidity and water freely in summer, sparingly at other times. Pests and diseases tend to be uncommon.

RHOICISSUS
* 7°C/45°F

There are about 12 species in this genus of South African climbers, two of which make useful houseplants for shady places in the home. *R. rhomboidea*, sometimes wrongly named *Cissus rhombifolia*, and popularly called grape ivy, has shiny, dark green foliage composed of three diamond-shaped irregular-edged leaflets. In the young stage, the leaves and shoots are covered with brownish hairs. The plant will reach at least 1.5m (5ft) if allowed, and when grown as a houseplant clings to supports by means of tendrils. The form 'Jubilee' has larger foliage and is even more vigorous, and is especially suitable for entrance halls and stair-wells. The cultivar 'Ellen Danica' has more distinctly serrated leaf margins.

Rhoeo spathacea (far left) and *Rhoicissus rhomboidea* (left).

R. capensis, sometimes called *Cissus capensis*, Cape grape, is of similar habit, but the foliage is singular, somewhat ivy-like but with less well defined lobes, and deep, shiny green. Both species can be kept to a reasonable height by cutting back drastically in spring. Young plants should have the growing tips removed to encourage plenty of basal shoots and discourage excessive height. The plants grow easily in any good potting compost and, although happy in shade, should not be given gloomy positions.

In summer, water freely and give overhead sprays with water. In winter, keep only slightly moist. Large plants may need potting-on into 25cm (10in) pots, and will then need bamboo canes or some other substantial support. In porches, the stems can be trained up wires. This genus is closely related to the genus *Cissus*, but can be distinguished by its simple tendrils. In cissus they are forked. Rhoicissus is also rather more tender than cissus and the recommended minimum winter temperature should be observed.

Pests and diseases are uncommon, but a watch should be kept for aphids and whitefly. Propagate by taking cuttings of lateral shoots in late spring, or use segments of main stems removed during pruning, allowing two leaf nodes.

RUELLIA MACRANTHA
** 15°C/59°F

This attractive plant has a shrubby habit, and reaches 90cm (3ft) in height. The leaves are spear-shaped, about 15cm (6in) long, dark green and corrugated. The flowers arise in clusters and are most attractive, from early in the year until spring. They are a purplish rose-pink colour and over 7.5cm (3in) long. This species likes a shaded position and moderate humidity, and grows particularly well in peat-based composts, with the addition of charcoal granules. The roots should be kept moist at all times, winter included. Potting is best done in autumn. Plants can be divided for propagation.

After flowering it is advisable to prune back the plant quite severely to form a neat shape. To root cuttings and germinate seed a temperature of 21°C (70°F) is necessary. This species is unsuitable for chilly homes or for where central heating is used without humidification. In chilly places it soon deteriorates, and the leaves may turn yellow and fall. Otherwise, troubles are unusual.

Some other plants often sold as ruellias have been reclassified under *Dipteracanthus* and will be found under that entry.

Ruellia macrantha.

SAINTPAULIA *(African violet)*
** 13°C/55°F

In recent years the African violet has
become one of the most popular houseplants. It certainly has much to offer.
It is an ideal size, neat and compact,
making an excellent gift plant. The
foliage is attractive and the flowers are
extremely beautiful, dainty and borne
freely over a very long period. It grows
well in the average home, and if well
cared for will live for a very long time.
There are about 12 species of saintpaulia, but those grown as houseplants
are progeny of *S. ionantha*, native to
coastal Tanzania. This plant has
beautiful single, vivid purple-blue
flowers, very violet-like, and with contrasting bright golden-yellow eyes. The
flowers are produced nearly the year
round. The leaves are oval and of velvety
texture. It is delightful to grow, and
there are now some excellent improved
seed strains.

The 'Fairy Tale' group are F_1 hybrids and
give flowers in the characteristic vivid
blue of the species, rich pink, and white.
'Amethyst' is also outstanding.

It is not difficult to grow these hybrids
from seed sown under window-sill conditions. The seedlings have F_1 hybrid
vigour and grow quickly. When sowing,
use a good seed compost and do not
cover the fine seed – it germinates better
if exposed to light, but not direct sunlight. For good germination a temperature of 18–21°C (65–70°F) is best. From
an early sowing, on a window-sill of a
warm room, it is possible to have flowering plants the first year, from autumn
onwards.

The number of named cultivars is now
enormous. There are now flowers in a
wide range of colours, embracing pure
white through various shades of pink,
carmine and red, to mauves, purples and
blues. There are bicoloured flowers and
some with picotee-edged petals, and
they may be single, semi-double or fully
double. There are also forms with fancy
foliage and a few with variegation.

Saintpaulias do not like being chilled. It
is wise to buy plants only during the
milder months of the year. Shops often
sell them in winter, and it is not unusual
for these plants to turn sickly after being
taken home. This is usually because they
have been subjected to cold or ill-
treatment beforehand. Many specialist
nurseries will not despatch plants until
weather conditions are suitable.

Some nurseries sell leaf cuttings of the
named cultivars for rooting at home,
and this is an inexpensive way to build
up a collection. The leaf cuttings usually
root easily on a window-sill.

Saintpaulias can be grown in 10–13cm
(4–5in) pots for a long time. They do well
in peat-based potting composts, but they
do not like excessively alkaline conditions. If the tap-water is hard and limy,
it is best to use clean rainwater.

The plants must have congenial warmth
and humidity. They enjoy slight shade to
good light, but should never be exposed
to direct sunshine.

Saintpaulias are absolutely ideal subjects
for growing in plant cabinets. They
respond extremely well to artificial light
culture, and the cabinets have the advantage of providing the humidity the
plants enjoy. In the home, saintpaulias
often grow especially well in bathrooms
and kitchens where there is warmth
coupled with humidity.

During summer, the plants can be
sprayed with a fine mist of clean rainwater from time to time. Hard water
must not be used, since it will cause
white spots and patches on the velvety
foliage, which cannot be wiped clean.

As the plants mature they can become
overcrowded by their leafy growth and
they then tend to flower poorly. They
form suckers around the parent plant
and these should be removed from time
to time. Tap the plant out of its pot and
cut away the suckers with a sharp knife,
leaving some roots attached. These suckers can then be potted individually for
propagation. Mature plants also form
side crowns, causing overcrowding.
These are little rosettes of leaves that
grow between the leaf axils – they can
be used for propagation, but in any case
they should be removed. The side
crowns can be removed with a pair of
finely-tipped scissors, such as vine or
nail scissors. They root easily if merely
gently pressed into the compost.

Propagation from leaf cuttings or side
crowns needs a temperature of 18°C
(65°F). The best time for potting is
spring. The plants should always be
watered sufficiently to keep the roots
moist. If through adverse circumstances the temperature falls much in
winter, water very sparingly. The plants

will often survive at temperatures much
lower than the recommended if kept
slightly dry. However, at low temperatures the plants cannot be expected to
flower well.

Aphids sometimes attack the plants, and
are best wiped off with a soft brush of the
kind used by artists. A similar tool can be
used to wipe off dust or fibres that may
collect on the velvety foliage after the
plants have been in the home for some
time. Low temperatures and low humidity will cause shrivelling and yellowing of the foliage. However, saintpaulias
often have a remarkable ability to recover from short-term ill-treatment.
Even if most of the leaves deteriorate,
they may send up new healthy growth
from the base if congenial conditions are
once again restored.

SALICORNIA
see page 158

SANSEVIERIA *(bowstring hemp)*
* 10°C/50°F

There are about 60 species in this genus.
Three forms are usually seen as houseplants; one is especially popular. These
are now regarded by some botanists as
all belonging to *S. trifasciata*, and as
being cultivars, but they are still listed
and regarded by many people as two
distinct species. The type species, rather
rudely called mother-in-law's tongue,
also has the name snake plant. The latter
is a better description, since the leaf
markings are reminiscent of that reptile.
The leaves are long, narrow and sword-
like, with sharply-pointed tips. They
form clumps which can become quite
dense in well-grown plants, and hold
themselves rigidly erect. The leaves have
irregular-edged wavy bands of green
and silvery-grey across the entire leaf,
from side to side. The favourite form,
'Laurentii', has similar markings, but
also a bold yellow border on each side of
the leaf.

The plant usually labelled *S. hahnii* but now recognized as another cultivar of *S. trifasciata*, is rather different. It forms a rosette of much shorter, wider and more oval leaves, which spread out. These are usually banded green and grey, but there is a more rare form with very wide creamy borders to the leaves. In both cases, the leaves reach 10cm (4in) long, and they are rather like dwarf forms of *S. trifasciata* and *S. t.* 'Laurentii' respectively, apart from their rosette-like habit. Sansevieria is a very misunderstood plant, and when bought is invariably very much under-potted. In nature it has a free root-run, sending out runners. If given a reasonably large pot it will do the same in the home and soon form a thick clump. It is a vigorous grower during the summer months, and can be watered quite freely. Summer is also a good time to divide the plants for propagation, using a very sharp knife to cut cleanly through the roots. Doing this in early summer gives the plants time to make active growth and become well established in their new pots before winter arrives.

Any peat-based compost suits these plants, but ensure that drainage is perfect. During summer, provide slight shade. The foliage is easily scorched behind glass when direct sunlight falls on wet or damp areas. In winter, give them full light. Innumerable plants are lost in winter through over-watering. It is vital to be very sparing with water, and often it is best not to water at all – certainly not during mid-winter. Wet roots at this time leads to rapid rotting and the whole plant turns yellow and dies.

The need for water can often be detected by close examination of the foliage. The leaves tend to curl to form a tubular shape if they want water, but even if this happens in winter, the amount given should be cautious and sparing.

In summer, the plants will not mind being left without water for a time, and can be left unattended for a week or more.

The only way to obtain more plants of the variegated cultivars is to divide them. However, plants are easy to raise from leaf cuttings taken in early summer, but these are most unlikely to have bordering of the foliage. Leaves that may have become damaged can be removed from close to the base, using a very sharp knife. Then cut the leaf into sections, each 5cm (2in) in length. Insert these in a propagator on a window-sill. The cuttings usually root readily and

new plants will arise from their base. The old piece of leaf then shrivels and can be removed carefully.

Provided care is taken over watering, sansevierias are quite easy plants to manage and do well in centrally-heated homes where the air may be too dry for most other houseplants. However, in low humidity the plants grow less fast.

Saintpaulias (below, left) and *Sansevieria trifasciata* 'Laurentii' (below).

113

SAUROMATUM VENOSUM
(syn. S. guttatum)
(monarch of the East, voodoo lily)
* 13°C/55°F

The sale of the tubers of this North-west Indian plant has become an annual event, usually in early spring. Despite this, few people seem to know much about the plant's characteristics or culture. As purchased, the plant takes the form of a flattish bulb. For the best results, buy the largest you can and check that it is firm and in good condition. Sometimes the plant is named *Arum cornutum*, and may appear in bulb lists under this title.

This plant has gained publicity because the tuber will flower without soil or water, and it is often given to children to grow as a novelty. The tuber can be gently pressed into a little sand in a saucer to keep it firm, and placed on a warm window-sill. Soon, a shoot will grow from the centre, and once this is seen things happen quickly. The shoot will form into a very strange arum-like flower, which strictly should be described as an inflorescence. It has a very long spathe, which soon grows too long to stay erect and therefore trails.

The spathe is purple-spotted and the inflorescence may often, at this time, emit a very unpleasant smell, like rotting meat. This attracts flies and bluebottles, which is just what the plant wants for pollination. However, whether or not this performance is an attractive one is a matter of opinion, and most people might prefer to put the plant outside during this period. Unfortunately many inexperienced growers, feeling a little cheated, discard the plant altogether after flowering. This is a great pity because the next stage is a really impressive and pleasing one. In any case, the inflorescence lasts for only a couple of days. If the tuber is now put into a 13cm (5in) pot of potting compost, planting about 2.5cm (1in) deep, and kept moist, another shoot will soon appear. This

develops into a strong, brightly spotted stem bearing a large palm-like leaf. This consists of a number of slightly glossy large leaflets borne on a ring-shaped stalk at the top of the supporting stem. The foliage lasts until autumn and during this time the plant is most attractive and unusual. When the foliage begins to die down, cease watering and let the pots become dry. The corm can then be removed and stored in dry sand for the winter, ensuring the temperature does not fall below 13°C (55°F).

Often a number of little bulbs (offsets) are produced, and these can be separated and individually potted for propagation. However, it may take some years for these to become large enough to give satisfactory results.

A suitable tuber should be at least 10cm (4in) across. During the leaf production stage, the plants can be well watered and if the tubers are to be saved they should be well fed with a liquid feed. Only aphids are likely to be troublesome.

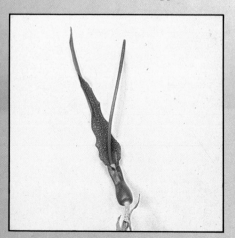

SAXIFRAGA *(saxifrage, rockfoil)*
* see text for temperatures

There are about 370 species in this genus, many being excellent plants for growing in pans in an alpine greenhouse. Many of these could be experimented with on window-sills, provided the situation is very bright and airy. Little more than frost-free conditions are required. However, the most popular houseplant is undoubtedly *S. stolonifera* (syn. *S. sarmentosa*), which is a very old favourite and has acquired a number of common names. For example, mother of thousands, strawberry geranium, pedlar's basket, and rowing sailor.

It is a creeping and trailing plant, sending out long runners with reddish stems. The foliage is roundish, with irregular edges, silvery veining, green above and reddish below, and slightly hairy. The form 'Tricolor' has the foliage variegated with creamy-yellow and pink, and is very pretty. Unfortunately, it is rather less vigorous and is best kept slightly warmer than the minimum 5°C (41°F) needed for the type species.

The plants are excellent for hanging pots or small baskets, and for pedestals or for trailing over the edges of troughs. A characteristic is that the stems produce numerous plantlets complete with roots, hence the name mother of thousands. These plantlets can be detached and used for propagation by potting them separately.

In the form 'Tricolor', plantlet production is very much reduced. Both these saxifrages should be given a shady posi-

tion and kept well watered and humid during summer. A spray with a mist of water from time to time is beneficial. A loam-based potting compost, such as John Innes, with a little extra washed grit, forms an excellent medium.

In winter, water should be applied very sparingly and the air kept drier. The best time for potting is spring, but when carrying out this operation do not press the compost down too firmly. In positions where there is too much light, the foliage may bleach and fall. However, the plants do not like excessive gloom. Of the many other saxifrages, one that is achieving more popularity as a houseplant is *S. cotyledon*, which is quite hardy and suitable for bright but chilly places in the home. It forms a dainty rosette of narrow foliage which has a lime-like encrustation along the margins. It is native to the Pyrenees.

A special attraction are the flowering stems that arise well above the rosette all summer. These bear graceful sprays of numerous pure white flowers and are very pretty. However, they sometimes need support and this is best done using thin split-cane, or very thin stiff wire. After flowering, remove the remains of the stems cleanly and put the pots outdoors, preferably with the pots plunged and where it is slightly shaded. New rosettes will usually form.

Before the first frosts, bring the plants back into the home and put them in a

Left: *Sauromatum venosum.*
Below: *Saxifraga stolonifera.*
Far right: *Schefflera actinophylla.*

cool place. The best time to remove young rosettes for propagation is in April and May. They should be treated like cuttings and rooted in a peat and grit mixture. Water sparingly at first and do not apply water freely until the cuttings are well rooted, which may take almost a year. This species likes a well-drained rather alkaline compost, and John Innes potting compost with some limestone grit added is suitable. A very desirable form of this species with white flowers daintily speckled with red can sometimes be obtained; the stems are more arching in habit.

S. stolonifera is liable to attack from aphids and whitefly. S. cotyledon is rarely affected by pests or diseases, but overwatering or bad drainage can soon cause yellowing and deterioration, and once roots begin rotting recovery is unlikely.

SCHEFFLERA
* see text for temperatures

This is a genus of small trees or shrubs with handsome evergreen foliage, originating in warm areas of the world. Some have showy flowers, usually crimson, but it is extremely rare for plants grown in pots to produce these. The species described here are very easy to raise from seed on a window-sill.

S. actinophylla, the umbrella tree, bears glossy green spear-shaped leaflets from the tops of stems, umbrella fashion. In young plants, the number of leaflets is about three, but this increases to five or six, and to more in mature plants.

In pots, the plant usually reaches 1.8m (6ft) after some years, depending on the size of container. Large containers will encourage much more extensive growth, but growth is very slow and a plant will remain useful in the home for a long time. Since it is happy in 10°C (50°F) minimum, it can make a very impressive plant for relatively cool places when grown to an appreciable size. Moreover, this species will do well in slight shade, although this does not imply gloom. In winter more light is preferable.

S. arboricola (syn. Heptapleurum arboricola) from South-east Asia, called green rays is very similar except that it is very much more compact and shrubby in habit. The full number of leaflets to each stem also seem to develop more quickly. It is a very deep, lustrous green, and the extra-shiny gloss is notable. It is a very striking plant set against a light background. S. digitata, from New Zealand, is also of a similar low-growing shrubby habit, and especially easy to raise from seed. The leaflets are not quite so pointed, but are toothed. This species will survive quite low temperatures if kept on the dry side during winter, and in mild areas of the country can even be grown outdoors, although a severe winter may kill it. Grown in pots it will reach about the same height as S. actinophylla. In all cases plants should be retained in no larger than 20cm (8in) pots for as long as healthy growth is made.

Potting-on should be done in spring and the plants kept moist at all times. However, if there is risk of cool winter conditions, watering should then be adjusted accordingly. Seed germinates freely at 21°C (70°F), and the seedlings should be potted as required.

SCHIZANTHUS *(butterfly flower)*
* 5°C/41°F

For many years this has been one of the most popular greenhouse and conservatory pot plants, usually in the form of various hybrids and cultivars. The true species, mostly natives of Chile, are rarely grown. Certain seedsmen have specialized in schizanthus and developed some magnificent strains, and schizanthus were at one time a feature of the great shows, like the Chelsea Flower Show, where great banks of these plants were exhibited with thrilling effect.

Schizanthus are very easy to grow from seed, but the older strains tended to grow rather tall and take up considerable space. The best results were obtained by growing them as a biennial, sowing in autumn and growing on over winter in frost-free conditions for spring flowering. These plants needed to have the growing tips removed a number of times to produce bushy growth. For anyone inexperienced in greenhouse techniques, results could be erratic and a show standard difficult to attain. Very recently all this has changed, with the introduction of some remarkable dwarf strains.

The new dwarf kinds can be sown in spring on a window-sill for late spring to summer flowering, and they need no pinching to induce bushiness, and no training whatsoever. A short time ago 'Dwarf Bouquet' and 'Hit Parade' were introduced. These are still excellent and grow to a height of 30–45cm (1–1½ft). The latest, 'Star Parade', grows only to about 25cm (10in) at the most, and is bound to become an especially popular pot plant for the home because of its sturdy and compact habit. Plants in bud will probably appear in shops in spring. The foliage is beautifully ferny and dainty, like the usual schizanthus strains, and the flowers have acquired the large size and amazing colour range of the giant forms. When in full bloom the plants are smothered with the delightful intricately veined and marked blooms, the appearance of which has also inspired the popular name of poor man's orchid, although they are really like small bright exotic butterflies. Every colour and combination is represented.

If you grow your own schizanthus from seed, it is best to put three or four seedlings to each 10cm (4in) pot. Just keep the plants watered and in a bright place. There is no need for any other cultural treatment.

If you grow the taller kinds in a greenhouse, they can be brought indoors for a while, but pinch out the growing tips early to induce bushiness.

After flowering, which will continue for many weeks, the plants can be discarded. Over-watering or erratic watering may cause the foliage to turn brown or yellow at the base. Protect the plants from direct sunshine and keep cool during the flowering period.

SCILLA
see page 142

SCINDAPSUS
** 10°C/50°F

This is a genus of climbing plants closely related to philodendrons, and they are grown in much the same way. *S. aureus*, which is now named by botanists as *Epipremnum aureum*, Devil's ivy from the Solomon Islands, is the one most often seen as a houseplant, and it has a number of forms with different leaf markings and colourings. The leaves are broadly spear-shaped, and in ideal conditions the plants can climb to at least 1.8m (6ft), sending out aerial roots.

As the plants mature, the leaves become more heart-shaped and the size increases three-fold to reach about 30cm (1ft) in length. Sometimes, these large leaves are rooted by nurseries and sold in this form. However, as the plant grows it will revert to producing small foliage and continue to do so until it matures. Many people buying these large-leaved rooted cuttings often imagine that it is their fault that a dramatic leaf size change takes place soon after purchase. The foliage of the type species is usually bright green with golden-yellow blotching. 'Marble Queen' is green with creamy-white marbling, as the name implies. 'Golden Queen' has almost entirely golden-yellow foliage. 'Tricolor'

Schizanthus hybrids.

Back, left and right: *Scindapsus aureus* 'Orange Queen'. **Front:** *Scindapsus pictus*.

has a mixture of green, gold, and cream speckling. Less frequently seen is *S. pictus*, the silver vine, from Java and Malaya, and usually grown in the form 'Argyraeus'. This is similar to *Epipremnum aureum* (syn. *Scindapsus aureus*) but with smaller leaves and shorter leaf stalks. The foliage is green, attractively blotched and spotted with silvery markings.

Scindapsus like warmth and humidity and slight shade in summer, with plenty of watering at that time. They are best grown up moss-covered supports, and enjoy being sprayed with a mist of water from time to time during the hottest months of the year. In winter, keep in much drier conditions, especially if temperatures tend to get low. Potting is best done during spring, using a peat-based compost with a little granular charcoal added. If plants become too large they can be cut back drastically during June. At the same time, cuttings can be taken from unwanted basal or tip growths. These need to be rooted in a temperature of about 21°C (70°F).

SEDUM
see page 164

SELAGINELLA
see page 139

SEMPERVIVUM *(houseleeks)*
* hardy

This is a small genus of hardy to half-hardy succulents, a few of which make extremely easy houseplants. In fact, the botanical name sempervivum is derived from the Latin meaning always alive. The leaves are succulent and form tight, symmetrical rosettes, and they have a variety of colours, shapes and textures. Sometimes there are very attractive flowers. Perhaps one of the most popular window-sill species is *S. arachnoideum*, the cobweb houseleek, from the Pyrenees. It forms green rosettes, often tinted red, and from around the tips of the leaves is suspended a fine, whitish webbing suggesting the common name. For pots, there is an especially fine variety, *S. a. tomentosum*, with more profuse webbing and larger leaves, but there are also a number of hybrids with other differences in colour and shape and they all soon spread out to form a clump. The flowers, borne in June and July, are a pretty carmine, but after flowering a rosette dies. This does not matter, since there are usually numerous young ones produced and a plant eventually forms a mat-like spread of growth if unrestricted. The flowers are formed in a starry structure, and are held well above the rosettes on 15cm (6in) stems clothed with small, succulent leaflets.

S. tectorum is the roof houseleek, so-called because it often colonizes old stone or tiled roofs of country buildings. It is very variable and there are numerous forms with differences in the leaflet colour. Those with reddish or purplish tints are very attractive as houseplants.

The flowers are pinkish to purple. A popular form called 'Commander Hay' is now thought to be a hybrid between this species and *S. marmoreum*. It has exceptionally large rosettes and the leaflets are a delightful, shiny, reddish-purple with green tips. The leaflets are rather spatula-shaped, with a small sharp point at their top edge.

S. soboliferum, now known as *Jovibarba sobolifera*, the hen and chickens houseleek, is another one popular for window-sills, and is native to Russia and Northern Europe. It has bright green rosettes, tinted orange-red in the best forms, but the greenish flowers are rarely produced. Its special characteristic is the freely-formed baby rosettes that appear over the parent rosette, presumably suggesting the common name. These can be removed and potted separately for propagation. *S × funckii*, a hybrid between *S. arachnoideum* and *S. tectorum* and possibly *S. marmoreum*, is very pretty with rosettes of downy texture and finely hairy, and flowers of a lovely rosy purple colour.

S. tectorum calcareum is attractive for its grey-green colouring, contrasting with purple-tipped leaflets, but unfortunately it rarely flowers. It is a pity that the sempervivums are so overlooked as houseplants, since they are easy to grow and will withstand considerable neglect. They should be given a bright position and are best grown in shallow pans or half pots, which must be well drained. Any of the modern potting composts are suitable, but add some sharp grit for good drainage. Propagation is easily effected by removing and potting the offsets. This is best done in spring. Pests and diseases are rare.

Sempervivum tectorum.

SENECIO (including cineraria)
* see text for temperatures

This is an incredibly large genus, including about 3,000 species. However, as far as houseplants are concerned, probably the most important is the cineraria, sometimes given the pseudo-botanical name of *Senecio cruentus*. However the plants known as cineraria are numerous cultivars, with a parentage involving the true *S. cruentus*, *S. heritieri*, and other species native to the Canary Islands, and are the result of many years of intensive breeding and selection. There are now numerous named seed strains offered, and the variety of size, form, colouring and flowering period, is considerable. In all cases, they are usually grown from seed as biennials and are quite easy to grow under greenhouse or conservatory conditions, with minimum winter temperatures little more than frost-free. They are often grown with calceolarias, as they need similar conditions and treatment. Cinerarias come into the shops from about December to spring and are best bought when the buds are just beginning to show colour. Most of them are dwarf and compact, and have a mass of daisy-shaped flowers in a wide range of glorious colours sometimes zoned with white.

In recent years, a double form called 'Gubler's Double' has been introduced, but the colour range is limited and less exciting and the flowers tend to be too heavy for their stalks. Various giant-flowered strains are available but are best bought as seedlings in autumn from nurseries and grown on over winter on a bright window-sill. These are at least twice as tall as the normal florists' strains and have an abundance of impressively large flowers.

A form called 'Stellata' is usually even taller and bears a mass of small starry flowers giving a beautiful effect. However, these plants are more suited to decorating a conservatory.

The culture and maintenance of cinerarias is almost exactly the same as described for calceolarias (page 64), but the plants are even more prone to wilting if given too much warmth and they are particularly prone to aphid attack. Kept cool, moist and shaded, cinerarias last a very long time. Like calceolarias the dwarf forms tend to flower earlier, and the giant types later. By selecting the various types, flowers can be enjoyed from Christmas to about early June. After flowering the plants should be discarded.

Two South African climbing species are pleasing foliage plants and remarkably ivy-like in appearance. They require a winter minimum of about 10°C (50°F) and ought to be far better known; both have yellow flowers in winter. *S. mikaniodes*, German ivy, has exaggerated ivy-type leaves, the points being extremely sharp. *S. macroglossus* is usually seen in the form 'Variegatus', in which the leaf shape is more typical of ivy and the colouring is green and golden-yellow. It has the common names Cape ivy and, because the leaves are rather waxy in texture, wax vine. Both these species can be trained to a considerable height up bamboo supports. In conservatories they can grow up into the roof and even along roof supports. They are similarly useful for garden rooms, and grow well in any of the usual potting composts. Plants required to grow vigorously to fill height and space will need potting on to 25cm (10in) pots. Give a slightly shaded place, but not too gloomy, and water well in summer. Keep the roots only slightly moist in winter. Scale insects are the most likely pest and should be removed promptly before infestation becomes severe.

Another species that has become popular for window-sills is *S. rowleyanus*. This is absolutely different from the other senecios described here. It is a mat-forming trailer useful for hanging pots, wall pots, and for pedestals, and is a very strange plant from South-west Africa. The leaves are succulent and almost spherical in shape and borne on long thread-like stems. This has led to the

obvious common name of string of beads. If examined closely each bead-like leaf will be seen to have a semi-transparent band and a tiny pointed tip. In autumn sweetly scented white brush-like flowers with purple stigmas are produced. Provide a bright position, water freely in summer and sparingly the rest of the year. The stems often send out roots freely and the plants can be propagated in spring by potting pieces of rooted stems, or by division. It is not fussy about potting compost, provided it is well drained.

S. bicolor (syn. *S. maritimus*) is often grown under the name of *Cineraria maritima* for garden bedding, where its beautiful silvery-grey ferny foliage makes a delightful contrast to many bedding plant flowers. For this purpose it is grown from seed sown early in the year. However, it is perennial and can make a useful foliage plant for winter decoration in quite chilly places in the home. Plants for potting can be bought from garden shops during spring and should be given 13cm (5in) pots. If kept for more than about a year or so the plants may become leggy. Yellow daisy-shaped flowers are borne profusely from summer to autumn, but they tend to be

straggly and, although pretty, have difficulty in competing with the exceptionally striking foliage.

For growing in pots the dwarf and neat form called 'Silver Dust' is specially recommended. For the first year it will grow little more than about 30cm (1ft) in height. The bright silver-grey colour of the plant is not common among house-plants and it is surprising that it has not become better known for this purpose. It looks especially impressive when combined with red-leaved plants or flowers, the combination of red and grey being most effective. Keep nicely moist in summer, but on the dry side in winter. Pests and diseases are unusual.

SETCREASEA PALLIDA
(syn. S. purpurea)
* 5°C/41°F

This is a small genus, one species of which has become widely grown as a houseplant because of its amazing ability to withstand neglect. It is *S. pallida* from Mexico, usually sold as *S. purpurea*, and also sometimes wrongly labelled as *Tradescantia purpurea*. It is a rather straggly trailer with habit similar

to tradescantias, to which it is related. However, by frequent removal of the growing tips of the stems it can be encouraged to produce an abundance of more erect new growth and acquire a more bushy habit.

It is unfortunate that this species is prone to untidy behaviour, because its foliage is a delightful purplish colour, not common among houseplants. The leaves are elongated and spear-shaped, about 15cm (6in) long, and slightly hairy. The colour below may be more carmine in some specimens and the best and richest colouring is obtained in positions of good light, but not in direct sunlight.

The plants can be used in baskets and hanging containers. In these they need more care to prevent the basal leaves on the stems from deteriorating, and watering should not be neglected. During winter the plants will survive almost freezing if kept on the dry side. In such conditions all top growth may be lost, but recovery is rapid with the return of warmth. Plants have been discovered in houses that have been empty for many months, and have grown again after being watered. Plants raised from cuttings in greenhouses have also been used for summer carpet bedding. From summer to autumn small purplish flowers are produced but these tend to be rather insignificant and do not compare with the foliage.

Division is an easy way to propagate. Troubles are rare.

Far left: *Senecio cruentus* (cineraria).
Below: *Setcreasea pallida.*

SINNINGIA *(including gloxinia)*
* 15°C/59°F

This is a genus of about 20 species of tuberous plants from Brazil and Argentina, the most important of which is the well-known gloxinia, and comprising hybrids and cultivars of *Gloxinia speciosa*. These are ideal pot plants with beautiful velvety foliage, extremely neat compact habit, and exceptionally showy trumpet-shaped flowers in glorious colours and colour combinations.

An important advance has recently been made with the introduction of F_1 hybrid seed. The plants are vigorous, easy to grow and quick to flower. From sowings made in January, good flowering plants can be obtained by early autumn. As this species does not demand maximum light, it is not difficult to grow from seed under window-sill conditions. The simplest and most convenient way, however, is to obtain tubers of the named forms in spring. For example, some good ones are 'Emperor Frederick' (bright scarlet with white border, very striking), 'Duchess of York' (violet with white border), 'Princess Elizabeth' (white with blue border), 'Red Tiger' (white, spotted red), 'Royal Crimson', 'Royal Pink', 'Mont Blanc' (pure white), 'Brilliant Scarlet', 'Tiger Red' (red flowers with wavy borders), 'Gregor Mendel' (double-flowered, usually reddish shades sometimes with white picotee edges to petals). Start the tubers into growth by immersing them in a bowl of moist peat in a warm place. Inspect them every few days and as soon as shoots are seen pot up in 13cm (5in) pots, one tuber to each. Set the tubers just level with the surface of the compost so that they are barely covered. Often it is difficult to decide which is the top of the tuber, but starting them in peat will soon reveal the areas sending out roots and where the shoots will spring from. All that remains is to keep the pots in a slightly shaded warm place.

Sometimes plants already potted and well under way are sold by garden shops and florists during early summer. If the more advanced stage is wanted, it is best to buy just when the first buds are beginning to open.

After flowering in autumn and when the foliage begins to die down, gradually let the pots become dry. Remove the tubers and store them in clean dry sand in a frost-free place over winter. Old tubers may become corky and they may flower badly. It is then best to make a fresh start. However, tubers can usually be kept for about three years or so.

S. regina is a species with boldly veined foliage quite striking for this alone. It is of Brazilian origin and bears beautiful purple rather pendent flowers reminiscent of streptocarpus. Presumably, the flowers have suggested the common name of Cinderella's slippers, although it is difficult to see why. Once known as *Gesneria cardinalis* but now regarded as *Rechsteineria cardinalis*, *Sinningia cardinalis*, the cardinal flower, can also be grown from seed, and there are a number of cultivars. The foliage is oval in shape and very velvety in texture. The flowers are brilliant scarlet and tubular in shape, borne in an erect cluster from summer to autumn.

A species that has recently had some publicity, and also easily raised from seed, is *S. leucotricha*, now known as *Rechsteineria leucotricha*, and given the strange common names silver song and Brazilian edelweiss. The foliage is delightfully silky and silvery-grey in colour, and the flowers, which are similar to *S. cardinalis* in shape, are a lovely orange-salmon shade. This species can form quite a large tuber, and it is not generally known that mature tubers can produce leaves and flowers without soil or water, and can be grown as curiosities like sauromatums or colchicums (see pages 114 and 145).

As well as from seed, most sinningias can be propagated by cutting up the tubers when shoots are forming, so that each segment has a shoot, and potting them separately. Some can also be grown from leaf cuttings and from cuttings of young shoots.

All sinningias like shade and moderate humidity, and should be kept nicely moist during their growing period. When producing leaves they can also be fed, especially if it is intended to save the tubers. Pests and diseases are not often troublesome, but overwatering may cause the tubers to rot. Chills will cause leaf yellowing and sickly or slow growth, and direct sunlight may cause leaf scorch leading to browning and shrivelling.

Sinningia (gloxinia) hybrid.

Sinningia (gloxinia) 'Emperor Frederick'.

SMITHIANTHA *(temple bells)*
* 15°C/59°F

This is a genus of only four species and they were once grown under the name 'gesneria'. These species are not now very often grown, since they have been crossed by plant breeders to produce a range of superb cultivars worth growing for their delightful foliage. This is of a lovely velvety texture and often subtly coloured, with an iridescent sheen or texture. The striking flowers are borne on long spikes above the foliage and often have colours giving unusual contrast to the foliage tints.

The form of the flowers and the country of origin of the species has also inspired the common name Mexican foxglove, although this does lead to confusion with the tiny *Tetranema mexicana* which has the same common name.

The plants are easy to grow from rhizomes, best bought from a specialist nursery, started into growth as described for gloxinias (page 120). However, it is better to start earlier, in February, and in a temperature of 15–18°C (59–65°F). The rhizomes can be potted singly in 13cm (5in) pots or three to a larger pot, but avoid mixing the named cultivars. The treatment from then on is much the same as for gloxinias, but singly-potted plants can have the growing tip removed when about 5cm (2in) of growth has been made. This delays flowering for a few weeks, but results in nicely shaped bushy plants.

It is important to water cautiously at first after potting, gradually increasing the amount given until leaf growth is well under way. Water should then be applied freely. Some recommended names are 'Orange King' (bright orange/yellow flowers; bronzy-green foliage), 'Scarlet Emperor' (scarlet flowers with golden-yellow throat and edged red), 'Abbey' (green foliage; peach flowers), 'Carmell' (red-tinted green foliage; cream flowers spotted red), and 'Cathedral' (green leaves; yellow-orange flowers). Flowering usually takes place from late summer to autumn.

During growth and flowering a moderately humid atmosphere should be maintained, and wide temperature changes avoided. After flowering gradually reduce watering as for gloxinias, but store the pots on their sides when dry in a place well free from frost. Next planting time the pots should be very carefully emptied and the rhizomes, which should have multiplied, separated and started as already described. Handle them carefully because they are brittle and easily damaged.

The species *S. zerbina* is sometimes sold as a houseplant when in flower, or almost so. The foliage is heart-shaped with irregular edges and prettily mottled in chocolate brown against an olive-green velvety background. The flowers are scarlet with yellow throats, and this species crossed with *S. fulgida* was used by Cornell University in America to produce some of the named forms already recommended.

Smithianthas are not particularly prone to pests or diseases, but chills, wide temperature changes, excessive sunlight, and a dry atmosphere, or overwatering, can bring about deterioration or poor growth.

SOLANUM *(winter cherry)*
* see text for temperatures

There are about 1,700 species in this genus but the one most important as a houseplant is *S. capsicastrum* from Brazil. This forms a neat little bushy plant and is notable for its bright red berries at around Christmas time. It is very often confused with capsicums (see page 65), which usually have more elongated fruits, and with *S. pseudocapsicum* which has smaller berries and smooth foliage. *S. pseudocapsicum*, of South-eastern American origin, is also often grown as a houseplant called Jerusalem cherry, and may be sold under the name of *S. capsicastrum*.

Unlike capsicums, the berries of both these solanums should be regarded as poisonous. There have been cases of death reported after children have eaten them, and care should be taken.

The solanums are usually sold in the shops when their berries are just beginning to turn orange or red. Often there is a gradual transition from green through yellow and orange to bright red. The plants are moderately easy to grow from seed, but do not set fruit as easily as capsicums, and they need to be sown earlier for Christmas display. About February is the best time.

Culture from seed is similar in other respects to capsicums, and 13cm (5in) pots should be the final size.

Solanums are especially prone to magnesium deficiency which causes sickly growth and yellowing foliage, which may tend to fall easily. Water from time to time with Epsom salts – 5ml (1 teaspoon) to 500ml (1pt) of water – as a routine measure. The plants are usually grown as an annual, but some people manage to save the plants for a number of years, keeping them frost-free and pruning back to a neat shape.

Pests and diseases are uncommon.

Solanum capsicastrum.

A smithiantha hybrid.

SOLEIROLIA SOLEIROLII
(syn. Helxine soleirolii)
(mind your own business, baby's tears)
* 4°C/39°F

This quaint plant, the only one of its genus, and originating from Corsica, has been a favourite on window-sills for many years, and is extremely easy to grow. In some mild areas it may survive winter outdoors, but is liable to be killed off by a severe cold spell. It forms a dense, creeping mat of tiny leaves borne on pinkish stems, which send out roots as they spread. In good conditions it can be very invasive and will creep down the sides of its pot or even spread to others if it gets a chance. It has been used as ground cover in greenhouses and to cover the surface of large pots in which large plants with long leafless stems or trunks, such as palms or greenhouses shrubs, are growing. It is also useful for wall pots and the edges of troughs or conservatory staging.

This is an excellent plant for growing amidst a collection of other plants, especially in a conservatory or a lean-to greenhouse. The small, attractive leaves cascade around the pots, helping all the plants to blend together and to create a unified picture. Once established, it grows quite rapidly.

This plant will grow well in slight shade or good light provided conditions are moist but by no means waterlogged. Excess water may cause rotting of the roots and stems. The plant grows vigorously in any of the modern potting composts. There is a form 'Aurea' with golden foliage and another called 'Argentia' with silvery leaves. Both are very pretty and can be grown with the type species to good effect. Propagation is by division in spring, taking pieces of the plant with plenty of roots coming from the stems.

It is unusual for this plant to have troubles of any kind, if treated normally.

Soleirolia soleirolii.

SPARMANNIA AFRICANA
(African hemp)
** 7°C/45°F

This South African plant is easy to raise from seed sown in spring, but may not flower until the second year. In pots it usually grows to about 90cm (3ft) in height by the second year, and often it is more convenient to discard old plants that become too tall, and start afresh.

The foliage is large and heart-shaped and of little special interest compared with other houseplants. The flowers, however, are rather unusual. They form umbels in May and June, and are white with a structure similar to St. John's wort. The central cluster of stamens is prominent and conspicuous and if gently touched spring outwards and back in a surprising manner.

The plants grow very vigorously in the modern potting composts and need a fairly large pot. They should be given a bright position and kept nicely moist in summer. In cool conditions in winter they may drop foliage, but they can usually be cut back and will send up new growth in spring. Some people prefer to use these new shoots for cuttings if facilities are available to root them. Plants so raised will usually flower the same year and make neat specimens. Sparmannias prefer less humidity than many other houseplants during summer and should be placed where ventilation is good. During winter keep the pots on the dry side, especially if conditions are cool. If given conservatory space and planted in a large pot or small tub, the plant can reach an appreciable size, often exceeding 3m (10ft) if there is enough height, and spreading out too. The somewhat hairy foliage and the white flowers with purple-tipped stamens can then look quite attractive. The leaves have also suggested the common name house lime. Pests and diseases are rarely troublesome, which helps to make this a very reliable plant.

Sparmannia africana.

SPATHIPHYLLUM *(peace lily)*
** 10–13°C/50–55°F

This is a small genus of tropical plants similar to anthuriums, and also related to them. Two have become popular houseplants although they are unsuitable for chilly homes and grow better where there is adequate central heating with humidification. However, they are usually more tolerant than anthuriums. S. *wallisii*, from Colombia, makes a neat pot plant with brightly shiny green spear-shaped leaves borne spear-like on long stems and forming a clump about 30cm (1ft) tall or a little higher in well-grown plants. The flowers arise on long strong stems from about May to August and consist of an erect catkin-like spike of tiny petal-less creamy-coloured flowers surrounded by a bold showy white spear-shaped spathe about 13cm (5in) long.

A hybrid called 'Mauna Loa' is a favourite. The exact parents are uncertain, although S. *floribundum* was probably involved. This hybrid is similar to S. *wallisii*, but the leaves are narrower and longer and the spathes larger, and the height may be up to about 60cm (2ft) when the plants are well grown. This hybrid, although a fine form, is not quite so easy and the minimum temperature of about 13°C (55°F) or a few degrees higher should be maintained if possible. Spathiphyllums must not be allowed to dry out at any time and a peaty potting compost with some charcoal granules added suits them. Provide slight shade and a high humidity in summer and spray the foliage with water from time to time. A position of good light should be found for winter and give a little less water, while keeping the compost slightly moist. Repotting is best done in spring and the plants can be propagated by division. They rarely have pest or disease problems, but deteriorate if chilled.

SPREKELIA FORMOSISSIMA
(Aztec lily, Jacobean lily)
* 10°C/50°F

This is a Mexican bulbous plant related to hippeastrums. It is notable for its remarkable flowers of rather orchid-like structure, deep blood-red in colour. The flowering time is often erratic and may be from spring to summer. Often leaves come before the flowers or at the same time, and these are unusually sparse and narrowly strap-shaped. The flower is about 10cm (4in) across and the structure is rather like that of a fleur-de-lis. The bulbs should be potted from February to March. When buying them, choose bulbs of good size, and firm when gently pressed. Small bulbs may not be of flowering size. Pot with the nose of the bulb well protruding from the compost, which can be John Innes or peat-based. Set one bulb to each 13cm (5in) pot. They can, of course, be grouped in larger pots if desired. After potting, give no water at first, then very little until the foliage begins to form. With the production of leaves watering can be increased accordingly, to compensate for the increased transpiration.

During the leaf stage the bulb can be fed, although if a nourishing potting compost has been used, such as John Innes No. 2, this need not be too generous. How the bulb is looked after at this stage determines its performance the next season. In autumn the pots should be gradually allowed to go quite dry and the bulbs stored dry for the winter. There is no need to repot bulbs that are kept, but they will need more feeding. Overwatering is liable to lead to rotting of the bulbs. This may also occur if they are damp in winter or stored at low temperatures. Sometimes offsets form around the bulbs and these can be removed for propagation.

STAPELIA
see page 161

STEPHANOTIS
see page 177

STRELITZIA
see page 178

Sprekelia formosissima.

Spathiphyllum 'Mauna Loa'.

STREPTOCARPUS *(Cape primrose)*
* 10°C/50°F

The true species, of which there are about 100 in this genus, are rarely now grown as pot plants. An enormous amount of work has been done on hybridization and the production of variants by chemical and physical methods, and it is these exceedingly beautiful named forms that are at present so popular. There are also some superb strains offered by the leading seedsmen. However, streptocarpus are not the easiest plants to raise from seed without proper greenhouse conditions.

For the home, it is better to buy young seedlings or plants, preferably when they are in bud or just coming into flower. These will be available from spring to summer according to the stage of advancement.

Established plants usually flower over a long period, extending from May to October, and often continuing well into winter. Streptocarpus belong to the same family as the African violet, and, ideally, rather similar cultural conditions are required. However, streptocarpus are less demanding with regard to winter warmth and strong plants will survive as low as 5–7°C (41–45°F) if kept on the dry side during the winter. The plants are also less demanding regarding humidity.

It is difficult to see how the common name arose, since the flowers are absolutely nothing like a primrose. They are rather trumpet-shaped and borne in groups on wiry stems well above the foliage. The plants send up these flowering stems in succession. There are large and small flowered forms, the latter types usually producing blooms more freely. There are numerous beautiful colours and colour combinations and there is often exotic markings and sometimes frilling of the petals. The John Innes Institute has done much work on the production of hybrids and there are many of them.

Unfortunately, the foliage of streptocarpus tends to be rather ungainly. It is slightly velvety in texture, very corrugated, elongated, curving downwards usually, and rather brittle so that it is easily damaged. Plants have to be moved with care and often it is wise to stand mature plants on a support so that the foliage can hang freely from the pot. These remarks may seem disparaging, but if the foliage is looked after it is not unattractive.

Good cultivars include 'Constant Nymph' (blue and purple flowers with dark throat veins), 'Maasen's White' (white mutant of 'Constant Nymph'), 'Albatross' (large-flowered mutant of 'Massen's White' with a yellow eye), 'Margaret' (purple and blue new hybrid notable for almost continuous flowering), 'Tina' (pink and magenta, prettily veined, compact foliage), 'Marie' (rose-purple, white throat, nicely veined, very compact), 'Fiona' (lovely pink with waved petals), 'Diana' (cerise with white throat), 'Paula' (reddish-purple, pinkish centre, neat habit), 'Karen' (magenta and dark pink with darker veining).

Streptocarpus grow well in any good potting compost, and usually a final pot size of 13cm (5in) is adequate. Water freely from spring to autumn, sparingly in winter, regulating the amount given according to temperature. Give a moderately bright position, but avoid direct sunshine. The foliage can become very easily scorched and will then turn dark brown and unsightly.

To ensure continuous flowering, promptly cut off faded flowers and remove stems when all the flowers supported have passed over.

Streptocarpus are most easily propagated by careful division of the roots in early spring. They can also be mutliplied from leaf cuttings taken from May to July. Cut a leaf into sections and insert in any of the usual rooting composts. New

Streptocarpus 'Purple Nymph'.

124

Above: *Syngonium podophyllum.*

plants will arise from the base. A temperature of about 18°C (65°F) is best for rooting, and the cuttings must be covered to maintain humidity.

Established streptocarpus plants enjoy moderately airy conditions although the air should not be too dry. Aphids are the most common pest, and generally the plants have few problems. It is surprising that streptocarpus are not more popular as houseplants, although they have long been highly prized for greenhouses and conservatories.

STROMANTHE AMABILIS
** 13°C/55°F

This plant is closely related to marantas and requires very similar culture and treatment (see page 95). It is of Brazilian origin and was a great favourite in the warm greenhouses of Victorian times. Lately it has been re-introduced as a houseplant. It makes a neat pot plant growing to about 30–45cm (1–1½ft) high. The handsome oval leaves are variegated with light and dark green herring-bone markings, often with silvery streaks.

Stromanthes thrive in the modern peat-based potting composts, but appreciate a moist atmosphere and should never be allowed to dry out completely. They are useful for the more shady parts of the home, provided the necessary warmth and moisture can be maintained, and grow well in groups with other plants. Propagation is by division of established clumps in spring or early summer. Pests and diseases are unusual, aphids being the most likely. Chills and erratic temperatures may cause the leaves to shrivel and turn brown around the edges. See also calatheas (page 63) and marantas (page 95).

SYNGONIUM PODOPHYLLUM
(arrowhead vine, goosefoot plant)
** 13°C/55°F

This plant resembles and is closely related to philodendrons, and needs exactly the same culture and treatment (see page 104). It is a very attractive climber, with sharply triangular arrow-shaped leaves. The two angles at the leaf stalk end often acquire a shape like rabbit's ears and it is rather surprising that a common name to describe this character has not been invented. In mature plants the leaf form changes to become trifoliate, then forming several lobes and becoming much larger, the central lobe being the longest – up to about 30cm (1ft) in length. The leaf colouring may also become much paler. In the type species the leaves are green and tend to be heart-shaped. The most desirable forms are 'Green Gold' and 'Imperial White'. These have the central portion of the leaves white to cream which changes to golden-yellow and eventually green around the leaf edges by a series of speckling. 'Green Gold' has the 'ear' effect, already mentioned, particularly emphasized. This species originates from Mexico and Panama and demands adequate warmth and humidity. It can also be grown as a trailer. Mature plants produce flowers (spathes) and these may be followed by fruits, but this is most unusual in the case of pot-grown plants. This plant is not quite so easy as philodendrons unless adequate warmth and humidity can be maintained the year round. In an unsuitable environment it has a startling habit of suddenly wilting and shrivelling with remarkable rapidity.

For propagation and general treatment see philodendron (page 104). If possible a few degrees higher than the minimum recommended should be maintained. Water cautiously in winter, as over-watering can soon lead to root rot. Repot in late spring when the plants are about to begin active growth.

Right: *Stromanthe amabilis.*

125

THUNBERGIA
* see text for temperatures

Thunbergia alata, black-eyed Susan, is a delightful South African climber, easily grown as an annual from seed sown early in the year. It starts flowering in the young seedling stage and continues to bloom with the utmost freedom until autumn.

The plant can be grown easily from seed sown under window-sill conditions. A packet of seeds usually gives a batch of plants with variously coloured flowers, including pale cream, pale orange, and vivid orange, with or without a jet-black eye. It is usually best to discard all those without the eye, and even all those without the best orange colour. It is the plants with the vivid orange, contrasting with a black eye, that are the most striking. Fortunately, this colouring usually predominates a batch. These plants are also the ones mostly sold as small pot plants by florists in late spring or early summer.

The plants can be grown up a fan of bamboo canes, or one of the plastic trellis-type supports sold for the smaller houseplant climbers, or put in hanging-baskets. Although the tendency is for the plant to climb, it can be persuaded to trail. Usually, at least three plants will be needed for a basket, and it is a help to fix the stems down to the basket sides at first as they grow. Pieces of bent wire can be used for this.

As a climber, the plant's height varies with growing conditions and may reach about 1m (3$\frac{1}{2}$ft) or more with average treatment, although far greater heights have been reported. Thunbergia grows easily in any of the usual potting com-posts. It will grow well in bright po-sitions, as well as slight shade, but too much light tends to bleach the flowers and cause them to pass over more quickly. If possible, remove all faded flowers and the seed pods as promptly as possible to encourage continuous flowering.

Keep the plants well watered through-out summer and maintain moderate humidity. If possible, spray the plants with a mist of water from time to time, especially under foliage. Try to provide a minimum temperature of 10°C (50°F). Unfortunately, this species is extremely prone to attack by red spider mites, and once an infestation has taken place it becomes very difficult to control the pest, which may also spread to other house-plants. Watch for any sign of yellowing foliage and inspect it through a powerful lens from time to time to see if the tiny spider-like mites, or their minute whitish round eggs, can be seen. Apart from this

Thunbergia alata.

126

specific pest, the plants are rarely troubled by others, or by diseases. At the end of the year, after flowering, the plants can be discarded.

Three other species may make interesting houseplants in certain circumstances. The most useful is probably *T. gregorii*, often confused with *T. gibsonii*. Although this is a perennial it can be grown as an annual in much the same way as *T. alata*. However, the plant is more vigorous and has much larger orange flowers – about 4cm ($1\frac{1}{2}$in) across – without an eye. If given a free run it will climb to a considerable height and is useful for stair-wells, porches or conservatories, provided the winter minimum can be maintained. If the plant is kept as a perennial it should be moved on to larger pots and at least a 20cm (8in) size will be needed.

T. grandiflora, an Indian species, is an even more vigorous grower, but is different in having even larger purple-blue flowers. It can be kept to a convenient size by drastic cutting back and pruning, but this does tend to inhibit flowering. This species ultimately needs a large pot. It makes an impressive conservatory or garden room plant, and is also suitable for a glass porch that can be kept warm in winter.

Of very recent introduction as a houseplant, and still needing some trial as a plant suited to this purpose, is the very lovely *T. laurifolia*, the laurel-leaved thunbergia. The common name of this species is suggested by the shiny, green laurel-like foliage. The flowers are very large and can reach about 13cm (5in) across. They are a beautiful lavender-blue, with a contrasting yellow throat, and are freely produced over a long period on mature plants. This species can now be bought as young plants, but these have to be grown on for about three years before they can be expected to flower. However, in the meantime the foliage is quite decorative in itself. This species is native to Malaya, but it is grown in most warm countries and is often a feature. As might be expected, moderate warmth is essential for its success and a winter minimum of about 15°C (59°F) is recommended. It is best given as much height as possible and grown up canes near a large window. However, this species will tolerate some shade.

TIBOUCHINIA
see page 179

TILLANDSIA
see page 152

TOLMIEA MENZIESII
(piggy-back plant)
* **hardy**

This hardy plant is the only one of the genus, and one of the easiest and accommodating of all houseplants. It is especially useful for the chilliest and most draughty places, where other plants might soon fade away. It originates from western United States and is a vigorous ground cover type of plant growing only about 15cm (6in) in height, spreading by means of creeping rhizomes. However, in pots it will form clumps and remain reasonably compact.

The foliage is pale green, slightly hairy in texture, and maple-like in shape. At the point where the leaf stalk joins the leaf a tiny plantlet forms. This eventually grows large enough to weigh down the parent leaf, and in the natural environment the plantlet will root when it touches the soil. When tolmieas are grown as pot plants those leaves carrying a plantlet can be removed by hand and placed in separate pots for propagation. The phenomenon of bearing these plantlets has also led to the common name of youth-on-age.

In summer, the plant produces stems about 45cm ($1\frac{1}{2}$ft) tall bearing spikes of greenish-white tubular flowers.

A shady position is suitable and if possible the plant should be raised on a low support to allow stems to cascade over the side of the container. Most of the plantlets seem to form at the ends of the stems. The plant is also suitable for small hanging containers or wall pots.

Tolmiea menziesii.

TRACHYCARPUS
see page 137

TRADESCANTIA *(wandering Jew, inch plant)*
* 7°C/45°F

This is surely one of the most popular and frequently seen of all houseplants, yet it is surprisingly not so often well grown. Untidy, straggly specimens with poor leaf colours abound.

The tradescantias are sometimes confused with the rather similar zebrina and may well be sold wrongly named by florists. In appearance these two plants certainly have much in common.

The tradescantias are usually grown in their variegated forms rather than as the type species. *T. albiflora* and *T. fluminensis*, both from South America, have a number of very pretty variations. *T. a.* 'Albovittata' has white striped leaves, narrower and more pointed than those of *T. fluminensis*. *T. f.* 'Variegata' also has white striped leaves, but with purple tinting below, and a golden-yellow colour often suffusing the upper surface. *T. f.* 'Tricolor' has pink, green, and white striping, and the form 'Quicksilver' has silvery striping.

A species of special note, often grown in conservatories but also useful in the home, is *T. blossfeldiana* from Argentina. This makes a fine basket plant and has much larger leaves than the other tradescantias. It has purple stems and foliage that is purple beneath and dark green above, slightly hairy, and often with a purple tinting. The flowers of this species are more showy than most. They are about 12mm (½in) wide, rose-purple with white eye, and borne freely in umbels from March to July. A form with cream-striped foliage is sometimes available and is also most decorative.

Most people grow tradescantias as trailers, allowing the stems to hang from raised pots, pedestals, wall pots, or baskets. With frequent removal of the growing tips when the plant starts growing in spring, they can also be made to produce more upright growth.

There is considerable controversy over the best method of culture, but it would seem that the finest leaf colours are developed with cautious watering. This is despite the fact that in its natural environment the plant may grow in rather wet soils. However, enough water should be given to provide nicely moist conditions for the roots. Another important requirement for best colour contrast and development is good light. So often the plants are tucked away in very gloomy places in the home. Direct sunlight should be avoided, otherwise the leaves may become scorched, but in dim places the plants tend to become pale and straggly.

Many tradescantias are expected to withstand temperatures far lower than they would like. They may survive if kept on the dry side, but will rarely thrive. *T. blossfeldiana* should preferably be given a few degrees higher than the minimum suggested, and also moderate humidity. In all cases chills will cause leaves to turn brown around the edges, and the same happens if the roots are allowed to become too dry. Even if plants have been drastically ill-treated, they usually send up new growth if all poor growth is cut back severely in spring.

The ease with which stem cuttings root is well known; they will usually root if merely stood in water. As old plants tend to become less decorative, reasonably frequent propagation to provide a supply of young plants is a wise procedure.

Most normal potting composts are suitable, and the plants rarely have troubles apart from aphids.

TULIPA
see page 143

VALLOTA
see page 145

VANDA
see page 175

VELTHEIMIA
* 7°C/45°F

There seems to be considerable botanical uncertainty about the number of species in this genus – probably only about two – and their naming. The bulb usually sold as *V. capensis* is claimed by some authorities to be *V. bracteata* (syn. *V. viridifolia*). Whatever it is, it would be worth the attention of plant breeders. It has distinct possibilities because of its easy culture, resistance to cool conditions, attractive foliage, and early flower spikes.

The flower is remarkably like a small red-hot poker spike (Kniphofia) and also resembles the flower of some aloes. The colour, however, is unfortunately rather dismal, being a drab pinkish shade. Even so, flowering as it does from February onwards, and lasting a fair time, it makes a particularly useful addition to the houseplant range.

Pot the bulbs in autumn, leaving the tips just above the surface of the compost. Set one bulb to each 13cm (5in) pot, and use any of the usual potting composts. Water cautiously at first and until the foliage begins to grow freely. The leaves, forming a rosette around the bulb top, are elongated and have attractively waved edges. The bulb is evergreen and can be kept very slightly moist the year round in cool conditions. In its native South Africa it flowers from July to September and grows in shady places. Water freely when the foliage is making active growth, but rest the bulb by reducing watering from summer to autumn. Trouble from pests or diseases is most unusual, and veltheimias can be relied upon to flower well.

VINCA ROSEA
see Catharanthus roseus

VRIESEA
see page 152

WASHINGTONIA
see page 137

Veltheimia bracteata.

YUCCA
* see text for minimum temperatures

Although there are a number of hardy yuccas, such as *Y. filamentosa*, the poisonous-rooted *Y. gloriosa*, and *Y. recurvifolia*, that can all be grown in pots as *young* plants, it is the tender *Y. elephantipes* (syn. *Y. guatemalensis*) that is usually sold by florists. Its popular name is spineless yucca.

Young plants of *Y. elephantipes* grow as a single stem, with a swollen base developing. The leaves are typical of the yuccas, being long and sword-shaped, sharply pointed, slightly toothed along the edges, and glossy green. Mature plants may branch at the base to produce a more shrubby habit. It can grow to a very considerable size but, although coming from Central America, is happy with about 7–10°C (45–50°F) as a winter minimum.

Y. aloifolia is similar to *Y. elephantipes* in appearance and treatment.

A cream-edged foliage form of *Y. filamentosa*, slightly less hardy than the type, is sometimes sold now as a houseplant. Its attractive foliage is also edged with fine filament-like hairs. It only grows to

Below: *Tradescantia fluminensis.*
Right: *Yucca aloifolia.*

about 60cm (2ft) and makes a compact pot plant.

All yuccas are best suited to a bright spacious entrance hall, stair-well, large porch, or similar place. They will thrive in any good potting compost, provided drainage is satisfactory (some extra washed grit can be added to the peat-based composts). Potting-on is best done in spring. The container size will range from about an 18cm (7in) pot to a small tub, according to the age and species. Watering should be generous when active growth is proceeding and sparing in winter. The more hardy species can be placed outdoors during the summer months for a time, taking care not to neglect watering. During this period they can also be fed with advantage. Mature plants, at least three years old, may produce striking spikes of creamy bell-shaped flowers.

Yuccas are remarkably free from pests, diseases, and cultivation problems if reasonably looked after. Propagation is usually from removal of basal suckers when they form. This is best done in spring.

ZANTEDESCHIA AETHIOPICA
(arum lily, calla lily)
* see text for temperatures

The arum lily or calla lily is a beautiful South African plant, hardy in mild moist places out of doors, and even in colder areas may sometimes be grown as an aquatic plant if covered with water in an outdoor pool during winter.

Pot up the rhizome-like roots in large pots, big enough to accommodate them comfortably, in spring or autumn. Use any of the usual potting composts with some charcoal granules added, water thoroughly and keep nicely moist at all times.

After flowering, from March to June, the plants can be placed outside, although the large glossy arrow-shaped foliage is quite handsome. A slightly shaded place is preferable. In winter, only frost protection is necessary.

The plants will lend themselves to gentle forcing in warmth for early flowering. This is sometimes done by nurseries to produce early flowers for cutting. When the plants are producing leaves freely they can be watered generously and fed with liquid feeds. In this case, it is quite in order to stand the pots in shallow containers of water which can be kept topped up.

There are a number of cultivars with slight variations of spathe colouring. 'Green Goddess' has green striping. 'Crowborough' is particularly good for pots, as it is rather more compact and is reputed to be exceptionally hardy.

Zantedeschia aethiopica is sometimes called *Richardia africana* and may sometimes be listed under that name. Anoth-er common name is lily of the nile. The flowers are among the most important for growing commercially for cutting.

Repotting of this species is best done in late autumn to early winter, although the roots are often listed in spring bulb catalogues. Look out for a dwarf form called 'Little Gem', which is particularly good as a houseplant. It grows to only about 45cm (1½ft), which is about half the normal. Unfortunately this form has recently become difficult to find.

A few other species may be encountered occasionally, including the yellow-flowered *Z. elliottiana*.

Z. aethiopica is rarely troubled by pests and diseases, although aphids are a possibility. In unsatisfactory potting composts, made with unsterilized garden soil for example, root rot may occur. This usually kills the plant.

Zantedeschia aethiopica.

ZEBRINA *(inch plant)*
* see text for temperatures

This small genus of trailers from Guatemala and Mexico very much resembles tradescantias and can be distinguished only by the flower structure. The two are often confused and the names mixed.

Justifiably popular is the attractive Z. *pendula*. The green leaves are marked by two silvery bands and have a lustrous crystalline texture above, purple beneath. A cultivar called 'Quadricolor' has white and purple striping.

Z. *purpusii* is rather different, with purple and olive green striping above and bright purple colouring beneath. It has the common name of bronze inch plant, but is now thought by some authorities to be a variety of Z. *pendula*.

All these zebrinas will survive temperatures much lower than the recommended 13°C (55°F) if kept on the dry side. Even if top growth is damaged by chills, new shoots usually arise with the return of warmer conditions. Their culture is much the same as for tradescantias (see page 128), but they are usually better in shadier places and are frequently used as ground cover under the staging in greenhouses and conservatories. However, they are especially suited to hanging pots or pots on pedestals. The stems usually trail down sufficiently far to hide the container and then make a sharp turn upwards, a growth formation that is extremely effective.

Zebrinas are remarkably free from pests and diseases, but chills or lack of water are likely to cause leaf browning and shrivelling.

Zebrina pendula.

ZEPHYRANTHES
(flowers of the western wind)
* hardy

Not all of these bulbous plants are hardy, but the one most frequently grown as a pot plant, Z. *candida*, from Argentina, is hardy outdoors in parts of this country. In pots indoors and with frost protection it has evergreen grassy foliage. The flowers are borne on wiry stems in autumn. They are at first crocus-like, but open to form pure white stars with yellow centres.

Pot the bulbs in spring, setting several to each pot, and using any of the usual potting composts. Water cautiously at first, and even when the plants are growing water should never be applied too lavishly. It is best to allow the pots to dry out very slightly before reapplying water. In winter little or no water is needed.

The first year of potting may not reveal the best show of flowers. The bulbs are seen with the most effect when they are left to crowd out their pots for a few years, but during this time they should be fed when making foliage, and not disturbed. Flowering will then be prolific and nice clumps will be produced during autumn.

Provide a bright position at all times and a reasonably well ventilated place. Since the rush-like leaves of this species are evergreen in the conditions of a cool room, it makes a useful foliage plant, undemanding regarding temperature. In some areas of the country, in the South and West especially, it has been used as an evergreen edging plant. However, a severe winter will kill off the leaves, although the bulbs usually survive and grow again.

Pest and disease troubles are rare.

Zephyranthes candida.

131

SPECIAL INTEREST PLANTS

PALMS & FERNS

Palms and ferns have been used to decorate homes for hundreds of years. These plants, which are early on the evolutionary scale, have been employed as houseplants for a much longer period than the traditional flowering types, and their graceful and elegant nature has impressed countless generations of plant enthusiasts.

The heyday of the palm was the Victorian era, when they graced many a drawing-room, rubbing shoulders with ferns and aspidistras which at that time were the backbone of indoor plant decoration. Even today there are few more pleasing sights than that of the aristocrat of all palms, *Howeia forsteriana* (previously called *Kentia*) standing in splendid isolation on top of a Victorian plant pedestal.

Besides doing duty as specimen plants – standing on their own – the majority of taller palms will also be the ideal background subject when a group of assorted plants are placed together. Whenever possible the dark green colouring of the elegant palms should be set off against light-coloured furnishings – light-coloured walls, in particular, making the perfect background.

Perhaps the least pleasing aspect of palms is their often high cost in comparison with other indoor plants. This is usually due to their scarcity value – there are always more customers than there are mature plants for sale. For instance, seed for *Howeia forsteriana*, which comes from the Lord Howe Islands, is always in short supply. There is the further complication in that almost all these plants are slow-growing, and occupy considerable space in commercial greenhouses.

Fortunately, the reverse is true of the popular parlour palm, *Chamaedorea elegans* (which may also be seen labelled as *Neanthe bella* or *Collinia elegans*). A considerable benefit is that seed is produced in many parts of the world, and the plants can be sold in small pots when they are about one year old.

The parlour palm is initially small, and an ideal subject for inclusion in containers housing a mixture of plants.

HOW TO GROW PALMS

Although palms originated from tropical regions and have, essentially, an exotic appearance, they are not difficult to care for as houseplants. Even in respect of temperature they are not demanding, and although there are some exceptions, most will do better at about 16°C (61°F) than they will if temperatures are maintained at very high levels.

In higher temperatures – in excess of 21°C (70°F) – where there is also a marked tendency for the atmosphere to be drier, it will be found that there is a much higher incidence of red spiders.

Good light is important, but strong sunlight should be avoided as leaf scorch may result if plants are placed close to a window pane in a sunny room. Glass has the effect of a magnifying glass – particularly frosted glass.

Right: *Howeia forsteriana* (left) and a collection of ferns.
Below: A typical fernery of the 1840s – in effect a lean-to greenhouse with no opening windows.

Compost

Loamless mixtures may be satisfactory for plants in their early stages of growth, but more mature specimens must have a richer and more durable mixture.

Many of the palms, *Phoenix canariensis* and *P. roebelenii*, for example, produce a large mass of light-coloured roots which in time become so numerous as they accumulate in the pot that they push the root-ball upwards and clear of the container. This should act as a warning that when repotting large palms it will be a futile exercise to use more modern loamless composts.

A mix of peat, leafmould and good loam in equal parts will then give excellent results for the majority of palms. However, there should be a tendency to increase the amount of loam in the mix for larger plants. To improve drainage, all mixes should have a proportion of sharp sand added.

Potting

With the majority of palms, good drainage is essential. However, *Microcoelum weddelianum* (syn. *Cocos weddeliana*) is an exception, as during its early stages it is frequently grown in pots without drainage holes. Normally, however, ensure that the pots have holes in the bottom and that they are covered with a layer of broken clay pots prior to the compost being placed in the base of the pot.

As a general guide to potting-on palms, move a plant in a 9cm (3½in) size pot into a 13cm (5in) pot; a plant in a 13cm (5in) pot can be moved into an 18cm (7in) pot; and one in an 18cm (7in) pot should be potted into a 25cm (10in) container, which may well be a tub of some kind. Palms should be potted much more firmly than most other houseplants, and after potting the soil should be thoroughly watered, then kept slightly dry for several weeks. However, at no time should the soil become excessively dry – being slightly dry for a few weeks after potting encourages the production of fresh roots.

An experienced grower of palms, however, knows full well that many of the more vigorous plants, such as *Caryota urens*, would very quickly outgrow the limited space of an average living-room. Even when their roots are confined to 25cm (10in) pots the caryotas, with their unusual ragged leaf edges, will attain a height of 4–4.5m (12–15ft). It is, therefore, obvious that it is necessary to keep the plants in small pots for as long as possible.

Root pruning

The stronger-growing palms, such as caryota and *Cocos nucifera*, can, as an alternative to potting-on, have their roots pruned, similar to bonsai plants. Root pruning of vigorous subjects can be quite severe – healthy plants will suffer a little but not unduly. The effects of root pruning in this way restricts growth and holds plants at a much more manageable size. For example a *Howeia belmoreana* over 50 years old may still be in a tub of 30cm (12in) diameter and be 3m (10ft) high.

Watering

When watering, pour water on to the top of the soil in sufficient quantity for the surplus to be seen draining through the bottom of the container. Waterlogged compost can play havoc with palms. Therefore, if water is seen to remain on the surface of the soil for any length of time it will be necessary to remove the plant from its pot so that the drainage can be checked.

Worms present in the compost produce casts which eventually block the drainage holes and cause the soil to become waterlogged. Similarly, poorly-drained compost containing too much loam and insufficient sharp sand can, in time, cause saturated conditions.

The most common reason for plants deteriorating is that the owner cannot resist the temptation to be forever watering the plant.

Feeding

Foliage may become discoloured as a result of insufficient feeding. Palms will need to be fed as soon as they have become established in their pots. In most instances, a policy of little and often is more beneficial than to give the plants heavy doses of food only occasionally.

Unless the plants are in especially favourable locations and growing during the winter months, it should only be necessary to feed them during the spring and summer.

Following potting-on into larger containers of new compost it should not be necessary to feed the plant for at least six months – that is, until the roots have well filled the new soil and are in need of additional nourishment.

Keeping palms healthy

Palms are not particularly troubled by pests or diseases, though red spider mite can be a problem in a hot, dry atmosphere. Scale insects might also be found. In spite of their tough appearance and texture, palm leaves are highly susceptible to many chemicals, so be careful in the choice of insecticide.

Because of the sensitivity of the leaves of many palms, particularly *Howeia forsteriana*, it is also wise to keep them well away from aerosols intended for furniture or for cleaning windows. Even leafshine products are best avoided – instead simply wipe the leaves with a damp sponge or cloth.

Easy palms to grow

Howeia belmoreana has typical palm leaves that in mature specimens may attain a length of 2.1–3m (7–10ft), with the serrated leaves drooping gracefully from the stout central midrib of the leaf. It is very much the palm court type of plant, with leaves spreading over a wide radius, which tends to rule larger plants out for all but high-ceilinged larger rooms.

More suitable for indoors is *Howeia forsteriana*, which has more graceful and upright growth, and is seen at its best when several plants are potted together in the same container. Although in ideal conditions this plant may attain a height of 4.5m (15ft), it will be found that by putting several young plants in the same container initially growth will be much less vigorous than if a single plant had been placed in the container. This is the most graceful and best suited palm for the modern home.

As a young plant, *Cocos nucifera* (the coconut palm) has attractive, upright leaves not unlike those of the howeia, but tends to become coarser with age. As with most palms – if seed is obtainable – it can be sown at any time of the year in almost any free-draining soil mixture, but will require a temperature in the region of 24°C (75°F) to induce germination.

An interesting aspect of this plant is that it can very occasionally be acquired with growth sprouting from what must be one of the largest seeds of all – the actual coconut complete with its outer husk in which it is protected on its tree.

The coconut, lying on its side and half exposed in the centre of a pot and with growth sprouting from one end, provides a very interesting and decorative plant. In its natural habitat, the plant may attain a height of 27.5m (90ft), and will develop into a substantial plant with roots confined to a pot. However, its development takes many years and plants can be both interesting and decorative over a long period prior to outgrowing their allotted head-room.

There are three phoenix palms that are occasionally grown. The best of these for room decoration is *P. canariensis*, which produces stiff, radiating leaves from a stout basal trunk. It is slow growing and compact.

Much bolder in appearance is *P. roebelenii*, with firm and generally spiteful leaf stalks. It therefore requires to be handled carefully. Also of interest is *P. dactylifera*, which is the date palm of commerce and grows to become a substantial tree.

A name to curl the tongue around is *Chrysalidocarpus lutescens*, also known as *Areca lutescens*, which produces clusters of small, bulbous basal stems that have an interesting yellow colouring.

When confined to pots, a maximum height of some 1.8m (6ft) can be anticipated. Foliage is slender and upright, and possibly injurious chemicals should not come into contact with the leaves. The windmill palm, *Trachycarpus fortunei* (also known as *Chamaerops excelsa*) is a familiar hardy palm in southern parts of Britain and an interesting plant to grow in a container. It has the advantage of occupying a position on the patio during all but the most adverse months of the year. Indoors, good light is essential.

Requiring shade from strong sunlight, *Euterpe edulis* is a palm that is making bold efforts to become popular. Its thin, rather sparse foliage, suggests that it has much to do to compete with the palms previously mentioned. Give it the same treatment as suggested for the howeias. Indigenous to California, *Washingtonia filifera* and *W. robusta* are plants that are occasionally available in Britain. They need modest warmth in the region of 16°C (61°F) to do well. As with the majority of palms indoors, less water is required during the winter months.

Opposite page: *Phoenix canariensis*.
Below: *Howeia belmoreana*, one of the taller palms for the home.

FERNS FOR THE HOME

These ancient plants bring an atmosphere of coolness and tranquility to the home. They are both bold and delicate plants, and although non-flowering have a distinctive charm not found in any other group of plants. It is now possible to buy a wide range of types for home decoration and, though they may vary in appearance, most require similar treatment.

In many instances, a bold clump of ferns of the same kind can be much more impressive than a collection of individual plants. In this respect several plants in a larger pot on a pedestal, or grouped in a hanging-basket, can provide a dominant and attractive feature in a spacious hallway or lounge.

How to grow ferns

At no time should ferns be allowed to dry out. Moisture at their roots and in the atmosphere surrounding them are important needs of all ferns. To provide these essential needs it is wise to plunge the pots in which plants are growing into larger containers filled with peat, sphagnum moss, or even wet newspaper. The essential requirement is that the material in which pots are plunged should be able to retain a reasonable amount of moisture.

Besides making arrangements for the area surrounding their roots to be moist, it is useful to have a hand sprayer with a fine misting nozzle. It can be filled with tepid water and regularly used to mist over the foliage.

Ferns, with their graceful and delicately-textured green, sometimes silvery-grey, foliage will need protection from direct sunlight.

Any drying out of the compost in which plants are growing, followed by exposure to direct sunlight, can play havoc with them. In fact, exposure to direct sunlight at any time is something that most fern plants can well do without.

Feeding of established plants is, of course, necessary, but avoid the temptation to make too heavy applications. It is better to give frequent and light feeds, than a few that are very heavy. It is best to feed ferns through their leaves by using a foliar feed applied through a handsprayer bottle producing a fine mist. Foliar feeds do not damage the tender root systems.

Composts and potting

Many ferns are acquired as reasonably large plants in relatively small pots, and it is wise to pot them on into larger ones. Delay in potting such plants will frequently result in them becoming starved of nourishment.

There are many potting composts available, but with ferns it is essential that the mixture does not contain any lime, and that it is open and fibrous.

The diversity of this family makes it difficult to recommend a mixture that will be suited to all plants, but it should be open and fibrous, and ideally contain equal parts of loam, leafmould, coarse peat, and sand.

Keeping the ferns healthy

Ferns are not too troubled by pests, but scale insects can be a nuisance. Also, mealy bugs often infest the more inaccessible sections of the plant. Leaves that are badly infested with scale insects should be removed completely, and a damp sponge used to wipe the scales forcibly from other leaves.

Easy ferns to grow

Of all the ferns used for indoor decoration, the nephrolepis in its many forms is the most important, and when properly cared for there can be few more satisfying potted plants.

The ladder fern (*Nephrolepis exaltata*), in its many fine crested and plumed cultivars, has few peers. In finer specimens the linear-shaped fronds are 60cm (2ft) or more in length, and a bright, fresh green in colour.

These plants are seen at their best when placed on a pedestal, or suspended in a hanging-basket. There are numerous excellent examples of this fine fern. Among the best are the Boston fern (*Nephrolepis exaltata* 'Bostoniensis'), *N. e.* 'Teddy Junior' and *N. e.* 'Whitmanii'. None of these is difficult to manage.

Similar in appearance to the nephrolepis, but with softer and less robust foliage that is also a paler shade of green, is *Microlepia setosa*. It requires similar cultural requirements as the nephrolepis. Another fine fern with densely clustered and delicate fronds of a pale green colouring is *Davallia fijiensis*, which can be most rewarding when seen as a solitary plant in a suspended macrame hanger.

The holly fern, *Cyrtomium falcatum* 'Rochfordianum', has, as its common name suggests, a holly-like appearance, although it is quite harmless to touch. Nevertheless, the leaves have the same glossy green appearance, and the plant itself is a fairly easy and robust grower. It is probably a little ambitious to consider the Australian tree fern, *Dicksonia antarctica*, among the genuine houseplants, but it is a possibility for the heated greenhouse that offers ample space. It is difficult to obtain, and is one of the true aristocrats among foliage plants, developing long, typical fern fronds on top of stout tree-like trunks. Its stately appearance gives the plant considerable character. Cool, moist conditions are really essential, as well as a compost that is free-draining.

At the opposite end of the scale, *Pellaea rotundifolia* is flat and compact, with dark green glossy leaves attached to wiry stems. It is an easy plant to grow. Totally different in habit, *Lygodium volubile*, also on wiry stems, is of a climbing habit and will quickly wind its way round any sort of framework. Give it good drainage, protect from sunlight, and keep reasonably warm.

There are numerous cultivars of the hardy hart's tongue fern, *Phyllitis scolopendrium*, with strap-like leaves. On account of its hardiness, this is an easy plant to manage in a cool room. *Polystichum setiferum* is another handsome plant with splendid foliage that will add much to any collection of ferns, and it is easy to grow.

Many ferns will grow more freely if attached to a tree branch and treated as epiphytes. The roots are bound in sphagnum moss and attached to the branch with plastic-coated wire, and thereafter kept moist. One of the best plants for this purpose is *Platycerium bifurcatum*, the stag's-horn fern, also known as *P. alcicorne*, which produces

flat leaves for attaching itself to trees. The fertile fronds are of antler shape and can be handsome in mature plants. One precaution when handling these plants is to ensure that the leaves are not damaged.

Asplenium nidus and *A. bulbiferum* are both attractive plants, with the former being the more difficult to grow. It needs shade and warmth to succeed well. The leaves are very easily damaged and should not be handled.

With their pale green and delicate leaves attached to wiry, dark stems, the adiantums, among which are the maidenhair ferns, are some of the most beautiful indoor plants. All of them need careful attention and a temperature in the region of 18°C (65°F). They need shade from direct sunlight, and moist surroundings. The plants should never be allowed to become starved as a result of remaining in small pots far too long. Pot them as soon as they are well rooted. *Adiantum raddianum* (syn. *A. cuneatum*), *A. capillus-veneris* and *A. tenerum* are all well established and dependable.

Among the pteris ferns there are many fine, dependable forms that are not difficult to care for, and can be put to many

uses indoors. Of these, *Pteris cretica* is one of the most popular. There are also many cultivars with green and variegated foliage, including *P. c.* 'Albolineata', with a central variegated stripe running through each frond, and *P. c.* 'Wilsonii', which has crested tips to the fronds. *Pteris ensiformis* 'Victoriae' is another fine plant worthy of inclusion in any collection.

The selaginellas belong to the family Selaginellaceae, but like asparagus plants (see page 58) they are commonly referred to as ferns. These plants form mossy clumps of green or variegated foliage, and are really best suited to the confined atmosphere of bottle gardens. Plants soon deteriorate should they become dry or neglected, so it is best to buy plants from a reliable source. There are a number of cultivars that are occasionally available, among them being *S. kraussiara* (syn. *S. denticulata*) and its golden form *S. k.* 'Aurea'. They require close, moist and warm conditions.

Opposite page: *Nephrolepis exaltata.*
Top left: *Polystichum setiferum.*
Below left: *Phyllitis scolopendrium.*
Below: *Platycerium bifurcatum.*

BULBS

Bulbs traditionally represent spring, and a bowl of bulbs in flower in the home at Christmas is always a welcome harbinger of the good things to come. In the home they can bring colour and cheer at a time when little else is in bloom, and some, such as hyacinths and *Iris danfordiae*, have the merit of fragrance.

It would be tragic, however, to consider only spring-flowering subjects, for there are excellent summer and autumn-flowering houseplants that can be grown from bulbs – including the magnificent lilies and vallotas.

Another great merit of bulbs as houseplants is their ability to flower under adverse conditions. Colchicums – incorrectly called autumn crocus – as well as the true autumn crocus will bloom even if the corms are loose on the window-sill with no soil or moisture. Obviously this is not to be recommended as a treatment for other bulbs, but once in bloom most of them can be used to cheer even the dullest corner of a room.

Although it is convenient to consider bulbs and corms together – they are usually bought from the same sources and treated in a similar way – their structure is totally different.

HOW TO GROW BULBS

Spring-flowering bulbs are traditionally grown in bulb fibre in bowls without drainage holes, and this is perfectly satisfactory if the bulbs are to be discarded after flowering, or planted outdoors for future years. But they will grow equally well in pots, pans or bowls of a loam-based compost such as John Innes No. 2, and this is a preferable method if you intend to grow the bulbs for another year. Obviously, particular care has to be taken to avoid waterlogging when growing bulbs in bowls without any drainage – whether using fibre or soil.

Planting in bulb fibre

Bulb fibre is basically peat with the addition of charcoal and oyster shell – but the right kind of ingredients are important so it is best to buy it ready-mixed. It only needs wetting before use; add sufficient water to make it damp, but not so wet that moisture can be expressed when squeezed in the hand.

Half fill a suitable bowl with the fibre, then position the bulbs fairly close together, but not touching each other or the sides of the bowl. Pack more fibre round the bulbs, completely covering small kinds such as miniature narcissi, *Iris danfordiae* and crocuses, but leaving the top 12–25mm ($\frac{1}{2}$–1in) of large bulbs exposed.

Be very careful never to let the fibre dry out while the bulbs are growing.

Right: Narcissi are a popular way of brightening a spring window-sill.

Hyacinths in glazed bowls should be potted in bulb fibre. Prepared bulbs should be chosen for early flowering. An odd number of bulbs looks best.

The tips of the bulbs should remain above the fibre, which should be nicely moist but not too wet. Press it down firmly around the bulbs.

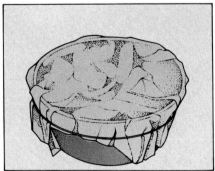

Place the bulbs in a dark cupboard, or outside plunged under a layer of peat or sand (to keep the bowls clean, protect with a sheet of plastic).

When the shoots are about 2.5–5cm (1–2in) high, bring the bulbs into the light. Keep the plants cool until the buds are visible.

Some bulbs can be grown in water, or on pebbles. Hyacinths are fun to grow in special glasses, while selected narcissi grow well on pebbles.

Planting in potting compost
The technique of planting in potting compost is the same as that for bulb fibre, except that good drainage material must first be placed in the bottom of the container.

If a deep container is used, daffodils can be planted in a double layer. Plant the lower layer about half way up the pot and cover all except the tips with compost, then place the upper layer of the bulbs *between* the noses of the first layer, and cover in the usual way.

Bulbs in water
The traditional hyacinth glasses seem to have been supplanted by plastic cups, but the fascination remains the same – especially for children.

Always choose a large hyacinth bulb – a prepared one will produce the most rapid results – so that it sits snuggly in the neck of the glass. The bottom of the bulb should sit just above the water, *not touching*.

Crocuses and some narcissi can be grown in water by placing them on pebbles heaped in a dish containing water in the bottom. If growing daffodils this way, choose 'Cragford', 'Paper White', or 'Soleil d'Or' – these have clusters of small flowers instead of one large bloom.

After planting . . .
All the spring-flowering bulbs should be kept cool and dark for at least seven weeks after planting. A cool cupboard in an unheated bedroom is suitable, or the pots or bowls can be placed in a polythene bag and placed outdoors with a covering of about 10cm (4in) of peat. The bag serves to make the job of cleaning the pots easier when they are brought indoors, and is essential to prevent bowls without drainage holes becoming waterlogged after heavy rain. A temperature of 5°C (41°F) is ample for root establishment.

Never put a bowl or pot of bulbs away and forget it for a couple of months – the compost and bulb fibre must be kept just moist. Once it dries damage may have been caused to the developing bud and it may not flower, even though the compost is kept moist subsequently.

When the shoots have developed sufficiently – about 2.5–5cm (1–2in) in the case of large bulbs such as hyacinths, obviously less with small bulbs – they should be brought into a temperature of about 10°C (50°F), in a position of good light. Although they can be used to brighten dull corners once they are in flower, poor light during the period of shoot development can be a significant cause of failure.

To produce balanced growth, give the pot or bowl a quarter of a turn every day; the trouble taken will be repaid by a more handsome bowl of bulbs.

When the flower buds can be seen the temperature can be increased to 15–21°C (60–70°F). A higher temperature will rush the bulbs too much, with a consequent loss of quality, or they may even fail to flower properly.

Feeding is not necessary unless the bulbs are required for planting out or growing on for another year, in which case they can be fed once a fortnight from when colour is showing in the buds and until the leaves have yellowed and died.

After flowering
It is not normally worth trying to propagate bulbs grown indoors, although the hardy kinds can be planted outdoors where they will probably flower and multiply again over the years.

If you intend to plant the bulbs outdoors, continue to water the pots or bowls after flowering has finished, until the leaves turn yellow, then plant them out.

If you are unable to plant them outside, do not attempt to force the bulbs another year – it is best to discard them rather than to face probable disappointment. Prepared bulbs lose the effect of treatment after flowering.

WINTER AND SPRING FLOWERS

Magnificent though some of the summer and autumn bulbs are, it is the winter and spring-flowering types that are inevitably the most widely planted.

Prepared hyacinths are naturally high on the list for Christmas flowering, and dwarf daffodils such as 'Tête-a-Tête' can be had in bloom in the New Year with very little heat, and if kept in a cool room will last in flower for weeks. A succession of unprepared hyacinths, crocuses, daffodils and tulips follows, with some of the charming smaller bulbs such as scillas, muscari and dwarf irises adding variety.

Daffodils

There is no difference between a daffodil and a narcissus. They are two names for the same family; narcissus is the Latin or botanical name, daffodil is the English name.

Trumpet daffodils are inevitably the most popular choice – and the yellow-flowered cultivars the most traditional. If you want a good traditional yellow trumpet try 'Dutch Master' or 'Golden Harvest'. An excellent bicolor for all purposes for pots, bowls, for showing or growing in the garden, is 'Trousseau', a white and buffy primrose.

More unusual and becoming more popular every year is 'Spellbinder', a shining rich lemon with a luminosity further enhanced after a few days by the trumpet becoming paler, almost white inside, leaving a smile of lemon around the lip of the trumpet.

For a good white, try 'Mount Hood', although the trumpet opens creamy, especially outside, and may take some while to fade to pure white. 'Empress of Ireland' is the leading white trumpet readily available.

Large-cup daffodils also make a bold display, and the stalwart 'Carlton' is a primrose kind that grows well in pots or bowls. 'Armada' is stronger in the stem and has large deep yellow and rich orange flowers.

Later-flowering kinds include the old but useful 'Carbineer', which is fine in pots and bowls provided it has plenty of light. Later still comes 'Feeling Lucky', which unfurls gold and orange flowers towards the end of the season.

A departure from the main stream of large-cupped cultivars is 'Ambergate'. This has a wide crown of deep orange-scarlet surrounded by a perianth of petals that are really golden and thoroughly suffused tangerine as if they had been dyed.

As a contrast to the incandescent brilliance of the cultivars just mentioned, try 'Binkie'. This opens lemon but then allows its crown to fade to white.

'Ice Follies' is an outstanding cultivar and a prolific bloomer. It has wide white petals and wide almost flat crowns of primrose fading to cream.

Of the white and orange large-cup types, 'Royal Orange' is a leap forward in extrovert flower-power, with an ample perianth of white and large wide somewhat frilled crowns painted a rich shade of orange. If bulbs are to be grown in bowls and then thrown away it is probably best to economize with the older and cheaper 'Flower Record'.

Probably more breeding work has gone into the production of pink-crowned daffodils than any other type. 'Mrs R. O. Backhouse' was the first to capture the public eye but has been long superseded. Of the cheaper kinds 'Pink Beauty' is neat with a longish crown. Outstanding inside and captivating outside is 'Passionale', a flower destined to be one of the few listed in catalogues for many years. Silky snow-white petals lie without the suggestion of a crease, behind an exactly proportioned crown of pure dog-rose pink.

Small-cupped daffodils tend to live under the dominant shadow of the large-cupped kinds, but many of them are

Left: Daffodils are always welcome.
Below left: Early double tulips.
Below: *Hyacinth* 'Salmonette'.

most lovely flowers. 'Birma' is a yellow and orange that can hold its own against many of the large cups. 'Altruist' is something quite different – its petals are smooth as porcelain but their colour is a creamy yellow that is lost under an even, pinky-orange rouging. The neat little cup is a distillation of orange-red.

The opening pure white petals of 'Aircastle' unfurl as large circles of glistening quality with a flat crown lightly shaded in lemon. After a few days the petals take on a lemon cast, an unusual and attractive metamorphosis. If you prefer your white flowers to stay white, 'Verona' is one that does this.

Double daffodils often arouse strong feelings, but if the idea of double daffodils does not appeal, try to view them just as flowers. Few cannot enjoy the Falstaffian good humour of the early double 'Van Sion', whose doubled trumpets may or may not belch out to form a rather tousled rose-like form. This has been known in Britain since the early 1600s.

Doubles grown indoors need a little more care with their watering and the heat given them. Avoid extremes otherwise the buds may fail to open.

The new doubles are altogether better plants. Most colours are now to be found. 'White Lion' is white and primrose and is a reliable kind.

Smaller daffodils should not be ignored, and the N. *cyclamineus* hybrids are some of the most worthwhile of all the family. 'February Gold' grows to 25cm (10in) and as its name suggests normally blooms early, even outdoors. 'Tête-a-Tête' is even smaller and earlier, and perhaps the longest in bloom of any daffodil; its 13cm (5in) stems carry one, two or sometimes three neat golden blooms. It is lovely in bowls or pots.

Several multiflowered cultivars are good for indoor work. 'Soleil d'Or' is the narcissus with lots of smallish yellow and orange, scented flowers that starts appearing in florists before Christmas. 'Bridal Crown' is white and cream and like an improved 'Cheerfulness'.

Tulips

Indoors, the huge tulips sometimes grown in the garden are difficult to manage, but it is worth trying some of the double earlies. Three or five bulbs in a 15cm (6in) bowl or pot can make a pleasing early spot of colour. They should bloom indoors from the second week in January to the middle of February, depending on cultivar. Because different cultivars may flower at different times always plant just a single colour in the one pot.

Darwin hybrids are really bold tulips, and 'Apeldoorn' is forced in millions for early flower. It is a deep scarlet, but sports now include 'Beauty of Apeldoorn' (golden yellow suffused red), 'Golde Apeldoorn', and 'Striped Apeldoorn' (a jazzy mixture of scarlet with yellow streaks and flashes outside but inside predominantly yellow striped with red). There are other lovely cultivars, but most of them are less suitable for indoor cultivation.

Some of the dwarf tulips usually associated with the rock garden also make good pot plants, provided they are grown in pots of sandy soil, and are kept in good light and not allowed to become too dry. The most popular dwarf tulips are Kaufmanniana and Greigii cultivars. Of all *T. greigii* hybrids the most successful is 'Red Riding Hood', a brilliant scarlet flower black-based and with beautifully marked leaves. The purple-striped foliage together with its name helps to make this an easy plant to remember.

Hyacinths

Hyacinths look as though they should be tender – their form is so perfect, the fragrance so heady, and the colours so rich. They would be welcome houseplants at any time, and flowering as they do from December to April, they are one of the finest bulbs for the home.

Crocuses respond well to pot culture if not forced too rapidly.

Lilium auratum.

Hippeastrum, popularly known as amaryllis.

The secret of a succession of bloom lies in a careful choice of cultivars and planting over a period of time. Plant prepared bulbs for December and January flowering and use unprepared bulbs to follow on. Not all cultivars are suitable for forcing. Plant early kinds in September for flowering at Christmas and in January, and later cultivars in October to bloom in February or March.

If a choice of bulb size is available, always select the largest for growing in glasses, but the second size will be adequate for bowls. Either size is suitable for growing in pots.

Multiflora hyacinths, which have several sprays of small but elegant flowers, are attractive when planted one bulb to a pot or three to a bowl, but secondary flower stems should be removed from the large-flowered kinds. If two or more spikes or sideshoots are produced, cut them off at the lowest point. If a secondary stem arises from the centre of the bulb it is best to pull it out forcibly.

No matter how tempting the idea may seem, never plant a mixed bowl of hyacinths – keep to one cultivar, otherwise it is probable that they will flower at different times.

Hippeastrums

The large-flowered hippeastrum hybrids, popularly known as amaryllis, are striking by any standards, and are constantly gaining in popularity. Given sufficient warmth, they are fascinating plants to grow, the flowering stem extending from the massive bulb at an amazing rate once growth starts – and rewarding with massive lily-like flowers. The flowering season can be spread from Christmas day to late spring by starting the bulbs into growth at different times. For early flowering specially-prepared bulbs should be planted as soon as purchased in the second half of October, and 18°C (65°F) maintained day and night. Timing and temperature is not so critical if the plants do not have to be in bloom so early, but 13°C (55°F) is really the minimum temperature these bulbs will be happy with; bottom heat is especially important, particularly during root formation before the shoot begins to develop.

Hippeastrums should be grown singly in a 15cm (6in) pot filled with John Innes potting compost No. 2. Half the bulb is left exposed.

Place the pots in a warm place – above a radiator is ideal – and keep the compost moist but not too wet until the bud can be seen. A warm, light place should then be provided until the flowers open, when a cooler spot can be found to prolong the flowers.

After blooming, keep the bulb growing strongly in a sunny spot, watering regularly and applying a liquid fertilizer every fortnight.

By June or July the pot can be placed outside and the growth kept active by watering. Only begin to withhold water gradually in August, when the pot can be brought indoors and the period of rest started. Cease watering by September, allow the leaves to die down, then cut them off. Keep the bulb, still in its pot, at about 10°C (50°F) until ready to start into growth again. The compost can be completely replaced each season or just the top half scraped away and replaced before starting the bulb into growth.

Small-flowered spring bulbs

Spectacular though the large-flowered bulbs can be, many of the smaller kinds have a charm of their own. Indeed, it is often when they can be viewed at close quarters in pots or bowls indoors that their full beauty can be most appreciated.

Chionodoxas have the common name glory of the snow – and this gives some indication of their charm. Outdoors the cheerful blue-on-white stars are among the first flowers to appear towards the end of winter, and indoors they are no less attractive. The bulbs are inexpensive so try six to ten in a 10cm (4in) bowl. Crocuses are traditional indoor bulbs, and there are almost no poor kinds. Only the large yellow Dutch hybrid type need to be treated with caution indoors – all the others can be planted with confidence. Any failures of the large-flowered cultivars can usually be ascribed to the compost drying out, too little time being given to root formation before being brought into warmth, or too much heat. Always hasten slowly; they flower early anyway.

The wild crocus species usually flower early. *Crocus chrysanthus* naturally blooms in February, and although the flowers are smaller than those of the Dutch hybrids there are many varied colours.

Most gardeners tend to associate irises with large border or waterside plants, but there are a few charming dwarf bulbous kinds that are superb in the home. Two of the best are *Iris reticulata* and *I. danfordiae*. The first is purple-blue with golden marks, and the second is vivid yellow. Both flower naturally in February, are about 13cm (5in) high, and delicately fragrant. These small irises are excellent in pots or bowls if grown with plenty of light and without too much forcing. Such bulbs are very rewarding, and should not be neglected because they are small.

SUMMER AND AUTUMN FLOWERS

To regard the end of the spring-flowering bulbs as the end of the bulb season would be to miss some of our most spectacular bulbous plants.

Lilies are frequently admired as garden flowers, but are all too seldom grown as houseplants. Yet the right kinds respond readily to pot culture.

The bulbs should be planted well down in 15cm (6in) pots, in a mixture of two-parts John Innes No. 3 to one-third peat. They are covered with 5–7.5cm (2–3in) of compost, and started in cool conditions – about 10°C (50°F). Once the shoots are about 7.5cm (3in) high the pots can be placed in an unheated greenhouse or a cool room, and watered sparingly. Once the buds are fully developed, bring into a warm room – 18°C (65°F) is ideal. Keep shaded from direct sunlight, and you will have a flowering pot plant to equal any.

It is best to start with easy kinds, such as *Lilium regale*, *L.* 'Enchantment', or *L.* 'Golden Splendour'. *L. regale* comes into bloom with white trumpets flushed pink or purple on the outside; 'Enchantment' has upright bunches of brilliant orange wide-open flowers decorated with a modicum of very dark spots; 'Golden Splendour' has wide-open trumpets of shining yellow. *Lilium auratum* also makes a spectacular pot plant.

Two excellent hybrids are 'Destiny', a pure lemon-yellow with minute brown spots, and 'Fire King', brilliant orange. After flowering, the pots should be placed in a shady spot outdoors or in a cool room until the growth dies down naturally. Never let the soil dry out completely, even when resting.

The Scarborough lily (vallota) is another wonderful houseplant, but this time it is not a true lily. It produces long, strap-shaped leaves and a stout stem, about 45cm (1½ft) high, topped with two or three, sometimes more, scarlet flowers. The blooms appear between July and September, but the bulbs should be planted the previous August or September in pots of John Innes potting compost No. 1. Plant the bulbs singly, using 7.5cm (3in) pots for small bulbs, but 15cm (6in) pots for larger bulbs of 5cm (2in) or more across. The tips of the bulbs should protrude from the compost. Keep well watered, but allow to dry gradually once the leaves have died.

The large bulbs should not be allowed to have all the glory. The colchicums, or autumn crocuses, are fun corms to flower indoors without soil. The large corms can be placed on a window-sill and the large, crocus-like blooms will appear in August and September. *C. autumnale* and *C. speciosum* are two widely used.

BONSAI

The word bonsai simply means a plant in a container. This can be a tree or a shrub or even forms of grass. However, it would be reasonable to assume that it is more readily understood as a tree or shrub that has been trained in a miniature form grown in a pot.

The art of cultivating bonsai trees and shrubs is considered a novelty in the West. However, they have been grown in China and Japan for 600 years.

Although their origins are shrouded in time, it would appear that the Chinese were the first to start transplanting small trees, found in the wild, into ornamental pots. Why they started pruning and training these trees to look like replicas of their giant cousins is not known. It has been suggested that it was more or less an accident – a tree that is small and growing in poor soil will inevitably grow at an accelerated rate if transplanted into a nutritious compost. After a while, these plants would simply outgrow the size of the container and have to be cut back for easier handling. In time, it was realized that pruning certain branches achieved a more artistic effect and so the art of bonsai had begun.

The original transplanted trees were probably Chinese – and bonsai is still practised there – but Japan has become better known as the country that developed the art and introduced the styles we know today.

STYLES

One of the original forms of tree resembled a pyramid, the trunk being absolutely straight and tapering towards the top, the branches forming the sides of the pyramid. This was followed by a style still used and called the formal upright. The trunk is straight and tapering with the branches evenly spaced around the tree – the whole giving rather a stylized effect. However, except with mainly evergreen trees, such as *Pinus* (pines) and *Juniperus* (junipers), this elaborate stylizing coupled with considerable bending and twisting of the trunks has now more or less given way to softer more natural forms.

It is difficult to give indications of the height of these plants, but as a guide some are still only 60cm (2ft) after 60 or so years.

There are still definite divisions of style when considering bonsai. The most popular form being the informal upright tree. Trees can also be trained to appear like a tree on windswept moorland, more or less parallel to the surface of the soil, and called the semi-cascade.

The cascade tree is one growing so that the top half of the trunk actually appears to grow downwards, sometimes reaching 60–90cm (2–3ft) below the top of the tree. This style represents a tree growing on a mountainside or cliff face.

Another style is a group of trees grown to look like a grove or small forest. With this form, perspective is very important. The largest tree is planted at or near the front of the group, with the smaller ones at the back. This gives a feeling of depth to the group. Groups can be any number, from two upwards. With the exception of two trees, these will always be planted in odd numbers, as it is difficult to achieve the right effect with even numbers.

POTS

The pots form the basis in which bonsai trees are grown. Except in a few instances, they must always have drainage holes to allow surplus water to escape and also to permit the circulation of essential oxygen around the roots. They should also be highly fired, so that they are resistant to frost damage. This is because for part of the year the plants should be stood outside in the garden or placed on a balcony.

The pot should be considered in the same way as the frame to a picture, not detracting from the beauty of the tree, but rather enhancing it. For heavy-looking trees like pines, heavy, rectangular and formal pots are often used. For forest groups, wide and very shallow pots are the best.

DISPLAY

One of the most important things to remember about bonsai trees is that they should not be considered solely as houseplants. Even if the tree originated in Japan, it should be remembered that the Japanese climate is similar to our own. Practically all bonsai trees benefit from a sojourn outside on a balcony or in the garden.

As this is the case it is worth constructing a raised table (size will depend on the number of trees) on a balcony or in a sheltered part of the garden. For ease of care, plastic, windproof netting or wooden laths can be erected over and behind the trees. This will help to protect them from excessive wind and sun.

This outdoor position should be regarded as their permanent home. Bonsai plants are not, by their very nature, houseplants, although they can be brought indoors for a short time – preferably not longer than four or five days. When they are indoors they should be given as much natural light as possible in a draught-free position that does not become too hot. After they have been admired inside they should be returned to the fresh air, when their place indoors may be taken by another tree.

In the winter it is very important that they should not be transferred from a hot lounge to a frosty atmosphere outdoors in one step. They should be gradually acclimatized to the cold by putting them in a cold room for a day and then by protecting their roots in a box of straw or peat for two or three days, when they rejoin their companions.

STARTING WITH BONSAI

There are a number of nurseries that specialize in the importation and growing of bonsai trees, and with their increasing popularity small displays of trees can often be seen in garden centres and the larger departmental stores.

Some of the trees for sale will be genuine Japanese bonsai specimens, others will be those grown in this country. When buying a tree, make sure that it is in good condition – looks healthy, not damaged, free from pests and diseases. Check that the pot has drainage holes and make sure that it is resistant to frost damage. If you would like to start a bonsai tree yourself, suitable subjects can often be found in garden centres. In this case, look for deciduous trees or shrubs with fairly small leaves.

Small trees growing in woods and moorlands can quite often be transplanted into a container. Before you attempt this, however, ensure that you have permission from the owners of the land. If you find a suitable subject and have

Top left: An 18-year-old cupressus over rock. Now about 25cm (10in) high.
Top: *Acer palmatum* 'Seigen', about 18 years old and 45cm (18in) tall.
Above: *Malus baccata mandshurica* (*Malus cerasifera*) in flower. This specimen is about 40cm (16in) tall and 18 years old.
Left: A 35-year-old specimen of *Juniperus chinensis*, now about 60cm (24in) tall.

147

been given permission to remove it, this should be done in the early spring, mid-February to mid-March, when the tree is still dormant. If the tree is little more than a seedling, two or three years old, it should be possible to remove it directly from the ground with little disturbance to the roots, except in the case of trees with long tap roots such as oak.

Shake off the surplus soil from around the roots, wrap them in wet moss or newspaper and put them in a plastic bag. At the same time, the top should also be pruned back to remove any crowded or spindly branches.

Make sure that your potential bonsai tree is kept moist during the journey home. If it has a lot of small fibrous roots near to the trunk, it can safely be planted directly into a container. If this is not the case, prune the roots back to within 15cm (6in) of the trunk and plant it in the garden for a year.

CARE AND CULTIVATION

Bonsai trees spend a major part of their life outdoors and it is essential for their general health that they are watered regularly. During the winter, the humidity and the increased rainfall will often be enough to keep a tree moist for weeks at a time during its dormant season.

During very hot spells in the summer, this will often be necessary at least once, and sometimes twice, a day. Never let a tree dry out, as only a few days without water can cause its death. It is preferable to use rainwater when available, but tap-water that has been allowed to stand overnight is perfectly adequate.

Every ten days to two weeks during the growing season – late spring to mid autumn – a weak, liquid fertilizer should be added to the water. All plants need nutriment for their growth and health. It is a fallacy to believe that bonsai trees are starved to achieve their smallness.

Regrettably, bonsai suffer from the same pests and diseases as other plants and trees, so watch for these too.

Keeping the top growth of the tree pruned back is important to maintain and improve the look of the tree and to stop the top growth becoming too large for the roots to cope with.

As most bonsai trees are hardy varieties, special winter protection is usually unnecessary even while the plants are standing outdoors. But hard and continuous frost can cause damage.

Right, above: A 45-year-old *Pinus parviflora*, still only 50cm (20in).
Right: Bonsai trees can be shaped with wire slightly less pliable than the branches (the technique is described in the text).

REPOTTING

Repotting a bonsai tree is sometimes considered a daunting task, but it need not be so. It is advisable to repot the trees in early spring before the leaves start appearing. Generally speaking, this is during March. If a tree is left too long without repotting it will become pot-bound. The roots grow, gradually filling the pot and the original compost is pushed out in tiny amounts until there is little left.

For young trees up to ten years old, repotting is necessary every one or two years. For older trees it can be anything from two to ten years. To decide whether to repot, first tap the edges of the pot gently so that the tree may be lifted out. If the root-ball appears to be a mass of roots then it is time to repot. First of all, tease the outer roots away from the root-ball using a pointed stick or even a 15cm (6in) nail, until approximately one-third of them around the outside and underneath the tree are hanging like a beard. Using a sharp and sterilized pair of secateurs or scissors, prune these back almost to the remaining root-ball, leaving a small fringe.

Wash out and dry the container and place small pieces of perforated mesh or crocks over the drainage holes. Follow this with a layer of sterilized grit and a thin layer of potting compost, pour this in around the sides of the root-ball and work it in with your fingers until you are sure there are no air pockets, and the tree is firm and stable.

If the tree is at all top-heavy it will sometimes be necessary to wire it into the pot, through the drainage holes, using gardening wire.

Water thoroughly and place in a protected position until the new roots start growing. Trees planted over rocks, so that their roots are in the soil, should also be repotted in this manner.

The compost for evergreen trees should be seven parts John Innes compost to three parts sterilized grit. For deciduous trees, eight parts John Innes compost to two parts sterilized grit.

When repotting groups of trees, this can be done in two ways. The easiest method is to treat the group as a single tree and proceed as previously described. The alternative is to remove the group from its pot and cut out complete segments of soil, as if cutting a cake, then proceed as previously described.

Trees planted directly into rocks cannot be repotted without breaking the rock and probably killing the tree. Fresh compost is added by considering the soil in which they are planted as a cake, and removing sections around the trunk of the tree. These are then filled with fresh compost.

TRAINING BONSAI TREES

Pruning a bonsai tree to maintain its health and make it look beautiful is necessary. During the winter and early spring, heavy branches that are dead or unnecessary should be removed as close to the main trunk as possible.

When pruning back a branch, make sure that the cut is made above a secondary branch or growing point. To maintain its health and to create a lovely specimen, it will be necessary to shorten all growth to the first or second leaf or set of leaves. Over the years, this will give you a tree with a strong trunk, firm branches and the twiggy outline of a tree in the wild.

Pines only need pruning once a year. This is done during spring when the new shoots have elongated enough for the needles to start sticking out. Two-thirds of their growth should be removed, leaving only two shoots at each growing point. Further shoots should be removed completely.

Spruce trees should be pruned in the same manner, as their new growth appears, but care should be taken not to damage the new needles.

Junipers, chaemacyparis and cupressus trees – which are evergreen trees with articulated needle-like leaves – should be pinched out with the fingers throughout the growing season to encourage full and bushy growth.

Trees that fruit and flower on the previous year's growth should not be pruned after the middle of July, except for their tips. Other deciduous trees can also have their leaves removed at the end of June, provided they are growing vigorously.

The main part of the leaf is cut off leaving the leaf stalk (petiole). This causes a false autumn and after a few weeks the petiole will shrivel and drop off. New leaves that are smaller and better coloured will then appear. If there is any doubt as to the health of a tree, do this on a small branch first to test how long it takes for the leaves to return. Most deciduous trees are suitable for this treatment, but not flowering or fruiting trees.

Correct pruning and training are essential to the well-being of a bonsai tree. Branches can usually be trained in any direction required by pruning to a suitably positioned bud. However, there are occasions when branches have grown away from the desired line and wiring or tying into position is necessary.

Wiring consists of selecting a length of wire about one-third longer than the branch to be trained and whose pliability is slightly less than the branch. The wire is twisted gently around the branch at an angle of about 45 degrees after anchoring the end nearest the trunk over another branch or looping it around the trunk underneath itself. It should now be possible to bend the branch carefully into the required position.

This wiring and shaping should only be done during June or July when the branches are at their most pliable. For deciduous trees, the wire should only remain on for four or five months. For evergreen trees that are slower to take shape, a year is often required.

SUITABLE SUBJECTS FOR BONSAI

When considering a potential tree to be trained as a bonsai subject, it is always best to choose a type with small needles or leaves, unless the tree is to be grown specifically for the flowers or fruit, such as flowering cherries or peach (*Prunus*) or a crab apple (*Malus*).

The following list of plants is not comprehensive, and there are many others that can be used.

Evergreen subjects

Pines (*Pinus*) need repotting every three or four years. They should have plenty of sunshine and only moderate watering. Allow only two shoots on each growing point and prune to two-thirds their length.

Junipers (*Juniperus*) should be repotted every two years. Never allow the plants to become dry. Always finger pick new growth to give shape.

Japanese cedars (*Cryptomeria*) can be treated as junipers.

Firs and spruces (*Abies* and *Piceas*) are repotted every two to three years. They need plenty of water and moderate sunshine. Prune the new growth as it appears by pinching and twisting out one half of the elongated buds.

Flowering subjects

Winter jasmine (*Jasminum nudiflorum*) is very strong and can be repotted at any time. Allow it almost to dry out before soaking thoroughly. Prune to shape, as required.

Peaches and cherries (*Prunus*) need repotting annually. Prune back two-thirds of each branch after flowering. The plant should not be excessively watered, but rather kept slightly dry.

Fruiting plants

Herringbone cotoneaster (*Cotoneaster horizontalis*) is repotted annually. Give ample sun and water. Although it is a well-known garden shrub, it is one of the easiest to train. It can withstand considerable wiring, but needs frequent pruning to keep it in shape.

Crab apple (*Malus*) needs repotting yearly into good compost. It requires a lot of water and moderate sunshine. Prune back one-third after flowering and stop the terminals on new shoots throughout the summer.

Firethorn (*Pyracantha*) is repotted annually. Do not allow the roots to become dry and set the plant in a sunny position for it to bear fruit. It is only necessary to prune the plant sufficiently to maintain an attractive outline and shape.

Deciduous subjects

Maples (*Acer*) are a large family of trees and shrubs, which need repotting yearly. Do not allow the roots to become dry and remember that harsh sunlight burns the leaves. Keep the plant in semishade. Prune young growth as it grows. Prune the main branches only in autumn, as they can bleed. Leaf cutting can be done in June.

Beech (*Fagus sylvatica*) makes a handsome tree and should be repotted every second year. Given plenty of water and sunlight. Prune as necessary, remembering the form of these beautiful trees.

Oak (*Quercus*) is not often used as the leaves are normally too large. The tap root, which is very vigorous, should be cut back each year during repotting. Ensure that the roots remain moist, and avoid very hot sun. Prune back hard during the growing season. Watch for insect attack and spray when necessary.

Elm (*Ulmus*) is repotted annually. Give sufficient water to keep the roots moist and place in a position with moderate sunshine.

BROMELIADS

Bromeliad is the word applied to any of the 2,000 or so species of plant that comprise the Bromeliaceae family. Perhaps the best known bromeliad is the pineapple, which is native to the West Indies. It is a bromeliad known as far back as the 15th century, and with the onset of widespread exploration it was not long before it was introduced into Great Britain. Its decorative shape gained it a place in the impressive fascias of many large country houses.

During the latter part of the 19th century, plant-hunting and botanical expeditions brought back to Britain many other attractive bromeliads. Some of the plants found their way into botanic gardens, and so initiated a botanical and scientific interest in the Bromeliaceae. From 1830 to 1840 several plants were recorded which are still popular today, such as *Aechmea fasciata*, *Billbergia zebrina* and *Vriesea splendens*. Today, a wide selection of bromeliads is available from specialist nurseries and an increasing number are available from florists, garden centres and large departmental stores.

BROMELIADS IN THE WILD

Bromeliads are native to many locations in the Americas, but as a result of botanical expeditions they may now be seen growing in many different countries. They can be seen in gardens and parks in areas such as Devon and Cornwall. Indeed, in areas of really favoured weather *Fascicularia bicolor* grows well outdoors.

They occur in their native areas in such contrasting environments, that inevitably there are plants for the home, greenhouse and office. From the humid rain forests of Brazil and Costa-Rica – growing among the large philodendrons and the twining orchids – are to be found a selection of bromeliads ranging from tiny epiphytes nestling in the rough bark of a giant tree to enormous urn-shaped plants 2.1m (7ft) across; these are quite capable of holding at least a litre (1.7 pints) of rainwater.

Across the States of the American Deep South, in areas of the Everglades and the Okefenokee Swamp, grow a different range of bromeliads. In such places grow the Spanish moss (*Tillandsia usneoides*) and the ball moss (*Tillandsia recurvata*). Grey in appearance, and with little or no root, these epiphytic plants hang from trees, telegraph poles, and even from the wires, existing on the moisture which is present in the atmosphere. These two species grow in such profusion that branches of trees break under their weight. These plants are of little use to the local inhabitants, and have little to offer economically, except perhaps for use as a filling for upholstery or a binder in the preparation of bricks.

In desert areas bromeliads are also in evidence. The savannah of Veracruz and the arid regions of Mexico provide homes for the small, hard, rosettes of dyckia and hechtia. While from the Argentine come clustering plants of the genus *Abromietiella*. The Andean mountain range and Peru have the largest bromelaid – *Puya raimondii*. This species will outlive most humans, taking what is our average life span before it matures to flowering size, about 10.5m (35ft) high. Using the puyas, large columnar cacti, or rocky outcrops for supports are the xerophytic tillandsias, attaching themselves to their hosts by wire-like roots. A xerophyte is a plant which has adapted to grow in dry conditions.

Rain forest bromeliads

Plants native to the rain forests or cloud forests are fortunate, as they luxuriate in what are virtually perfect conditions for their growth – high temperatures and humidity, diffused light and little air movement.

Every tree is covered by some form of plant life, be it mosses, lichens, ferns or aeroids. In such an environment, the growing medium is of little importance and bromeliads will be found almost everywhere – on living trees, fallen logs, the forest floor, and even growing upon each other. The urn-shaped forms of vriesea and guzmania sit resplendent in niches formed by large branches, their tangled roots securing them to the bark. Decaying logs, adorned with multi-hued fungi, provide platforms on which sit the glossy-leaved nidulariums and neoregelias. The moss-covered remains of tree stumps make a fitting green backcloth to the many varied forms of earth stars (cryptanthus).

Intermediate bromeliads

If it were possible to have an escalator in the rain forest and to proceed to a higher level, the changes in the plant life would be quite noticeable.

On such a level, termed an intermediate area, the intensity of light and the amount of air movement increase, humidity is less, and the temperature fluctuates. The climate of such an area is similar to that of an average English summer.

These tougher conditions mean that the plants, too, must toughen up to survive. There the bromeliads exist as epiphytes, alongside orchid cacti, zygocactus and rhipsalis. The roots of such bromeliads are harder and stronger than those produced by the plants at lower levels, and they form a strong anchorage to the trees. No form of nutrition is gained by the plants from this union. Instead, they have evolved a method by which they collect what nutriment is required. The rosettes of leaves form tight, upright vases. These vases retain rainwater, insects and leaf debris which fall into them. Small birds perching on the plants add their own form of manure and the whole concoction forms an excellent brew on which the plants exist.

The thick leaves are scruffy, spitefully spined along their edges, and the brighter greens of the rain forest bromeliads have been replaced with a mixture of dark greens, greys, browns and purples, exotically striped or mottled with lighter colours.

Other bromeliads in these intermediate areas are bulbous shaped, with tapering, tendril-like leaves which are channelled to guide the droplets of moisture to the centre of the plant.

Desert bromeliads

Bromeliads have even adapted to the rigour of the deserts. The types to be found there are in the form of low-growing rosettes of hard, dark-green leaves, or grey tomentose. The leaves are edged with spines.

Their way of life is terrestrial, absorbing small amounts of moisture and mineral salts through a normal root-system. In

Neoregelia carolinae are often called nest plants because of their central cup.

an attempt to avoid strong sunlight, the plants have drawn themselves down into the dusty terrain. Alternatively, in the case of the more fortunate ones, they manage to grow in the shade of larger plants or grasses.

BROMELIADS AS HOUSEPLANTS
The sheer range of shape and form make bromeliads interesting plants for the home. There are many different types of rosettes – in most cases stemless – and they range in size from minute plants 12mm ($\frac{1}{2}$in) or so in diameter to species far too large for the home.

The forms of leaf vary immensely. Simple strap-shaped types are displayed by vrieseas or guzmanias, while billbergias have stiff, upright vases. The genus cryptanthus has flat, crinkly leaves, and acanthostachys has leaves of a hard, pendent form, reaching 60cm (2ft) in length. In the genus neoregelia can be found a variation from hard-leaved vases to flat rosettes of leaves, softer in texture.

The tillandsia have such a large assortment of types that a collection of this genus alone warrants an interest. There are large plants with thin, strap-shaped leaves (*T. lindenii*), bulbous species with rolled leaves (*T. butzii*), tufted plants which resemble silver grasses (*T. filifolia*), spiral-shaped types which are powdery in appearance (*T. balbisiana*), and octopus-like forms which glisten with a covering of scales (*T. seleriana*). Plants dependent on an epiphytic way of life rely on a covering of specialized organs called trichomes. These are absorptive organs acting in a way similar to minute sponges – absorbing atmospheric moisture. Although most bromeliads possess trichomes, they are found in higher concentrations in xerophytic types of tillandsia.

The leaf coloration in bromeliads is interesting. In the billbergias there is a chocolate and grey combination (*Billbergia zebrina*), yellow and grey dappling (*B. 'Fantasia'*), green with white (*B. porteana*), and olive to purple (*B. vittata*). As its name implies, *Vriesea hieroglyphica* has dark figurations on a light green background, and *V. gigantea* (syn. *V. tesselata*) appears translucent when the light filters through its leaves. *Aechmea chantinii* has silver striping on a darker base colour, while *A. orlandiana* is a mixture of green, brown and purple.

The many forms of cryptanthus have a tendency to hybridize easily, giving an unbelievable mixture of multi-coloured variants and the pinkish tinge on a cream-and-green combination makes the variegated form of *Ananas bracteatus* a favourite of many people.

The flowers of bromeliads range from the insignificant to the breathtaking – even in different species of the same genus a contrast can be found. In *Tillandsia usneoides* the flowers are small, yellow tinged white and will go unnoticed unless the plant is viewed closely. However, *T. cyanea* has a most colourful purple and pink inflorescence.

Dyckias produce their orange flowers on stalks, but the small, white flowers of cryptanthus are almost hidden.

Sadly, the red to pink and blue flowers of the billbergias are short lived. On the other hand, the aechmeas produce long-lasting blooms from the dark purple flowers pendent on a carmine stalk as with *A. fulgens*, to the pyramid-shaped pink-and-blue inflorescence of the distinctive and attractive *A. fasciata*.

Neoregelias and nidulariums are termed *nest plants*, as the tiny blue to mauve flowers sit nestled in the central cup. In some species, such as *Neoregelia carolinae* 'Tricolor', the central area of leaves flush a striking scarlet as a prelude to flowering. In contrast, the vrieseas gain the epithet flaming sword plants, referring to the 60cm (2ft) lance-shaped inflorescence of red bracts and yellow flowers. In the genus of the soft-leaved guzmanias, the dominant colour of the flowers is white, but the contrasting colouring of the bracts – yellow, green and orange – make these plants an asset to any collection.

It is the varied nature of these plants that makes them so interesting.

Vriesea hieroglyphica.

Cryptanthus bromelioides 'Tricolor'.

Billbergia nutans.

Good plants to grow

Only a fraction of the bromeliads discovered are grown by plant enthusiasts. This is because many natural environmental conditions cannot be reproduced. Some plants' natural conditions are too demanding, but fortunately these are in the minority. With the ones which are readily available it is not difficult to assemble a good, representative collection of easy culture. Then, if the interest in the group matures, specialist nurseries have less common species.

The following list comprises plants that are obtainable without too much effort – and they will provide an assortment of attractive leaf types and flowers.

Plants from the rain forests: *Aechmea chantinii, A. 'Foster's Favorite', A. fulgens, A. orlandiana, Ananas sugenaria 'Striatus' (syn. A. bracteatus 'Striatus'), A. comosus 'Variegatus', Cryptanthus beuckeri, C. bromelioides 'Tricolor', C. fosterianus, C. zonatus, Guzmaina lingulata, G. lindenii, G. minor, G. musaica, G. monostachya, G. zahnii, Vriesea carinata.*

Plants from intermediate areas: *Aechmea coelestis, A. fasciata, Billbergia 'Fantasia', B. nutans, B. porteana, B. windii, B. zebrina, Cryptanthus acaulis, C. bivittatus, Neoregelia ampullacea, N. spectabilis, N. tristis, Tillandsia bulbosa, T. butzii, T. caput-medusae, T. recurvata, T. usneoides.*

Plants from desert areas: *Dyckia brevifolia, Tillandsia baileyi, T. ionantha.*

Ananas comosus.

Tillandsia lindenii.

Ananas comosus 'Variegatus'

153

CULTIVATION

The cultivation of bromeliads is no more difficult than any other group of plants, and in some ways they are far easier.

As with all plants, some consideration should be given to the conditions required by the bromeliads. Prime importance is to treat each plant as an individual, and not to classify a complete genus as requiring one specific treatment. For instance, *Vriesea splendens* is a shade lover, yet *V. espinosae*, looking like a tillandsia, favours good light. Selected types can be grown to match the conditions available or the types can be mixed, varying their position. This method can be seen to advantage in the bromeliad collection at Kew Gardens, London. There, the plants are grown in a natural setting, some in shade, others in a brighter position, with a few epiphytes on the lower portions of cork-bark 'trees', others perched high up. In this way, a natural balance is achieved which is pleasing to the eye and beneficial to the plants.

Growing media

Most of the forest bromeliads grow as epiphytes with the minimum of material around their roots. Therefore, whatever medium is used it must be open, with good aeration and ample drainage.

A soil-mix used for most pot plants is not suitable, as it will cloy and sour the plant. A base mixture of peat should be employed, with an addition of some granulated charcoal. This can be opened up by using sphagnum moss, osmunda fibre, pine tree needles, or the expanded larva products as used for hydroponics, in a one-to-one ratio. A point to note when potting the plants, is that they need to be planted firmly; if the compost is suitably moist when potting, it can be firmed around the plant.

Species from the deserts will fare well if grown in a mix of equal parts loam, sand and peat.

The xerophytic tillandsias are not suited to pot culture and are best attached to rough-barked branches such as elder, cactus skeletal wood, or cork bark. They can be positioned with the minimum of sphagnum or osmunda placed around the roots, and then secured with plastic-covered garden wire. After a few months of growth, the plants will produce new anchorage roots which will embed themselves into the wood.

Light

Light is one of the most important aspects of bromeliad culture, as the amount and intensity given to the plants has a great effect on their appearance. The soft-leaved plants from the rain forest prefer semi-shade, and too bright illumination will cause burning of the leaf tips and edges. Plants from the other areas require good light, with some sunshine. This light helps to retain the striping and variegation which, in shadier conditions, would be lost, so taking away some of the natural beauty of the plants. The desert-growing genera and the small, grey tomentose epiphytes enjoy good light intensity, with sunshine, preferably in a south-facing window. To make the plants really feel at home, some form of artificial lighting can be employed for a few hours during the short days of winter.

Watering

The amount of water required will depend on the type of plant. Those from rain forests should never be allowed to become dry. Spraying the plants daily with a fine mist helps to maintain a good level of humidity, without the plants becoming excessively wet around the roots.

Plants with a harder leaf texture should be allowed short periods of dryness. Those with a central vase can be filled with a small amount of water, except when it becomes obvious that a flower bud is imminent or that the flower may become infected by mildew.

Naturally, the genera from a desert environment require less moisture – a weekly watering in spring and summer, reducing the amount in autumn and winter, depending on the temperature of the room in which the plants are grown. With tillandsias mounted on wood, misting is sufficient, the frequency being varied according to the season. During the period of rapid growth, misting in the morning and evening is favoured. However, in the cooler months, once or twice a week will suffice. A dry area plant will never be lost through being under-watered. In fact, all of the bromeliads can safely be left for two or three weeks. Where possible, rainwater should be used, as in some areas the tap water can be rather alkaline and this tends to leave a residue on the leaves, making them unsightly.

Temperature

Fortunately – in these days of high fuel costs – bromeliads are very adaptable with regard to the degree of heat they require. In the home, where heating is available, no further allowances need be made for the plants.

The most demanding plants are those from the rain forests, preferring 18°C (65°F) as a minimum. Those types with a harder leaf texture are less particular, and if something like 10°C (50°F) can be maintained they will grow quite well. If, in an emergency, the temperature drops slightly, the plants should come to no harm, especially if the soil is kept rather dry. *Fascicularia bicolor*, a native

of Chile, is hardy and can be grown as a garden plant in a sunny position – on the rockery or in a large tub on the patio where, even when covered with snow, it should survive.

Feeding

As with the majority of houseplants, the amount of growing medium contained in the pots has limited capabilities over a lengthy period. With bromeliads, where maturing takes some years, it is advisable to administer some form of fertilizer, particularly where it is evident that a plant is approaching flowering. A good proprietary brand of an organic feed can be used.

With the vase types and earth stars, dosage and concentration can be as recommended for pot plants, and given during their active period of growth. Additionally, a dilute solution – one-third of the concentration – can be added to the water in the central cups occasionally.

Feeding of the desert varieties is less advisable, but can be done once or twice during the period of active growth. Although the air plants tillandsias appear to receive no nutrition in nature,

they usually have a covering of dust particles which provide some food. Dilute manuring in the warmer part of the year will be appreciated.

Pests and diseases

In their natural habitat, the bromeliads fall prey to many setbacks. However, under cultivation the situation is easier. Two types of pest that may be encountered are those prominent in attacking cacti and succulent plants, namely mealy bugs and scale insects.

The mealy bugs generally infest the more tomentose plants where they can go undetected in the axils of the leaves. Scale can be a problem with the larger plants, such as the neoregelias and aechmeas.

Chemical controls are available (see pages 25 to 29) but it should be remembered that the plants absorb moisture through the leaves, and care must be taken in treating the problem. If possible, a more personal touch should be given. Both of these pests can be removed from the plants, using a cocktail stick tipped with cotton-wool soaked in methylated spirit. The removal of the scale insects should be done with

Above: A selection of tropical bromeliads in a natural-looking setting.
Opposite page: *Vriesea carinata,* also known as *Tillandsia carinata,* is a native of Brazil.

care on the plants that have a powdery bloom to the leaves, as this is easily removed, making the plants unsightly. House spiders, while not being classed as horticultural pests, can be a nuisance, as they tend to make webs across the central cups of the larger plants. All that is required here is to remove them bodily.

Horticultural diseases that affect the Bromeliaceae are few. A fungal disease can attack plants of aechmea when grown in a commercial quantity in nurseries, but will not be found in small collections.

One problem that might arise will be with the neoregelias and nidulariums. After flowering, the remains in the central cups might develop to the fruiting stage and if too moist will be susceptible to fungal attack. Remedial steps involve removing the remains and flushing out the cups with methylated spirit before rinsing thoroughly with clean water.

Generally, however, problems are few.

PROPAGATION

Bromeliads can be propagated from offsets or seed. Offsets produce flowering plants more quickly, but seed offers the possibility of more plants.

Seed. Seeing a plant in flower may give you the inspiration needed to try producing plants from seed. Some species, such as *Vriesea splendens*, are self-fertile, but in those plants which are not, pollination can be induced. In the case of the billbergias, pollination must be effected quickly due to the short life of the flowers. Then, again, there are those species whose flowers open only at night. Temperature is another aspect that will affect pollination. In some cases, the seed is set by the aid of insects. When the fruits have been formed they can be collected and the seeds squeezed out. They can be rinsed in a mild disinfectant, teased out and dried. The seed of most genera will remain viable for several months, after which germination may be retarded.

The variation in the shape of the seeds is extensive, from the flat forms produced by dyckia, the thin seeds of pitcairnia to the small parachutes of tillandsia and vriesea.

The compost used for germination should be fine, without any lumps or large granules, and have a buoyant consistency. Sieved peat is a good choice, with some finely-chopped sphagnum moss added. The inclusion of some granules of charcoal helps to keep the mix sweet. It is preferable to well moisten the mix before adding it to the trays, rather than water after sowing, which could mean that the seeds float together on the surface.

Another method utilizes synthetic sponges that are used about the house. The sponge is soaked thoroughly and the excess water allowed to drain off. The seed is sprinkled on the sponge and enclosed in a polythene bag. After germination, the sponge can be sliced into portions containing a number of seedlings and these portions placed into a compost. Some of the small tillandsias will germinate quite well on bundles of pine needles, on blotting paper, or most materials that have a good moisture content.

As with most seeds, the temperature for germination must be high, 21°–24°C (70°–75°F). The seed-trays should be covered with glass sheets and if bottom heat is available, so much the better. Depending on the species sown, germination should be completed in six to ten days. When the seedlings are evident, it is wise to cover the glass lids with paper to reduce the light and deter the algal growth that can be a problem.

A close watch should be kept on the moisture of the compost, as drying out at this time could be fatal for the seedlings. As the growth progresses, the seedlings can be allowed to have stronger light intensity, with the removal of the glass covers to give good air circulation. Again, avoid any drying out.

When the seedlings have reached 2.5cm (1in) or so in height, they can be transferred into smaller communities, given more air and perhaps a spray of fungicide to prevent damping off.

As the growth progresses, dilute fertilizer can be applied. Later, when it is noticeable that the characteristics of the plants are established, they can be potted into a particular compost. Specialized treatment with regard to light and water can then be given.

Seed of some species can be bought from seedsmen specializing in uncommon plants.

Offsets. The time taken for the different genera of bromeliads to mature to flowering size varies depending on the species and the cultural conditions the plants receive.

Some plants, cryptanthus for example, will mature in three years. Larger growers, like aechmeas and vrieseas, can take something like five years, and slower-growing genera may not mature for seven years or more.

The propagation of plants vegetatively by offsets or cuttings means that it is possible to have mature plants earlier than by seed, showing their natural characteristics and colourings earlier.

Another point is that to obtain a true-to-type plant, such as the man-made *Cryptanthus* 'It', *Neoregelia* 'Red of Rio', and *Vriesea* 'Mariae', vegetative propagation is more reliable than seed, since in some cases the flowers are sterile and produce no seed. This accounts for the high prices demanded for these cultivars.

The bromeliads are monocarpic, this means that each plant will produce flowers and then die. As with the houseleeks of our rockeries, offsets are produced either singly or in profusion, while the adult gradually dies away during the following months.

Obviously it is not necessary to remove offsets from the parent plant, unless for commercial interest or exchange, for nothing looks better than a clump of four or five plants emanating from the same rootstock, particularly when all the heads are in flower together.

It is fortunate that most of the bromeliads are on the fleshy side or else xerophytic, so that there is no fear of the offsets drying out between the time that they are taken and the time that they are rooted. With this prospect in mind, it

means that it is possible to have cuttings sent from other parts of the globe, without any fear that the plants will succumb should there be any undue delay in the mail.

The best time to root the offsets is obviously in the period of rapid growth, spring to summer. However, any time will be suitable if the room is heated. If the container of offsets is placed on a radiator, to provide bottom heat, rooting will be hastened. The peat and sphagnum mix used for seed germination will also be suitable for rooting offsets, or mica-flake products can be used.

The methods of offset removal are different from one genus to another. In the genus *Cryptanthus*, the small plants will appear around the centre of the mature rosette; they are very delicately attached and are removed easily, even accidentally. If one batch of offsets is removed, the plants will produce more.

The genus *Billbergia* has species that produce young plants on stolons, a hard form of stem that radiates from the parent plant, usually hanging over the side of the plant pot. Here, a sharp downward snap gives a clean break.

In plants of the genus *Aechmea*, the young shoots are produced closer to the parent plant, and it will be wiser to let the shoots attain some length before separating them. Removing the plant from its pot will give easier access.

The harder-leaved neoregelia produce stolons or runners, but the soft-leaved types and the nidulariums complicate matters somewhat as their offsets grow nearer to the centre of the plant. It will be easier to allow some of the leaves of the old plant to die away before making any attempt at removing the offsets, by which time they will be a better size and more conveniently handled. The problem created by the vrieseas is that the new shoot, unfortunately just the one, appears between the leaves of the old plant, thus it is just as well to leave it on the original rootstock. The best method to gain an increased number of plants of this genus is by seed. The genera *Cryptbergia* and *Fascicularia* are so prolific that they require nothing more than splitting up the clump to gain complete plants.

With tillandsias propagation could not be easier, since they can exist for months without roots. Offsets are wrapped in moss and wired on to the chosen position on the branch. With *T. usneoides*, nothing more is required than to pull off a few strands and to hang them somewhere.

Aechmea fasciata, a striking plant with attractive leaves and long-lasting flowers.

156

CACTI & SUCCULENTS

Succulents have many virtues. They are able to withstand a dry atmosphere, do not demand constant attention, and can certainly be left on their own for a week or two. But best of all they are delightfully attractive. Their beauty does not depend solely on their flowers – albeit often short-lived – but also on their attractive shapes and spines.

Cacti belong to the Cactaceae family, which is only one of several groups of succulents, and are succulents as much as any of the others. But many enthusiasts tend to give the cacti special rank and talk of cacti 'and other succulents'.

Succulent plants can be considered to be the camels of the plant world – for they are able to store water to help survive periods of droughts. The water is stored in large cells in the stems and leaves. Having stored the water it is important not to lose it by excessive transpiration,

and therefore many succulents are leafless. The thickened stems are often able to photosynthesize and produce plant-building materials; and the plant exposes the minimum surface to the drying effects of wind and sun. Some succulent plants have leaves which are relatively small and very thick; those with more delicate leaves shed them in the dry season. The stems and leaves of succulents often have a waterproof, waxy coating to reduce water loss.

It is not necessary to travel to foreign places to find succulents. Some grow in temperate climates, and Britain has a few, such as the stonecrop (*Sedum anglicum*, and glasswort (*Salicornia europaea*). The stonecrop grows chiefly on dry, stone walls and the glasswort in salt marshes, where there is a shortage of fresh-water. Only plants with efficient water storage systems could survive under these conditions. However, succulents cultivated

as houseplants originate from the warmer, arid regions of America and the Old World.

Succulent plants do not grow in absolute deserts where there is no water. However, some will survive arid regions where the rainy season lasts for only a few weeks or even days in the entire year. Many more succulents are found in semiarid grasslands, where the surrounding vegetation affords shelter from the burning sun. Others grow on cliffs and the rocky slopes of mountains, where any rain quickly drains away or evaporates. There are even succulents growing on the debris which collects on trees in tropical forests. Such plants are called epiphytes, using the tree only as a support, not obtaining water from it.

Right: *Opuntia microdasys.*
Below: An old illustration demonstrating the perennial charm of cacti.

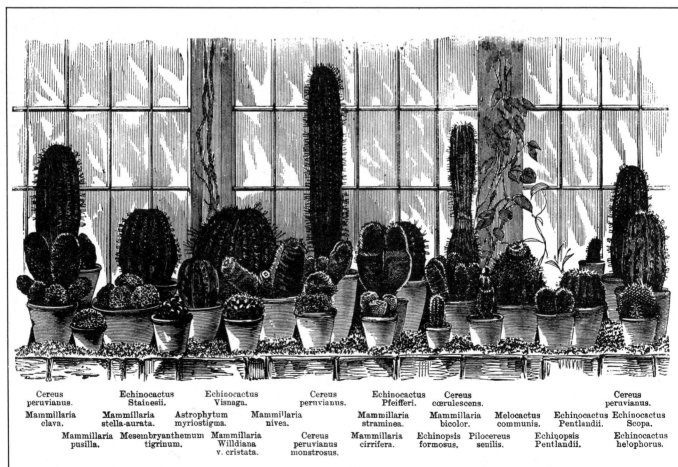

Cereus peruvianus.		Echinocactus Stainesii.		Echinocactus Visnaga.		Cereus peruvianus.		Echinocactus Pfeifferi.		Cereus cœrulescens.				Cereus peruvianus.
Mammillaria clava.		Mammillaria stella-aurata.	Astrophytum myriostigma.		Mammillaria nivea.			Mammillaria straminea.		Mammillaria bicolor.	Melocactus communis.	Echinocactus Pentlandii.	Echinocactus Scopa.
	Mammillaria pusilla.	Mesembryanthemum tigrinum.	Mammillaria Willdiana v. cristata.		Cereus peruvianus monstrosus.		Mammillaria cirrifera.	Echinopsis formosus.	Pilocereus senilis.		Echinopsis Pentlandii.		Echinocactus helophorus.

SUCCULENTS FOR THE HOME

The range of succulent plants in cultivation suitable for home decoration is vast, and would burst the bindings of even the largest tome. Therefore the plants described here have been selected for their suitability for most homes. However, do not be discouraged from attempting to grow a plant not mentioned, as success can be assured if the general principles described under cultivation are followed. The more difficult and rarer plants are unlikely to be found except in specialist nurseries, so there is to some extent a safeguard against attempting the almost impossible!

The Aizoaceae family

This is an immense family of plants whose members show varying degrees of succulence. All of them are leaf succulents – water being stored in thickened leaves – and the flowers superficially resemble daisies.

Some of the hardier species have been introduced into Europe. In Cornwall and the Isles of Scilly the shrubby lampranthus makes brilliant patches of colour in local gardens. Carpobrotus (the Hottentot figs) are found growing on the cliffs of South Wales and Cornwall. The long, prostrate stems are covered with large sabre-shaped leaves, and they have large, purplish flowers. However, it is the smaller, more highly succulent species which are best indoors.

One of the interesting characteristics of members of the Aizoaceae family is their 'ancestral memory'. They may be raised from seed in this country, but their growing period will be the same as their African relatives. If the rainy season in their homeland is from November to March, they will grow in the English winter. Certain species have never ever flowered in cultivation here because the light intensity in winter is never sufficient to stimulate bud formation.

Two very good species are *Faucaria brittenae* and *Glottiphyllum arrectum*. These are compact little plants with fleshy leaves on short stems. Both have deep golden flowers. Faucarias grow in the summer and flower in late summer and early autumn. They are commonly called tiger's jaws, since the leaves have soft, tooth-like projections along their edges. Glottiphyllums grow in late summer and flower in autumn or early winter. Outside their growing period these plants should receive little or no water.

Slightly more difficult to grow are the stone-mimicry plants, the lithops. These consist of two thick leaves pressed closely together to form a compact, circular or oval head. The flattened tops of the leaves vary in colour – grey, brown or fawn – and are often attractively mottled and spotted, closely resembling the stones among which they grow in their native habitat. Their growing period is our summer and the yellow or white flowers are produced in autumn. Among many attractive species are *L. aucampiae*, *L. bella*, and *L. helmutii*.

Another group of stemless plants is the conophytums, growing and flowering in late summer and autumn. They have compact green heads, often prettily speckled, and a range of flower colours. Good species are *C. frutescens* (orange) and *C. tischeri* (purple). Both conophytums and lithops are plants of the more extreme deserts, and must have the maximum light possible. They need to be positioned in a south-facing window and should, preferably, spend some time out of doors during the summer. During the resting period (that is when not in growth), the plants should be kept dry. The old leaves will shrivel and new ones will develop, obtaining their moisture from the old ones. When the old leaves have completely shrivelled, revealing the bright new leaves, it is time to start watering the plants. After flowering, water less.

Above: *Stapelia variegata.*
Above left: *Glottiphyllum arrectum.*

The Stapeliads

The family Asclepiadaceae is widely distributed over temperate and tropical regions of the world, and they are by no means all succulents. The succulent species are collectively called stapeliads, and in their native habitats are found from Spain to India. But the greatest number of species come from Africa. Stapeliads are stem succulents – the thickened stems have taken over the process of photosynthesis. Minute awl-like leaves arise on the new growth of some species, soon shrivelling and falling as the stem matures.

Stapeliads are found in areas where there are no bees, the flowers being pollinated by flies and have an appearance and odour to attract these insects. They are frequently of a brownish or purple colour, sometimes hairy and in some species have a decided smell of decay – hence the common name of carrion flowers. In Britain, however, few species seem to attract flies, and most have little or no odour obnoxious to human noses.

The five-petalled flowers of stapeliads have a starfish-like appearance, and some may reach a considerable size.

Stapeliads need a warm, dry atmosphere and a winter temperature of 10°C (50°F), or more. This makes many of them ideal houseplants and, indeed, some specialist growers with greenhouses will bring their stapeliads indoors in winter in order to save on heating costs. They do, however, need rather special care in watering as they have a tendency to rot if over-watered, and particular care should be taken never to allow the compost to become soggy.

Huernias are small stapeliads. They are short-stemmed plants, producing small-ish flowers from the base of young stems. Good species are the red-flowered *H. aspera* and the striped *H. zebrina*. Both are quite easy, but *H. aspera* must be the easiest stapeliad in cultivation – it appears to be almost indestructible.

Stapelias themselves are probably the best known of this group and if watered carefully and not allowed to become too cold in winter they should cause little trouble. They are mostly larger than the huernias, with larger and more showy flowers. *S. hirsuta* (so named because of its hairy flowers) is frequently seen in cultivation. Another good plant is *S. variegata*; the spotted flowers are very striking, but it must be admitted that these in particular do have a somewhat unpleasant odour.

The Cacti

The outstanding popularity of cacti among succulent plants is to be understood, if only because of the fascination of their spiny appearance and brilliantly coloured flowers. There are over 2,000 species of these stem succulents, all native to the American continent, although some have been introduced to other warm regions of the world, where they have been growing outside for many years. Large specimens of prickly pears (*Opuntia* species) are familiar plants along the Mediterranean coast and Spain. Cacti may be distinguished from all other succulent plants by the presence of the areole. This is a small, cushion-like structure found on the stems and from which appear the spines and flowers. The areole is characteristic of the family, although it is not always easy to see, particularly in those species which have no spines. These spineless species, however, are in the minority, and most cacti are spined. A few of these species are so fiercely armed that handling them must be undertaken with caution. Others have only soft bristles. In general they have no leaves; some opuntias have tiny awl-like ones on new growth, which eventually drop off. There are one or two exceptions and one rather uncommon cactus, *Pereskia*, has persistent leaves resembling those of a wild rose.

The flowers of cacti are usually of an open bell shape and they are always stemless (unsuitable as cut flowers!), coming in all colours except blue. Many of the night-flowering species, including most echinopsis, have white flowers with a sweet, lily-like perfume. Most cacti flower in the early summer, and although individual blooms do not last for long, a plant may remain in flower for weeks or months.

There are many myths about cacti, the most persistent one being that they flower only once in seven years. This is nonsense – a mature cactus flowers annually, if well treated. But when selecting a cactus, it is important to select one which reaches maturity in a few years, not a species that does not do so until it is about 15m (50ft) tall and 50 years old. For horticultural purposes, cacti may be divided into two classes; those which grow in tropical forests, supported by trees, and the desert and semi-desert plants.

Forest cacti. These make ideal houseplants, as they grow naturally in places with partial shade. In forests they are found in pockets of leaf debris trapped in tree branches. These cacti are less succulent than those of the desert and usually have flattened stems, often segmented.

161

These segments are often erroneously called leaves, but they are true stems – the plants have no leaves.

Very popular plants in this group are the rhipsalidopsis and schlumbergeras. They consist of a large number of small segments. Their brightly coloured red or pink flowers are carried at the ends of segments. Rhipsalidopsis bloom in spring. *R. gaertneri* is popularly known as the Easter cactus.

Christmas cacti are a familiar sight in florists' shops in December, and the common name covers a number of hybrids of these winter-flowering cacti. True species are not grown, except by some specialists, but they all belong to the genus *Schlumbergera*. The most usual flower colour is cerise, but hybrids exist with pink, red, and even white blooms. The most spectacular epiphytes are the epiphyllums, or orchid cacti. They have long, strap-shaped stems. At their edges,

large, brilliant flowers appear, usually during early summer. Again, true species are rarely cultivated, but there are many beautiful hybrids with flowers in shades of red, white, orange, and pink. Most of these hybrids have been given cultivar names, but it is usually necessary to visit a specialist nursery to buy named plants. The ones most commonly seen are the so-called Ackermannii hybrids, with brilliant-red flowers. These are among the easiest to grow and flower. Although the word epiphyllum literally means *on the leaf*, these cacti also have no leaves, only stems.

All these forest cacti need more warmth and water in the winter than those of the desert types.

Desert cacti. Among the smaller-growing desert cacti which flower easily in pots are the echinopsis. They are nearly globular plants with long, tubed flowers, often sweetly scented. Good

species are the night-flowering *E. eyriesii* and the day-flowering *E. polyancistra*. Both of these have white flowers, but there are a number of horticultural hybrids with flowers in vivid shades of yellow, orange, pink, and red. Most of the echinopsis readily form offsets from around their bases.

Many of the gymnocalyciums make suitable houseplants because of their comparatively small size. *G. bruchii* is a genuine miniature cactus which flowers when 2.5cm (1in) across, producing small, pink blooms. The plant itself quickly forms a small clump, and when all the heads are in bloom it is a most attractive sight. This cactus is sometimes encountered under its older name of *G. lafaldense*.

The mammillarias, with their circlets of small flowers around the tops of the plants, have always been popular cacti in cultivation. There are over 300

Above left: *Notocactus mammulosus.*
Above right: *Mammillaria zeilmanniana.*
Left: *Rhipsalidopsis gaertneri.*

species, and a few specialist collectors grow no other plants. Their flowers are usually red, pink, or whitish. As a general rule, the red-flowered plants are more difficult to flower, but one exception to this is the exceedingly beautiful *M. zeilmanniana*, which will flower when about 2.5cm (1in) in diameter, and rapidly forms a clump. A good, white-flowered species is *M. trichacantha*. But most of these cacti are well worth trying indoors. One point to remember with them is that they always flower from the previous year's new growth, so that if they have not grown well one year they will not bloom the next.

Notocacti are globular-shaped and carry their usually yellow flowers on the top of the plant's body. Most of them are quite hardy and can survive the British winter, provided they are dry during this period. Nevertheless, they can certainly be grown as houseplants. *N. mammulosus*, one of the best-known, is very attractively spined, and *N. crassigibbus* must have the largest flowers of any in this genus.

If space is limited, the miniature rebutias will give great pleasure. These plants will often flower in their second year from seed, when less than 2.5cm (1in) across. The flowers, sometimes forming a complete ring, are produced from around the base, and one of the most beautiful is the orange-flowered *R. calliantha* var. *krainziana*. The salmon-pink flowered *R. haagei*, with its finger-like stems, is also very desirable. But any

rebutia is well worth growing and there are plenty to choose from.

One cannot leave the cacti without at least mentioning the prickly pears, or opuntias. Most species rapidly become too large to make satisfactory houseplants, but the popular *O. microdasys* and its varieties *albispina* and *rufida* make attractive specimens when young. They may be re-started from cuttings when they become too large or straggly. The small *O. spegazzinii*, a species with long cylindrical stems, will flower freely in a 7.5cm (3in) pot but it does not have the elegant form of a well-grown *O. microdasys*. All opuntias need care in their handling because of the glochids (minute, barbed bristles) growing from the areoles. These can be particularly troublesome in the case of *O. microdasys*, as being spineless it appears harmless, but it is not.

The Crassulas
The Crassulaceae family is distributed world-wide, but the half-hardy specimens grown in collections come mainly from Mexico and Africa. In areas where there is little danger of frost, such as the Isles of Scilly, aeoniums can be cultivated in gardens. The Crassulaceae are leaf succulents; the thickened leaves of many species are covered with short hairs, giving them an almost furry appearance; others have a waxy coating or a white meal. The ones with a meal-like appearance often have highly coloured leaves – the colour showing through the layer of white powder – and need to be handled with great care otherwise the coating will rub off, leaving a permanent bare patch on the leaf. Crassulaceae

flowers are either small bells or star-shaped and arranged in clusters. The colours are mainly red, yellow, orange, pink or white.

Most crassula species in cultivation come from South Africa, but they are easy to grow and flower even under the grey skies of northern Europe. A few, such as *C. arborescens*, are small shrubs. This makes a very attractive pot plant, but does need space. On a smaller scale, *C. falcata* with its large head of scarlet flowers has always been a popular florist's plant. The cultivar 'Morgan's Beauty' is a hybrid between *C. falcata* and another species. It is a true miniature and in the spring almost stemless pink flowers are formed in the centre of the rosette of leaves.

The most beautiful of the Crassulaceae are the echeverias; the plants in cultivation are all Mexican. The miniature *E. derenbergii* or painted lady makes a delightful pot plant and is very free-flowering. A more recent introduction, *E. shaviana*, also grows and flowers readily in cultivation. One hybrid which is not too large is 'Doris Taylor'. This plant has beautiful furry leaves and pretty orange flowers in spring.

A delightful species for a hanging-basket (although it may also be grown as an ordinary pot plant) is *Kalanchoe pumila*. This little specimen comes from Madagascar, and like many kalanchoes it grows and flowers during our winter and needs the heat of a living-room at this time. The whole plant, leaf and stems, is covered with a dense white meal, which makes an attractive background for the pink flowers which appear in late winter. Another plant, really needing a hanging-basket, is the Japanese *Sedum sieboldii*. This has trailing stems and pink flowers, but these are produced in autumn. Possibly the most beautiful of the sedums is *S. hintonii*, with tiny egg-shaped leaves covered with white hairs, giving the whole plant a furry appearance. It also has the added bonus of flowering in the winter. This is one plant that should be watered with caution; while flowering it needs to be left dry, since this is the time when it is prone to rot.

This is, of course, only a small selection of the many attractive houseplants in the family Crassulaceae.

The Euphorbias

The family Euphorbiaceae is vast, and has world-wide distribution. There are over 400 succulent species found in the warmer parts of the world, particularly the African continent.

Euphorbias are stem succulents, but they are not necessarily devoid of leaves. Some species have quite large, non-succulent leaves during the growing period; these usually fall during our winter. Those plants with fleshy, spiny columns closely resemble the taller cacti. This is an interesting example of parallel evolution. It is, however, easy to distinguish a euphorbia from a cactus – the euphorbia has no areoles, and where there are spines they are more like rose thorns. Also, all euphorbias have a milky sap which exudes from the slightest cut or prick. The resemblance to milk is only superficial – great care must be taken not to get it near the mouth or eyes, as it causes a severe burning sensation.

Euphorbia flowers are tiny, often no more than 5mm ($\frac{1}{4}$in) across and usually greenish in colour, although some species have vividly coloured bracts around the flowers, giving the impression of large petals. The non-succulent poinsettia (*E. pulcherrima*) is a good example of this. Although many euphorbias form shrubs or even reach tree-like proportions in their native state, they are slow-growing and may be kept as pot plants for many years.

The crown of thorns, *E. millii* (formerly *E. splendens*), is a popular florists' plant, and although it is scarcely succulent, it is by tradition included in collections of succulent plants. It is one of the species with highly coloured bracts, usually red but there is also a yellow form. If kept warm in winter it will keep its quite large leaves throughout the year.

Two of the smaller cactus-like euphorbias are *E. aggregata* and *E. submammillaris*, both South African plants. Their stems are attractively spined.

164

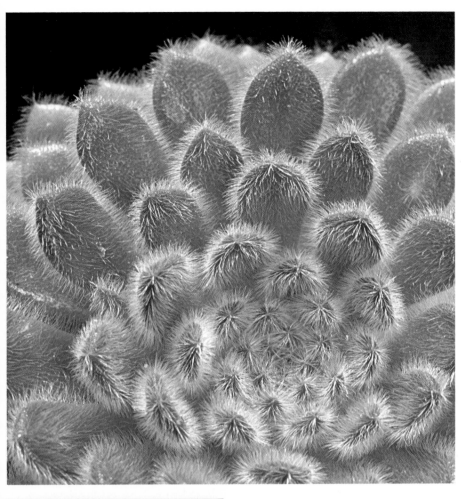

Far left: *Sedum sieboldii* 'Roseum', a charming, cascading plant.
Far left, below: *Euphorbia millii*, previously known as *E. splendens*.
Left: *Echeveria setosa*, a particularly distinctive succulent.
Below left: *Aloe jacunda*, an easy, free-growing plant.

HOW TO GROW SUCCULENTS

The successful cultivation of succulent plants in the home is not very different from that of other houseplants, although for some reason they have attracted a number of myths and misconceptions about their cultivation. The poor, dried-up, half-dead specimens often to be seen on window-ledges have given rise to the idea that they are dull, ugly, and difficult plants. Nothing could be further from the truth, and if given reasonable attention they will thrive and flower well, and continue to do so for many years.

Composts

While any old, hard soil will not do, succulent plants are, in general, quite tolerant about their compost. The main essential is that it should be well-drained and never waterlogged – but this applies to most houseplants. There is no need to buy special compost for succulents. John Innes potting compost No. 2, or a peat-based loamless type are suitable for most plants, including succulents. A few succulent enthusiasts like to mix about one-third of sharp sand or grit into the standard compost to improve the drainage, and this is an advantage if it is convenient to do so, but is by no means essential.

Potting and potting-on

Florists sometimes sell cacti and other succulents in what are somewhat unnecessarily called cactus pots. The feature of these is that they are small. Any plant bought in a pot less than 5cm (2in) in diameter should be potted-on at once into one of at least this size, since the very small pots dry out too quickly and give virtually no root room. The most popular pots are plastics, but clay pots are quite suitable, the main difference being that plants in plastic pots need less frequent watering than those in clay ones. Although it is possible to grow succulents in decorative pots with no drainage holes, it is not advisable unless the grower is very experienced and careful with watering. If decorative pots are required it is better to use them as outer containers for conventional pots. One piece of broken pot over the drainage hole is all that is needed for a clay pot. Nothing is needed for a modern plastic type, which normally has a number of small holes.

The Lily family

The Liliaceae includes many well-known garden plants, such as hyacinths, lilies and tulips, yet there are also succulent members from the drier regions of Africa. The most popular genera in cultivation are *Aloe*, *Gasteria* and *Haworthia*. None possess a bulb, and they are all leaf succulents.

Aloe flowers are tubular, usually on long stalks and in nature are mostly pollinated by birds. The leaves, arranged in rosettes, exude a thick juice when cut. *Aloe jacunda* is a freely-growing dwarf plant. The best-known is undoubtedly *A. variegata*, the partridge breast aloe. Aloes occur in partial shade among bushes and therefore adapt very readily to room cultivation.

Gasterias make ideal houseplants. They are small and like the shade, turning an unpleasant red colour if exposed to too much sun. The thick, shiny leaves are usually arranged in two rows. The flowers are very small (shaped like a miniature stomach, hence the name gasteria) and carried on longish stems. The plants are grown for their attractively mottled leaves and one of the prettiest is *G. maculata*, with white spots. Haworthias are also small plants, most of which like partial shade. The thickened leaves are usually arranged around the stem in a rosette and the small, white flowers are carried on long, thin stems, but add little to the beauty of the plants. Many haworthias are winter-growing and these should be kept moist at that time. If haworthias are repotted during their resting period it may be found that the roots have dried and shrivelled. This is quite normal; the plant will produce new roots when it starts into growth again.

With over 160 species of haworthias, it is difficult to choose only a small number, but *H. margaritifera*, *H. reinwardtii*, and *H. tesselata* are good.

When to pot-on

A vigorously-growing plant will need potting-on annually, others can spend two years or so in the same pot. If there is any doubt, it is merely necessary to remove the plant from its present pot and examine its roots. If tightly packed around the sides, the plant should be replaced in a size larger pot, and fresh compost added. Otherwise, as much old compost should be shaken from the roots as possible, without damage, the pot thoroughly cleaned and the plant replaced, again with fresh compost added as necessary. Spiny plants, such as most cacti, can be gently held in a folded strip of newspaper whilst handling for potting.

Watering succulents

The successful watering of succulent plants is much the same as for other houseplants. In spring and summer, soak thoroughly and do not water again until the compost has almost dried out, and never allow the pot to remain standing in water. The difference is that these plants will usually survive even if watering has been neglected. But they will not grow and thrive under such treatment if prolonged. It is impossible to say just how often water is needed, as this will depend upon the conditions in the room. Generally, much less water is needed as winter approaches.

Most cacti prefer to rest during winter and their pots should not be soaked at this time. Instead, just dip the pot in water every few weeks to prevent the compost completely drying out. If this happens, the fine root hairs will be destroyed, delaying growth in spring. Exceptions here are the Christmas cacti and other forest cacti (rhipsalidopsis and epiphyllums) which need to be reasonably moist at all times. Other succulent plants can be given a little water in winter, particularly if the room is warm and the plant appears to be still in growth.

The rather specialized watering of the lithops and conophytums is mentioned under their section of the Aizoaceae family.

The best way to water all these plants is to stand the pot in water until the compost is quite wetted, and then remove and allow to drain. With a large collection, this is not practicable and plants will have to be watered from above, taking care not to wet the leaves.

Situation

Just where in the room to keep succulent plants is important. Apart from aloes, gasterias and haworthias, and the forest cacti, which all prefer some shade from the summer sun, they should be put in the sunniest window possible, which means that north-facing windows are really not suitable, except for the plants just mentioned. Because window light is one-sided, the plants should be turned every few days to prevent them showing one-sided growth. If possible, put your plants outside in the open during late spring and summer, as direct sunlight is beneficial – but still remember those with a preference for shade. Plants should never be placed near a radiator.

Temperature

Normal room temperatures during spring and summer will suit succulent plants if they are kept inside at this time. During winter, however, most cacti prefer a colder rest and if they can be transferred to an unheated room they are likely to flower better the following year. But, if no cold room is available or, as is quite natural, you want to keep all your plants in the living-room to cheer you in the winter, it would be unreasonable to suggest otherwise. But if a cactus which should flower well fails to perform, it is worth trying a colder situation the following winter. The forest cacti, together with the rest of the succulents, can certainly be kept in the living-room in winter.

Feeding

All succulent plants will appreciate a fortnightly feed while in active growth, and those growing in a loamless compost will need regular feeding, since the soil nutrients are quickly exhausted. Liquid feeds should be high in potassium, such as those used for tomatoes.

Pests and diseases

There are really no pests specific to succulent plants, but any pest affecting other houseplants can also affect them. The most common are mealy bugs and root mealy bugs. These can be controlled most effectively by proprietary systemic insecticides, used strictly according to instructions.

The most common disease is rotting of the stems or roots, usually due to over-watering or poorly-drained soil.

Propagation

Cuttings and offsets. Most succulents can be propagated from cuttings, although some root more readily than others. One general principle which must be observed with cuttings of all these plants is not to pot up immediately, but to allow the cut end to dry for a period of a few days to a week, depending on the area of the cut, to allow a callus to form – otherwise there is risk of rot. They can then be potted up in a sandy compost or a peat and sand mixture, and kept slightly moist.

Once new growth starts, it can be assumed that the cutting has rooted. The best time to pot it is during the active growing period of the plant, usually spring and summer.

The actual method of cutting obviously depends upon the type of plant. Usually a piece of stem 5–10cm (2–4in) long is about the right length.

Long stems, such as those of epiphyllums, can be cut into smaller portions, each of which should root and send up fresh shoots.

In the case of segmented stems of plants, like the Christmas cacti, a portion consisting of one or two segments is chosen. One segment or pad of an opuntia will usually root.

Succulent leaves, such as those of echeverias, will often take root if gently pressed into the compost, or even laid upon it. Euphorbias, with their milky latex, are rather difficult – the cut ends should be dipped into water to clear the latex before the usual drying-off.

Many cacti, notably echinopsis and mammillarias, readily produce offsets which can be carefully removed, if overcrowded, and used for propagation. If the offset can be pulled away, without actually cutting, it can be potted into a pot of compost straight away.

Raising from seed. Seeds of succulent plants are often available and should be sown in a seed compost.

Most seeds are small and should be scattered over the surface of the compost – larger ones are pressed into the surface. A glass or plastic cover is needed until germination starts. The seed container is best watered from below, the compost being kept moist, but never waterlogged. A temperature of 21–25°C (70–77°F) is necessary for good germination and if this can be maintained, March or April is the best time. Alternatively, it is advisable to wait until June. Light is not needed for germination but as soon as the young seedlings appear, in about 10–14 days, they must be exposed to diffused light, but not direct sunlight. The glass or plastic cover should be removed.

Young succulents can usually spend a year in the seed container before being transplanted. Do not expect all of the seeds to germinate. Commercial seed is not always fresh, and stale seed germinates badly or not at all. However, usually at least some plants will result and raising these plants from seed is so fascinating and economical that it is well worth the effort.

BOTTLE GARDENS

The cultivation of plants in bottles or Wardian cases is a revival of a popular Victorian fashion which developed from the unexpected results of an experiment and subsequent research carried out by Dr. N. Ward early in the last century. He was an ardent, but thwarted, gardener who yearned to grow ferns, but he was unsuccessful with them and assumed that this was due to the smoky atmosphere of the dock area in London where he lived.

He was also a keen naturalist and wishing to observe the emergence of a sphinx moth from a chrysalis, he buried one in some moist earth in a glass bottle with a metal lid. Some time later he noticed a seedling fern in the bottle. The fern thrived and was left in the bottle for over four years, until the lid rusted and the plant deteriorated.

Bottle gardens can provide
a charming setting
for a surprisingly
large range
of houseplants.

He noted that the moisture given off by the leaves, also some rising from the damp soil which condensed on the inside of the glass, trickled down to the soil, so keeping the latter damp and the atmosphere within the glass at a constant degree of humidity.

He deduced that other plants would grow in similar conditions – a humid atmosphere and protection from dust or smoke as well as draughts, or extreme changes of temperature. Dr. Ward experimented with other bottle gardens and a wide range of plants and subsequently developed elaborate fern cases known as Wardian Cases, which became a feature of many Victorian drawing rooms.

Bottle gardens

The traditional bottle gardens with stoppered tops – so producing a closed and humid atmosphere – are well suited to growing moisture-loving plants such as ferns and small rushes with resilient and water-repelling leaf surfaces. However, many bottle gardens now sold are not of this traditional nature, and contain soft-leaved flowering plants which would soon be damaged in a totally closed environment. Bottles containing such plants are left unstoppered and therefore do not benefit from a re-circulatory water system. They are, therefore, just a method by which to display plants in an attractive manner.

The information given here refers to the stoppered and traditional type of bottle garden.

In a bottle with a narrow neck it is best to start with small, young plants of a type that will not crowd the container too quickly. Also it is important to select plants that will flourish in semi-shade and a moist atmosphere. Limit the choice to plants which are non-flowering and need very little attention.

Containers. The containers can be of a variety of shapes and sizes, from small flasks to large carboys. In fact, any rigid and transparent container can be used. Preferably the container should be of clear glass and free of decoration. The neck must be large enough to enable the plants and soil to be inserted. Glass containers are better than plastic, as drops of moisture adhere to plastic and tend to obscure the plants.

Before starting to plant the container, wash it out and ensure that it is thoroughly clean and dry.

Planting. First, using the funnel, cover the base of the container with a mixture of charcoal and pebbles. Its depth will, of course, depend on the size of the container – a large carboy needs 6.5cm (2½in). Then add a thin layer of peat, and enough compost to accommodate the roots of the plants.

The most dominant plant should be positioned near the centre, and to avoid introducing any insect pests into the bottle, shake each plant free of soil and inspect it carefully. Make a depression in the compost's surface with the looped wire, and using the same tool lower the first plant, roots downwards, into the hole. Then cover the roots, using the same tool, and firm down. Repeat this operation until all the plants are arranged to your liking.

Brush off any compost left on the foliage or the glass and then spray with tepid water from a fine syringe, using enough to wash the foliage and the sides of the glass. Then put in the stopper.

It may take several hours for the moisture to seep through to the base and for the plants to transpire. If the atmosphere is humid enough to condense, then to roll down the glass leaving this clear, a balance has been achieved and this sequence will be repeated daily. However, it might be necessary to syringe

again the next day. If the atmosphere is saturated the plants will not flourish. In this case, the stopper should be left off to encourage evaporation until the correct balance is achieved and the bottle can then remain closed.

The plants can remain in the bottle for several years. However, often one plant starts to dominate the bottle and pruning is required. If the plants do eventually resemble a jungle, replanting is the only action to take.

Selecting the plants. For the carboy, or larger bottle, any of the following ferns can be used: the maidenhair fern (*Adiantum capillus-veneris*), delicate fan-shaped leaflets on wiry black leaf-stalks; small lady fern (*Athyrium filix-femina* 'Minutissima'); the bladder fern (*Cystopteris bulbifera*), well-divided fronds; the common polypody (*Polypodium vulgare*), a widespread native fern with blunt, undivided leaflets; and the well-known hart's tongue fern (*Phyllitis scolopendrium*), with tongue-shaped leaves.

Some of the popular foliage houseplants can add considerable interest, even though some of them may need to be kept in check or removed after a year or so. The earth stars (cryptanthus) are charming subjects, and the aluminium plant (*Pilea cadierei* 'Nana') can be quite striking. Fittonias also have delightful foliage and appreciate the humid atmosphere – but choose a small-leaved form. Two popular foliage plants that can be introduced provided you are willing to prune regularly are the creeping fig (*Ficus pumila*) and ivy (*Hedera helix*) – but use only small-leaved cultivars of ivy.

It is even feasible to grow a palm in a large container! The parlour palm, *Chamaedorea elegans* (*Neanthe bella*), grows only slowly and can be potted up to grow on elsewhere once it becomes too large.

For the smaller container the following

are admirable, but perhaps less well-known. *Acorus gramineus* 'Pusillus' is a small rush-like plant of rich green, growing 2.5–5cm (1–2in) high; *Asplenium trichomanes* (maidenhair spleenwort) is an engaging little plant about 7.5cm (3in) tall sometimes found on old stone walls, but it also grows freely in a moist atmosphere; *Blechnum penna-marina*, about 5cm (2in) high, has a creeping rhizome which sends up, at intervals, fronds of very dark green with a wavy margin.

Selaginellas, sometimes called moss ferns, although botanically they are neither, have the delicacy of the moss and a fern-like structure. There are several good kinds for bottle gardens, including *S. apoda*; (syn. *S. apus*) which has tiny fronds forming a 5cm (2in) hummock of brilliant green, *S. pallescens* (syn. *S. emmeliana*), with erect fan-shaped fronds of ethereal beauty 15–25cm (6–10in) high ('Aurea' is a golden form), *S. martensii*, has broader, lacy fronds.

For the smaller bottle some of the mosses, can make an enchanting miniature landscape – with no expense, only the time needed to collect them.

Above right: If the atmosphere is too humid, remove the stopper to encourage excess moisture to evaporate more quickly.
Right: When the correct moisture balance has been achieved and the glass remains clear, insert the stopper.

Below: The basic equipment for planting a bottle garden: charcoal and pebbles for drainage, sterilized compost, peat, a funnel with flexible tube, small paintbrush tied to a cane, and a stiff wire with looped end.
Below left: Use the funnel to position the compost, and the looped wire to insert the plants. After brushing the glass clean, carefully syringe the plants and glass with a fine mist of clean water.

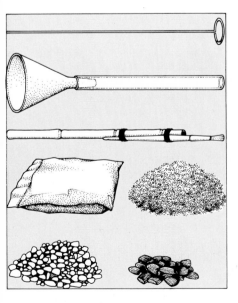

ORCHIDS

For many years orchids have enjoyed a reputation for being the most exotic of greenhouse plants. Their cultivation can be traced back to the middle of the last century when the first tropical orchids were brought to the western world. Now they have become the ultimate in houseplants.

As more and more people seek to grow something really different they are turning to orchids, and realizing that they can be grown with ease once their basic cultural requirements are understood.

The modern hybrid orchid is the type most suited to the home. These have been bred over many generations, and are derived from the species, many of which are now very rare. The hybrids are tolerant plants which grow in a variety of surroundings with the minimum of attention, and reward the grower with large, flamboyant blooms. Many of the flowers last for eight to ten weeks.

A number of these hybrids are winter blooming, producing a fine display of flowers during the worst months of the year. By careful selection, it is possible to have blooms the year round.

These plants vary tremendously in size and shape, and small and compact plants can be found to fit most window-sills. For sun rooms, there are the large-growing varieties which require good sized tubs and grow into enormous plants, 30cm (1ft) or more across and producing flower spikes over 90cm (3ft) tall. Many small species will grow in indoor growing cases.

The whole orchid family is extremely large, but the plants that can be grown indoors successfully come from a very limited selection, and it is from the numerous hybrids from a few genera that the best houseplants are to be found – yet the choice is immense.

THE INTRODUCTION OF ORCHIDS

Tropical orchids were relatively unknown in the western world until the 18th century. Many famous names became involved with the introduction of orchids, among them Captain Cook and Charles Darwin.

The first orchid to be classified was named *Epidendrum*, meaning *upon a tree*. This species, now known as *Encyclia cochleata*, was then called *Epidendrum cochleatum*. It arrived in England in 1786 and bloomed the following year. It was not until the 19th century that collectors went specifically in search of new and hitherto unknown orchids.

Early collectors were employed by the first commercial orchid nurseries, which came into existence to meet the demand for these new plants. There was a great rivalry between collectors, who stripped the orchids from the trees and despatched them in their tens of thousands – a regrettable onslaught.

The losses of plants during their journey to England were tremendous. Also, many perished in the hot steamy greenhouses of the early Victorians. It was years before they realized that many orchids require cool and airy conditions, but gradually these requirements began to be understood as experience was gained through trial and error. In those early days, very high prices were paid for the finest specimens and the growing of orchids became a status symbol.

During the first half of the 19th century, more and more new varieties arrived in Britain from the tropics. Each new variety caused more excitement than the last, and when they flowered, awards by The Royal Horticultural Society were showered upon the finest of them.

In 1856, the first man-made hybrid bloomed, and by 1885 so great had become the interest in orchids that The Royal Horticultural Society held the first-ever orchid conference in London. By this time, the hybrids were beginning to outshine the species, and while many of the imported species could now be acquired for a few shillings, the price for the latest hybrids could still be many guineas.

Around the turn of the century calanthes were the the great favourites. The Victorians grew them in their thousands and decorated drawing-rooms with their blooms during the festive Christmas season. Many hybrids were raised from them at that time, and a few are still available today.

It was much later that the potential of the cymbidium hybrids was realized. Today, they are the most popular orchids in cultivation.

Orchids in the wild

In their wild state, orchids grow all over the world as epiphytes and terrestrials living in trees or on the ground. The most flamboyant are the epiphytes, which grow on trees – not as parasites but as air plants. This means they take nothing from the host tree, but merely take advantage of living in the air and using the tree as an anchorage.

These plants have evolved in the warmer parts of the globe, where protection from cold is not necessary and there is constant moisture in the air. Therefore, their feeding requirements are meagre, and they exist on nothing but water and what can be derived from bird droppings and debris collecting in the axials of the branches. These epiphytes could not survive in colder climates where exposed roots could be damaged by frost, and it is in tropical forests that they have thrived in limitless quantities for millions of years.

Most epiphytes produce pseudo-bulbs or false bulbs, which are swollen stems, at the base of the plant. These pseudo-bulbs enable the plant to store sufficient water for its needs, and will carry it safely through long periods of drought.

Pseudo-bulbs vary considerably in their size and shape, but all form the same function. The bulbs carry the leaves, which can vary considerably in size and number. The bulbs outlive the leaves by several years, so that a plant will consist of bulbs with and without leaves at any one time.

A few orchids are deciduous and shed their leaves each year, retaining only the bulbs to sustain the next season's new growth. This appears from the base of the last completed pesudo-bulb and is followed by the formation of the new roots, which serve the plant in two ways. They are the means by which the plant can absorb moisture from the atmosphere, at the same time giving the plant anchorage on the tree.

The flowers of these orchids may appear on long spikes from the base, from the apex of the bulb at the base of the leaves, or from the sides of the bulb, depending upon the type. These bulbous plants are known as sympodials.

A further method of growth is adopted by some epiphytes, which consists of a

Above: Charles Darwin (1809–1882) was involved with the introduction of many orchids, as well as a wide range of other plants.
Right: An old print from *Practical Gardener*.

sepal

petal

column

sepal

lip (petal)

Top: Orchid flowers are very variable in shape, but they all have the same basic structure of three sepals and three petals. The sepals usually look like petals, while one of the true petals is often modified into a conspicuous lip.
Above: *Paphiopedilums*, the famous slipper orchids, produce solitary flowers on tall stems. Unlike many orchids they do not produce pseudo-bulbs.

single vertical rhizome which is continually growing and producing leaves from the apex, which form in pairs each side of the rhizome. These orchids are referred to as monopodials. Another method of growth adopted by epiphytic or terrestrial orchids is known as diopodial, and produces a series of bulbless growths with broad, rounded leaves. The growths are joined by an underground rhizome similar to the sympodials.

The number of terrestrial orchids (those which grow on the ground) probably outnumber the epiphytes (tree orchids), but they are generally less showy and are not cultivated to the same extent. Also, many do not adapt to cultivation as readily as the epiphytes. The typical terrestrial orchid has a single stem arising from underground tubers which serve the plant in the same way as the pseudo-bulbs of the epiphyte. These plants grow on grassy plains and in the cooler climates of the world, reaching almost to the arctic. Most of them become dormant during the winter or dry season, with a relatively short growing season.

CULTIVATION

The culture of orchids indoors is not so very different from that of other houseplants, and most of their requirements are easily understood. An orchid will continue to grow and repeat its annual cycle of growth indefinitely, and can be regarded as permanent.

When large enough, they can be divided, although this should be done only if they become unmanageable – the larger the plant, the better the display of flowers. It is, therefore, a mistake to reduce a plant by too much division, and prevent it from flowering for a number of years.

Compost and potting

One of the biggest differences between growing orchids and other houseplants is the type of compost needed. The majority of cultivated orchids are epiphytic, or have been bred from epiphytic species. For this reason, they must be grown in an open, free-draining compost. If you have not previously grown orchids, this may be the first time you come across bark compost. It is fir bark that has been ground down to form small chunks, and is sold by orchid specialists.

While this bark forms the basic ingredient of orchid compost, on its own it is too dry, and it is difficult to keep it evenly moist. Therefore, a small percentage of sphagnum peat is added. The more peat that is added, the wetter the compost becomes. Therefore, if you tend to excessively water your houseplants, you would require very little peat in your orchid compost – and *vice versa*. In addition, a small amount of charcoal should be added to prevent the peat making the compost too acid, which can be observed by the appearance of green algae on the surface.

Potting orchids in this compost is very easy, although it may take a little getting used to because of its unusual composition. Orchids are generally in need of repotting about every other year, and when repotted they should be given just sufficient room in their new pot to allow for a further two years' growth.

Overpotting is a big mistake. The plants will look unsightly and out of proportion with their pot, and there will be too much expanse of compost around the roots, which will remain too wet for long periods, resulting in overwatering of the plant. Therefore, always use as small a pot as possible and place the plant with its new growth facing towards the rim with space in between.

A plant should be repotted when the new growth can be seen, about 2.5–5cm (1–2in) high at the base of the last completed bulb, usually during spring. An orchid is in need of repotting when the leading bulb has reached the rim of the pot and there is no room for the next growth. Alternatively, repot if the plant has pushed itself over the pot rim by an abundance of roots below.

With monopodials, check whether the compost is firm and sweet. If a finger can easily be pushed through the compost it has deteriorated to an extent where it should be replaced, and the plant repotted.

Compost that has become sour – showing a green algae surface – also needs to be replaced. It is not always necessary to remove all the old compost before repotting. Very often, where there is a good root-ball and the compost remains intact, the plant can be repotted without further disturbance. Where the compost has deteriorated it must be removed by shaking it from the roots.

Dead roots should be cut off and the longest of the live ones trimmed for easy insertion in the pot. A few leafless back bulbs can be removed at this stage. These are the oldest bulbs at the back of the plant, and they should be removed if there are more of them than green bulbs in leaf. Otherwise, they should remain on the plant. Deciduous plants with leaves on the leading bulb only can safely be reduced to four good sized bulbs without affecting the flowering of the plant. The bulbs should be removed by severing them with a sharp knife, through the rhizome.

When this has been done, the plant is ready for repotting. A layer of crocking material should be placed in the bottom of the pot, to allow for good drainage. Broken polystyrene tiles are ideal for this. On top of the drainage material place sufficient compost to allow the base of the plant to be on a level with the rim of the pot. The space between the plant and pot can then be filled with the compost and firmed down with the fingers. A potting stick is not necessary. The plant should now be firmly in place with the new growth sitting on the surface of the compost and not buried. After repotting, the plant should not be watered for a few days, giving the severed roots a chance to settle down. During this time, the leaves should be sponged daily or as often as possible until normal watering is resumed.

Watering

An orchid plant in growth should not be allowed to become completely dry at any time. The aim should be to keep the compost evenly moist, bearing in mind that it is very open and well drained. When watering, a maximum of water should be poured on to the plant, most of which will run straight through the pot. Therefore, make sure your plant has received sufficient water in one application. If necessary, flood the pot several

times to ensure it is thoroughly wetted. Overwatering in such an open compost is difficult, unless the plant is left standing in water, in which case it will quickly become sodden with loss of the roots through drowning.

Underwatering is far more common indoors where plants often dry out quicker in the drier atmosphere. The first sign of an underwatered plant is a shrivelling of the pseudo-bulbs, usually from the rear. In severe cases, the leading bulb will shrivel, causing a slowing up of growth and functioning of the root system, when the whole plant will become limp. From this stage, it will take a little time and continuous sponging of foliage to restore the leaves, while copious supplies of water to the roots will be required before they become active again and the bulbs regain their plumpness. Good, plump bulbs are the sign of a healthy plant; shrivelled bulbs are usually caused through underwatering, although it may be by overwatering.

In the case of overwatering the roots drown in the sodden, airless compost and are unable to support the pseudo-bulbs, which shrivel from the lack of moisture supplied to them. In both cases, it is best to repot the plant which has suffered into fresh, damp compost immediately, paying careful attention to its watering requirements from then on.

Feeding

Orchids should be fed in moderation only. By their very nature they are unable to cope with large quantities of artificial feed. Feeding, therefore, should be kept to the minimum. Any phosphate or nitrate-based food is suitable for them. It should be given only during the spring and summer months, when there is sufficient light available to warrant the extra food supply.

Feeding should start gradually, as the days lengthen into spring, adding a liquid feed at about every third watering. This dosage can be increased during the summer to every other watering, with an additional foliar feed about once every ten days. As summer turns into autumn, gradually lessen and then discontinue all feeding until the following spring, when it can be resumed.

Only strong, healthy plants should be fed. Do not feed sickly plants or newly-repotted plants until their new roots are showing.

Resting

Orchids that have completed a season's growth and are resting will require little or no water during this period. When an orchid is at rest, all growth stops and the roots cease to take up nourishment for the bulbs.

Some orchids have resting periods of up to four months at a time, while others have so short a rest it can pass unnoticed. A resting orchid may discard part or all of its foliage at the commencement of its resting period, or it may retain all its foliage. Most of the orchids suitable for indoor cultivation are evergreen and retain their foliage for several years. They usually shed one or two leaves at a time from the older bulbs.

Provided the bulbs remain plump when resting, there is no need to give water, but should shrivelling occur, particularly in the younger bulbs, one application of water is usually all that is required.

Some orchids may need two or three waterings over their period of rest, while others will need nothing until the new growth is seen. The commencement of this new growth indicates that the plant has once again started to grow, and normal watering can be resumed.

Orchids that are resting should always be given as much light as possible. This is important, to ripen the bulbs prior to their flowering the following year.

Special tips

Most orchids are shade-loving plants and although they require sufficient light to induce normal flowering, they must not be exposed to direct sunlight through a glass window. This is far too strong for them, and yellowing of the foliage and possible sun-burn will result. Sun-burn will show up on the leaves as black or brown areas, and can only be removed by severing a leaf, which is not always possible with a plant that carries only a few leaves.

Insufficient light, however, may lead to non-flowering.

Greenhouse pests that attack orchids growing in greenhouses are not usually found in the home, and pests are very few and far between. More harm to plants can be done indoors when a plant is knocked over. Damaged areas will become wet and should first be dried with a paper tissue and then dusted with a sulphur preparation to assist drying.

Many orchids retain their foliage over a number of years. As a result, old leaves will occasionally become 'tipped', showing black ends. This is usually no more than a sign of old age, and for appearance they can be neatly trimmed.

Orchids dislike cold draughts and exposure to direct heat. Keep the plants well away from draughty areas and sources of heat. For example, do not stand plants over a radiator or the television set.

Cymbidiums are beautiful plants but best suited to a spacious sun-lounge.

ORCHIDS FOR BEGINNERS

Of the whole orchid family, only a few types are in cultivation, and of those even fewer are suitable for growing indoors. The following orchids can be recommended as those most likely to succeed indoors. They are among the easiest to grow, and produce the most beautiful and rewarding flowers. However, they cannot be grown all together, but are suited for different temperature ranges, and should be grown where conditions are suitable.

Cymbidiums have long been regarded as the beginner's orchid. In a greenhouse they are ideal, but indoors they can be rather space consuming and are best suited to a spacious sun lounge. Large plants can require up to 30cm (12in) pots, and the handsome plants produce rounded pseudo-bulbs, each carrying many long and narrow leaves.

The flower spikes appear towards the end of summer and grow to a height of 90cm (3ft) and will require support from a long cane. The flowers, a dozen or more on a spray, come in all colours, from white, through pink to red, bronze, green and yellow. The lip is nearly always of a contrasting colour and these beautiful blooms will last up to ten weeks. They can be cut individually and worn for a special occasion, or cut as a spray and placed in water. Cutting off flowers reduces the strain on a plant, which will grow and flower better the following year.

Miniature cymbidiums are also available and are more easily coped with indoors. While they lack the bulkiness of the standard cymbidiums, they produce smaller flowers, every bit as attractive and in a multitude of colours.

There is an extensive range of named hybrids, and the beginner may do better to order by colour choice rather than name. All orchid nurseries will have their own particular cultivars.

Cymbidiums should be watered throughout the year and kept at a minimum temperature of 10°C (50°F). If they are kept much warmer than this at night it may affect flowering. The maximum summer temperature may rise as high as 30°C (85°F).

Odontoglossums are wonderfully showy orchids; they make smaller plants than cymbidiums and can be accommodated in under 15cm (6in) pots. The odontoglossums are closely related to a number of other orchids, including cochliodas, miltonias and oncidiums, with which they will readily inter-breed to produce many different named hybrids. The most popular of these are odontiodas, odontonias, odontocidiums, wilsonaras and vuylstekearas.

These orchids are often collectively known as odontoglossum types. The main difference is that they are far more robust than pure odontoglossums and are ideally suited to indoor culture. They all produce neat, bulbous plants with a few leaves. The flowers are carried on long, arching sprays in a multitude of colours and colour combinations, often with several colours of dramatic design contained in one flower. Their flowering season is not regular and a well-grown plant can be flowered approximately every nine months. The large, attractive blooms can vary tremendously in their shape, and will last up to ten weeks at any time of the year.

While a few of the species are grown the more robust hybrids are better suited for indoors. A minimum temperature of 10°C (50°F) is ideal, with shady conditions in the summer when the temperature should not rise above 18°C (65°F) for any length of time. These plants should be watered throughout the year and fresh air is always important to them.

Cattleyas are the largest and most flamboyant of all orchid blooms. These plants are related to laelias, brassavolas and sophronitis, and intergeneric hybrids are available that combine the beauties of the different types. The most popular types are laeliocattleya, brassolaeliocattleya and sophrolaeliocattleya. The first two named produce large plants, often requiring up to 25cm (10in) pots, with stout, club-shaped pseudo-bulbs, each carrying one or sometimes two thick, broad leaves.

The flowers emerge from the top of the bulb at the base of the leaf, where they are enclosed in their young stage by a protective sheath. Several large, frilly flowers are produced at a time, the colour ranging from white, through pink to the most beautiful mauves and purples, with yellow and green occasionally seen. The sophrolaeliocattleya types produce smaller plants, which can be contained in 15cm (6in) pots. Their colour is rich red and mauve hues.

Cattleyas and their allies produce an abundance of thick roots, which will often trail out of their pot, but this is quite natural. They have two main flowering seasons, spring and autumn, although not all plants will bloom twice a year. Their blooms will last for up to three weeks on the plant.

Cattleyas enjoy fairly warm conditions and their winter night temperature should not drop below 13°C (55°F) which can rise on summer days to 26°C (80°F). Their leaves should be sponged regularly, then they will keep a high gloss. They require a semi-rest during the winter, without allowing the bulbs to become shrivelled.

The cattleya species are rare collectors' items, and have no place in the home. Numerous fine hybrids are available which have a built-in tolerance of indoor conditions.

Paphiopedilums are the famous slipper orchids, and are among the most well-known and best loved of all orchids. The plants do not produce pseudo-bulbs, but have a series of growths, often with beautifully mottled foliage which makes them an attractive foliage plant when not in bloom. Their flowers are produced singly on a tall stem. Most of the cultivars suitable for indoors are not excessively large and can be accommodated in 15cm (6in) pots.

The handsome blooms come in a variety of colours and colour combinations.

Extreme left: *Odontoglossum grande*.
Far left: *Coelogyne orchracea*.
Above left: *Brassolaeliocattleya*.
Above: *Paphiopedilum* 'Hoopla'.
Left: *Laeliocattleya* 'Resplendent'.

These include green and white, purple and green, bronze and brown and pink and green. They are extremely long-lasting and can remain in bloom for over ten weeks. Their flowering period is mostly in winter.

Both species and hybrids are available, and they can be grown in a cool or warm atmosphere. The cool-growing types prefer a winter temperature of 10°C (50°F) while those requiring warmth (usually indicated by their mottled foliage), do best at a minimum of 13°C (55°F). They are shade-loving orchids, and should never be exposed to direct sunlight. They are ideally suited to indoor growing cases when they should be kept evenly moist all the year round. Lacking pseudo-bulbs, it is a mistake to allow them to become too dry at any time of the year.

Phalaenopsis are the beautiful moth orchids, whose beauty cannot be rivalled among the warmer-growing types. They are most suited to indoor growing cases, where a high temperature can be maintained. This should not drop below 18°C (65°F), to grow them successfully. The plants produce few leaves and never become too large. Their growth is monopodial and one or two new leaves are produced each year. Strong aerial roots are often produced outside the pot. They flower on long arching sprays any time of the year, often blooming twice. Their colours are restricted to pink and white. The hybrids are more suitable than the species.

From this selection can be built up a fine collection of indoor orchids, with a variety of bloom to flower throughout the year. This collection can be extended with a few carefully-chosen true species, which are easily cultivated and have exceptionally showy and dainty flowers. The following orchids are of modest size, and all require cool conditions with a minimum temperature of 10°C (50°F).

Coelogyne ochracea is a delightful plant that blooms in spring, and is grown for its fragrance. It produces sprays of small, white and yellow flowers. It requires a winter's rest and plenty of light.

Dendrobium nobile is a tall, caned plant that enjoys plenty of light and will bloom in spring with clusters of mauve-pink flowers along the length of its canes. It requires a winter's rest and plenty of good light to grow well.

Brassia verrucosa produces graceful sprays of elegant, green flowers with long, narrow petals and sepals. Its fragrant blooms are produced in early summer. It requires a semi-rest in winter, for good results.

Vanda cristata is worth growing. Most of the vandas are hot-growing, sun-loving orchids with no place in the home. However, this small-growing species is the exception to that rule and can be grown in any well-lit position. Its striking green-and-red flowers are produced in clusters during spring and summer. It requires a slight rest during winter.

Odontoglossum grande is a very striking species, producing its large, showy blooms during autumn. The flower spike may carry up to four bright yellow and chestnut-brown blooms. This plant likes a winter's rest, when it can be completely dried out and given full light.

175

FLAMBOYANT PLANTS

Many of the houseplants grown in the home, trapped in small pots and kept in captivity, are never really able to display their full glory. In the wild they may reach magnificent proportions, but in our homes never produce the glorious flowers they do when in the wild. Some of the more flamboyant and colourful plants, although native to the sub-tropics, have become extremely popular for growing outdoors in those countries with a reasonably mild climate.

Many of these plants also thrive in our homes, and most do not demand high temperatures. They grow especially well in modern homes where there are large picture windows. If the heat loss can be reduced by double glazing, they grow even better. Such plants also thrive in public buildings, offices and shops where there is space and the temperature is congenial most of the year.

These plants have long been prized for decoration in greenhouses and conservatories as well as home extensions. Most can be kept reasonably compact by suitable culture and judicious pruning.

BOUGAINVILLEA

One of the easiest, and by no means the least colourful, is bougainvillea. Unfortunately it is of little interest when not in flower. Moreover, what appears to be the flowers are three brightly-coloured bracts – the true, central flower is insignificant. However, these bracts remain brilliant for several months, summer to autumn, and are borne in great profusion, so creating a most striking sight. The plants literally glow with colour – rich red, purple and orange shades predominating.

There are about 16 species of bougainvillea, most of them scrambling climbers of shrubby character and originating from South America. There are a number of delightful and attractive hybrids. A common name sometimes applied to these plants is paper flower.

Undoubtedly, the best bougainvillea for room cultivation is B. glabra and its cultivars. These can easily be kept from invading their surroundings, and have the great advantage that they will give lots of colour as a small and young plant.

By suitable training, they can be kept compact and bushy and dissuaded from rambling. Its species has bracts in various shades of dazzling red and purple. The fine hybrid B. × buttiana is interesting, because it was found growing in a Colombian priest's garden by a Mrs. R. V. Butt early this century, and is presumably of natural origin. It is now sold as 'Mrs. Butt', and bears very large crimson to magenta bracts. Several variants – probably sports or mutants – have arisen and are also most desirable acquisitions.

Young plants can be grown in 15–20cm (6–8in) pots, John Innes potting compost No. 2 suiting them very well. If you wish to restrict development, snip off the tips of the stems when they reach 15cm (6in) long in their early stages. This encourages the free production of more shoots to give a bushy habit. These shoots can then be allowed to grow as much as space permits. If a plant with a taller habit is wanted, provide a cane for support to the desired height. Usually, about 1.2–1.5m (4–5ft) high is advisable. Allow one or more stems to grow up the support, securing where necessary. Side-shoots on the main stem, or stems, should then be cut back to about 15cm (6in) from the main shoots.

A position in good light is absolutely vital for bract production. Keep the plants well watered in summer, spraying them regularly. In autumn, when flowering is over, reduce watering and rest the plants. In winter, give only sufficient water to prevent the compost drying out completely. In March when growth begins again, watering can be gradually resumed.

Although it has to be done for convenience, bougainvilleas do not like being continuously cut back. In conservatories they are best allowed as much freedom as possible. Train them on wires or on a wall trellis.

Propagation can be effected from cuttings taken in summer, but they need about 21°C (70°F) for rooting. The seed is easy to germinate, although it is a gamble whether a plant will be produced up to the standard of the named hybrids. However, seed saved from fine forms is well worth trying, and is certainly a cheap way of obtaining plants.

STEPHANOTIS

Another climber to which the name flamboyant can be applied is *Stephanotis floribunda*, popularly called the wax flower because of the texture of the flowers. It is also called the Madagascar jasmine because of the exquisite and powerful scent of the flowers. This species frequently appears in florists' shops as a houseplant, and is then usually in flower and trained around and over a wire loop. The leaves are evergreen, bluntly spear-shaped, thick, green and shiny, making the plant usefully decorative the year round. The flowers are tubular, with flared petals at the tip, giving a starry effect. They are borne in clusters, and are waxy white. These flowers are borne very freely from May to October on well-grown specimens, and their fragrance alone gives an enormous amount of pleasure. One small plant fills the home with scent.

Although when bought this plant is relatively small, it is able to reach at least 3m (10ft) in height, climbing by means of its twining stems. If height and space allow, it is a good idea carefully to disentangle the stems from the wire loop and pot into a larger pot equipped with stout bamboo canes. This species also makes a superb conservatory plant, but its temperature requirement is a minimum of about 10°C (50°F) in winter, and preferably a few degrees higher.

The plant grows extremely well in the modern peat-based potting composts, and in summer should be given moderate humidity and slight shade. It needs to be freely watered.

By keeping the plants in relatively small pots, their growth and development will be slowed down, which is helpful when limited for space. However, if this is done the plants must be fed properly during their growing period, using a balanced houseplant fertilizer. Restriction of the pot's size also tends to increase the freedom of flowering.

In winter, reduce watering to maintain only moist conditions for the roots. If kept on the dry side the plants may survive temperatures much lower than the minimum recommended. They will probably lose leaves and become tatty-looking, but resume growth with the return of warmer conditions in spring. However, too much chill for too long is very risky and the plants may die.

Opposite page: *Bougainvillea.*
Below: *Stephanotis floribunda*, the popular Madagascar jasmine.

OLEANDER

Oleander, sometimes called rose bay, and botanically *Nerium oleander*, has many romantic associations. It is freely grown around the picturesque beauty spots of Mediterranean regions, as well as in the sub-tropics and the Orient. In this country it may survive outdoors in very sheltered parts of the South and West, and on the Isles of Scilly. Although it is a shrub that will reach a considerable size, it can be flowered easily in small pots. Seedlings, for example, will flower in the third year from sowing, in 18cm (7in) pots.

The plant is extremely easy to grow and has pleasing, slightly shiny spear-shaped evergreen foliage, as well as a wonderful show of flowers from summer to autumn.

There are a number of types bearing large clusters of flowers in rich red to purplish shades, pink, and white. The blossom may be single or double. There is also a cultivar with smaller but very tight double flowers, and a form with cream-variegated foliage and pink flowers. Anyone with a spacious conservatory, little more than frost-free in winter, could form a most attractive collecton of these plants.

Neriums are also extremely useful for cool porches, entrance halls or foyers, provided the light is good.

The plant grows well in any of the usual potting composts. It often grows naturally in very moist soils, and should be watered well from spring to autumn. In winter, very little water is needed, usually just enough to prevent drying out. If the temperature is very low, watering should be even more sparing.

Where space is limited the development of neriums must be checked by drastic cutting back after flowering. New shoots will arise from the base. It is important to remove the shoots that grow from the bases of the flower trusses promptly. If this is not done the plants soon become large, straggly and ungainly. Even with constant cutting back and pruning, moving on to a 25cm (10in) pot or small tub is usually necessary. It is a good idea to raise new plants from time to time, to replace old, large ones. Cuttings taken in summer usually root easily even if stood in a jar of water. Sometimes, a flower will produce an elongated seed pod, which will ultimately burst open to reveal the seeds with silky hairs attached to aid distribution by the wind.

STRELITZIA

There is one plant which can be singled out as having created world-wide fascination. It is the bird of paradise flower (*Strelitzia reginae*) which, once seen, is

never forgotten. It is a native of South Africa and belongs to the banana family. The derivation of the name Strelitzia is of interest. The plant was named in honour of Princess Charlotte of Mecklenberg-Strelitz (1744–1818), who later became Queen to George III of England. The dedication was made by Sir Joseph Banks (1743–1820).

Its spectacular appearance cannot fail to give the impression that it must have demanding cultural requirements, and jungle-like preferences. Indeed, in many gardening books it was – and still is – described as a stove plant. This means only suited to a very warm greenhouse. In fact, this is a complete nonsense. In the Isles of Scilly the strelitzia is hardy. It is also surprising to discover that it is one of the easiest houseplants to grow. Moreover, it will delight you with its amazing flowers at Christmas time, as well as in summer.

The plant is clump-forming, growing as rather fan-shaped groups of foliage. The leaves are large, stout, bluntly spear-shaped, evergreen, and borne on long, stout stems spear-fashion. The flower, formed at the top of a strong, long stem, is designed by nature to be pollinated by a tiny honey bird. This bird has bright colouring similar to the flower. The bird alights on the blue stigma, transferring another flower's pollen from its breast. To obtain nectar from the base, the bird moves down the stigma and when bending to drink collects pollen on its breast feathers from the conveniently

positioned anthers. So the process is repeated from flower to flower. The entire flower is shaped like a bird's head, hence its common name. The plumage consists of showy orange sepals, this colour contrasting strikingly with the bright blue stigmas. Both sepals and stigmas rise up out of a sheath-like structure which is held almost at a right angle to the supporting stem, thus creating even more the striking appearance of a bird's head.

Well-grown plants produce two or more flowers twice a year at the times already stated, and this assumes they are growing in 25cm (10in) pots. The flowers are long lasting and can be cut for floral decoration.

Young strelitzia plants are now sold by a number of nurseries. When received, they should be given pots just large enough to take the roots comfortably. Any of the usual potting composts can be used.

Plants will not flower until they have reached maturity. From seed this may take from about three to five years. Before flowering, the plants will have to be large enough to demand 25cm (10in) pots. Flowering may be encouraged by keeping the plants slightly pot bound, but feeding must not be neglected during summer. If plants tend to be reluctant to flower, a little superphosphate incorporated with the upper layers of compost in spring may help. Once flowering begins, it will usually be repeated every year afterwards.

The plants will eventually need dividing. This is best done in early spring. It may be quite a mammoth operation and the plant is best cut through with a very sharp knife, since this does less damage to the very fleshy roots than attempts to pull them apart, which may cause bruising and lead to rotting.

TIBOUCHINA

Because of its exquisite flowers, like giant purple-blue pansies with satin-like petals, borne from summer to autumn, *Tibouchina semidecandra* has long been a highly-prized conservatory plant, and has now been introduced as a house-plant. In a modern home, with large picture-windows, it will grow quite well. It is still widely listed and known by this name, but should be correctly called *T. urvilleana*. Although native to Brazil, it is easy to grow with a minimum temperature of about 7–10°C (45–50°F). In those countries with a climate mild enough outdoors, it forms a handsome, large shrub inspiring the popular name glory bush. As well as a profusion of glorious flowers, about 10cm (4in) across, the velvety dark-green leaves may give reddish tints in autumn where conditions are cool. The plant is then only semi-evergreen.

As a houseplant, tibouchina can be conveniently accommodated in 18cm (7in) pots, using any of the modern potting composts, preferably a rich one such as John Innes potting compost No. 3. Give one or more bamboo canes as necessary for support, and secure the stems as they grow. If the plant is a young one bought in spring, it may need stopping to encourage several shoots which subsequently should be trained up canes. If possible, give young plants a minimum temperature of 10°C (50°F).

Plants grown in conservatories or garden rooms are best trained up a wall trellis and given either large pots or small tubs, or planted in a border.

During summer, give very slight shade and plenty of water. In winter, keep only very slightly moist. Proper pruning is important if the plants are to be kept within bounds. If in small pots, cut back drastically in February by reducing the main stems by about two-thirds and lateral shoots to two pairs of buds or leaves. Plants given a free run in conservatories need only be cut back to a convenient size, although the lateral shoots should be reduced to two pairs of buds or leaves, as for smaller pot plants.

Opposite page: *Nerium oleander,* better known as the oleander.
Above left: *Strelitzia reginae.*
Left: *Tibouchina semidecandra.*

179

GROWING FOOD INDOORS

Few pleasures are as great as serving family and friends with food grown at home, and even if you do not have a garden, it is possible to grow some fruit and vegetables indoors, as well as certain herbs.

The area at the sides of windows can be utilized by placing glass shelves on brackets there, and this helps to extend the productive area.

Glass shelves positioned near a window, or secured to a glass door, afford additional space for plants, and enable them to grow in areas where there is plenty of light.

Garden rooms, sun lounges and light frost-proof porches are ideal places to raise food plants. However, there are a few points which should be checked. So far as the kitchen is concerned, the kind of heating used for cooking is critical. Gas, oil and coal fumes do not suit many plants, and some will fail to thrive if there is the merest trace of any of these in the atmosphere, although natural gas is less harmful than the old coal gas.

The intensity of light is important. Most food plants need a sunny window-sill, and will become drawn and spindly if set in a dark position.

Many herbs will grow happily on a sunny window-sill, including mint, marjoram, parsley, chives and thyme.

THE PLANTS

Raising plants from seed gives great pleasure, and fortunately most of the plants discussed in this chapter can be grown this way. The contents of a seed-packet often produces more plants than required so therefore only sow part of a packet. However, it is as well to note that the viability of the seed decreases with age. Many home gardeners might consider buying established plants to be easier and cheaper where only a few plants are required but many of the specialized plants for the home are only obtainable in seed form.

It is not convenient – or even possible – to raise by seed all of the plants required. For instance, although chicory and rhubarb are easy enough to force indoors, usually only those people with gardens can produce the mature roots necessary for this purpose. Obviously, the indoor gardener with no garden has to find a source of stored roots. Some garden centres and shops sell both these. Seedlings are usually transplanted into progressively larger pots, but not all seedlings tolerate or need transplanting. The herb chervil, for instance, tends to sulk if moved. The practice for such plants is first to sow the seed very thinly directly in the final pot, and later to thin out crowded seedlings when large enough to be handled.

Some plants are best sown in successional batches. Among the herbs sown in succession for a continuous supply are oregano, summer savory, basil, chives and lemon balm. The pungency is quite strong in the young growth of these herbs. On the other hand, it is the fairly mature plants of parsley that have the best flavour.

Herbs and other plants grown indoors will never be as lush as those outdoors. However, their value is that they are near at hand and fresh.

Herbs

It is essential to remember that herbs are not houseplants proper. Some houseplants are able to tolerate low light levels, but herbs are usually from sunny climes and need lots of light. Even if this is not direct sunlight, it should be strong daylight or the plants will become spindly and drawn, rather than producing lots of leaves.

Basil is at its best indoors when young. It should be grown by successional sowings of the seed. Keep the seedlings warm, their soil moist, and provide as much sunlight as possible. It is not always easy to grow the seedlings on to

large plants, and careful watering of the pots is needed. The plants seem to resent being constantly picked when grown indoors.

Chervil is a fast-growing annual that never makes robust plants. It is best sown in succession. A packet of seed will suffice for several sowings.

Chives are easily grown from seed by successional sowings. They germinate easily and grow quite well on a warm window-sill. Leave the seedlings unthinned. As soon as the foliage becomes long enough, it can be cut. Take off 2.5–5cm (1–2in) of the tips using a pair of scissors. It should be possible to cut-and-come again as the clipped 'grass' grows.

These seedlings will grow into more mature plants. They can be divided in autumn for forcing early in the year, or in spring for use during summer.

To divide a mature plant remove it from its pot and examine the roots. The plant is really a cluster of tiny bulbs, which can be pulled apart and small groups potted as separate plants.

Mint. Although spearmint is the mint most often seen, the round-leaved woolly type has a much better flavour and is the more highly scented of the two.

Mint grows quite well on almost any window-sill, in sun or shade, as long as it can be kept close to the glass, where the light is strongest.

When grown in a pot, it does best when kept standing in a shallow saucer of water. Fill the pots to one-third of their depth with drainage materials (shingle will do), and then fill with compost.

Mint roots can be lifted from the garden in autumn or in early spring. Fill the pots with the string-like roots and pack soil between and around them.

Mint can also be grown in water – like a hyacinth bulb. Wash the soil from the roots and place a bunch in a glass jar. Keep the leafy portion well away from the water. If necessary, keep the foliage above the water by placing a few stones, or some shingle or sand, on the base of the glass, along with a nugget or two of charcoal to keep the water sweet. From time to time add a weak plant food to the water.

Parsley, a biennial, is an adaptable plant, well suited to growing in pots. One to five plants in a 15–20cm (5–8in) pot will allow room for the long, strong roots. However, terracotta parsley pots, in which many plants grow from holes in the side of the vessel, are popular, though not so practical. Herbs other

than parsley can also be grown in them. Marjoram, thyme, summer savory and parsley, alone and mixed, do well in such containers. When mixed, the parsley should be at the base; if grown at the top it shades the other herbs.

Parsley pots can present problems unless properly prepared. To prevent the water cascading from each hole when the pot is watered from the top, bringing the soil with it, there should be a core of drainage material such as sand or gravel.

First, pour in soil, reaching to the holes nearest the base. Insert a hollow tube with its base resting on the soil, its top protruding well above the rim (a length of hose or pipe, even a slim liquid cannister will do) then, pour the drainage material into this. Before removing it, plant the seedlings, one to a hole, roots laid inside, tiny seed leaves on the edge of the hole (no seed leaves should ever be buried) and the true leaves outside the pot. Pour in more soil, so that the roots are covered and the level reaches to the next layer of holes. Repeat and contine this until the pot is filled. Plant three seedlings around the top edge.

Pour water into the tube until the soil is uniformly moist, then carefully remove the tube. Always add water through this drainage core at the centre of the pot.

Alternatively, simply fill the pot with soil in the usual way and water from the base only, by keeping the pot standing in a shallow plate, not a deep saucer, kept filled with water.

Parsley seed is notorious for taking up to six weeks to germinate. However, indoors it germinates much more quickly if the seed-box is placed in a propagator or enclosed in a polythene bag and kept in a warm place. Seed can be sown at any time for growing indoors.

Chicory

When growing naturally, this green-leaved plant has bitter leaves, but if grown in the dark during winter, the forced leaves are pale, sweet and crisp. There are two ways of forcing chicory indoors. The roots can be set in a large pot of soil or compost, and covered with an upturned pot of the same size (to ensure no light enters, block up the drainage holes of the upper pot). Alternatively, place a black plastic bag over the rim of the pot. In each case, the chicons (plump young shoots) have room to grow and light is excluded.

Place the pot in any convenient area – the porch, hall, or garden room. It can also be hidden from view under the stairs, in a broom cupboard, or in a cupboard under the kitchen sink. Instead of using pots, the roots can be placed in a strong box and covered with a strong, black plastic bag. Even the box can be dispensed with and the roots grown in the bag.

Chicory roots should be parsnip-shaped, and of equal lengths (cut them from the base end, if necessary), about 20cm (8in) long and 5cm (2in) across the top.

Any clean ordinary soil will do for pot culture, but the chicons will stay cleaner if this is topped with a layer of horticultural sand.

Begin by putting a little soil in the pot, and then stand three or more roots upright 10cm (4in) apart. Pack soil around them, leaving the top 2.5cm (1in) of the root protruding.

Water the soil until it is moist but not sodden and allow it to drain. Cover to exclude the light.

A temperature of 7°C (45°F) should be maintained, and it can safely rise to 16°C (61°F). Avoid rapid fluctuations.

The higher the temperature the quicker the chicons will mature. Forcing should normally take from five to six weeks. Discard the roots once the shoots have been cut. To maintain a succession of chicons, plant at weekly or fortnightly intervals. For the box or bag method, use moist peat. When using a bag, first pack peat into the base, so that it stands firmly, aiming for a depth of 7.5cm (3in)

or so. Plant the roots as previously described. Close the bag in such a way that it does not fall on to the crowns. A cane inside on each side will keep the bag upright.

Cucumbers

Because cucumbers need special conditions when grown in a greenhouse, it may be surprising to learn that they can be grown in the average home. In recent years plant breeders have produced many new cultivars, including one for window-sill culture – a hybrid known as 'Fembaby'. It produces only female flowers, which means that each one should develop into a cucumber.

'Fembaby' accepts the drier conditions that prevail in the home, and is resistant to mildews which beset this vegetable and cause growth to become stunted. The plant is small, only 90cm–1.2m (3–4ft) high, and produces 20cm (8in) fruits. It can be grown on a sunny window-sill in a 20–25cm (8–10in) pot. Unlike most plants, the pots for this cucumber should be kept standing in a deep saucer or bowl holding about a litre (2 pints) of water, topped up every day. The leaves need spraying daily, more than once in hot, dry weather.

The best method of training is to fix three supports, one in the middle of the pot. The plant is then trained up this central cane. When it reaches 90cm (3ft), its tip is pinched out. It will then develop sideshoots, two of which should be allowed to grow down the other canes, one to each.

If the shoots appear to go on growing, their tips can be trained across the pot and back up the cane on the other side. The first 60cm (2ft) of stem is trimmed of its leaves, an operation which forces the plant to produce flowers on the main stem, and subsequently cucumbers. Sideshoots should be kept pinched out.

Seed can be germinated at any time of the year at about 27°C (81°F). Mid to late summer is recommended as the time to begin raising a winter crop. Sow each seed individually in small pots, preferably peat ones.

When the seedlings have produced three to four leaves, move them to their final pots. Keep the plants in a temperature of at least 18°C (65°F) by day during those early stages. Later, they will tolerate a lower temperature, about 15°C (60°F).

Mushrooms

While many of the green-leaved food plants are decorative in some way, others are not, although they usually make up for this deficiency in some other fascinating way. This is certainly the case with mushrooms.

Most people, having grown an indoor crop of mushrooms successfully, continue to cultivate them. And mushrooms have the advantage in that they can be grown out of sight and tucked away. The choice of place to put them is often limited, because apart from needing to be warm, 15–18°C (60–65°F), and dark, it should also be well ventilated. In addition, once the mushrooms appear, the atmosphere should be kept humid by spraying the soil with water through a fine mister.

Mushrooms are grown from spawn, not seed. The most convenient way for the home gardener to grow mushrooms is to buy a kit, which has a container (usually a bucket or plastic bag), and properly-prepared compost impregnated with the spawn. Instructions for use usually come with the kit.

Generally, the value of the entire crop of mushrooms is about equal to the cost of the kit. The profit – and this is a real one – is that the mushrooms grow a few at a time and can be eaten fresh.

Children find mushrooms an exciting crop, being able to go each day to watch how they develop and to pull (never cut) the largest specimens.

Strawberries

It is possible to grow strawberries indoors when they are commanding high prices in the shops. Strawberries are not only delicious to eat, they are lovely to look at and fun to watch develop from the sight of the first flower bud to the last berry. Fortunately, most cultivars flourish quite happily in many different kinds of containers, so long as they have a depth and width of at least 23–25cm (9–10in). A row of large, matching pots, each in its own neat saucer on a sunny window-sill is an attractive feature.

There are other containers that can be used, such as terracotta strawberry pots, which are similar to parsley pots. The new tower pots, which consist of a number of cylindrical containers each with a hole for a plant, fitting neatly and tightly one into the other, are decorative and space-saving. The tower can be as high as convenient. The tower is easily handled for turning daily so that all the plants receive an equal amount of light. Strawberries can be grown indoors all the time, but it is not the best method. The ideal way is to keep the containers outside until the plants are ready for forcing. As the large strawberries are divided into summer and autumn-fruiting types, this means that the first

Cucumbers and mushrooms, strawberries and rhubarb – all are surprisingly easy to grow in the home.

type should be brought indoors in mid-February and the second in early September. They need gentle heat, not more than 16°C (61°F) from March onwards. Once the plants have fruited, they can go back outside to recuperate.

It is possible to grow them a second year, but for a really heavy crop it is best to begin with fresh plants each year. Runners can be taken from plants in the garden, or plants bought from specialist strawberry growers.

Containers must be well drained, and the potting compost should be lime-free. Cultivation entails ensuring that the compost never dries out, although it must not become sodden. The plants should be fed with a liquid fertilizer every fortnight, following instructions.

Once the plants bloom they need to be pollinated, because there will not be the bees and other insects indoors to do this job naturally. This is done with a soft paintbrush, taking the pollen from the centre of the flower and transferring it to another flower.

Children enjoy growing the little alpine strawberries, which can easily be raised from seed. Incidentally, the seed germinates erratically, so do not be in a hurry to discard the compost.

Plant one alpine seedling to a small pot and gradually pot it on into larger pots.

Rhubarb

The beautiful, magenta-pink stalks of forced rhubarb are delicious substitutes for fresh fruit for pies and desserts at a time when these are scarce or expensive. The forcing season is from November to February, and one root (or crown as it is called) will yield a worthwhile crop. Two- to five-year-old crowns are best for this purpose. Whether these are lifted from the garden or bought from a garden centre, they should have been exposed to frost for a few days.

To do this, leave them lying on the open ground for a few frosty days.

Rhubarb should be forced in warm, dark, moist conditions in a temperature of 13–24°C (55–75°F). One crown is usually enough for a single large pot, tub, box or black plastic bag. If you want a continual supply, plant the crowns in a monthly succession. Ordinary soil or peat can be used. Water this after planting and keep it moist, but never sodden. From time to time check that the roots have adequate moisture. Pull out (not cut) the stems as they are ready, and cover the plant again to encourage more stems to grow.

The roots can be planted outdoors later. It will take time for them to recover from forcing, but eventually they will be productive again. Do not force again.

Sprouting vegetables

This is child's play, in more senses than one – nothing could be easier. Seed is readily available from many sources. The types of plant used for sprouting include alfalfa, beans of many kinds such as mung and soya, fenugreek, millet, sesame, sunflower and cereals such as oats, wheat and rye. Some of the these are to be found in mixtures, others are sold separately. Approximately, 15g ($\frac{1}{2}$oz) of seed will develop into 140–225g (5–8oz) of shoots, depending on the kind. There is also mustard and cress. Except for the latter, seeds should be grown in a warm, dark atmosphere. A suitable environment is attained by using a glass jar covered with muslin or similar material. Children enjoy growing these vegetables because they see the results so quickly. Give them small jars and a little seed. Place the seed in the jar. Cover the top with muslin, held in place with an elastic band. Fill the jar with tepid water poured through the muslin, then shake the jar to moisten all the seeds; drain the water away through the cover, and repeat this three times. Lay the jar on its side in a warm place, such as on a radiator shelf, or in an airing cupboard, for four or five days. Sometimes the seed will germinate in less time. Rinse the seeds twice each day with tepid water. If you like to see

green sprouts, lay the jar in sunlight for the last day.

To prepare the seeds for cooking, float the sprouts so that the seed husks fall away. Drain and serve raw or cooked, Chinese-style.

Instead of glass jars, it is also possible to buy specially designed plastic sprouters, some of which have two layers, one of which takes very small seed such as alfalfa. Some have as many as six trays, so that several types of vegetable can be grown at the same time.

Mustard and cress production engages children, and there are many easy ways in which this crop can be grown. Incidentally, mustard germinates first, and is often the only one grown. The seeds can be spread on moist rag or tissue laid in a saucer and kept damp. Horticultural show exhibitors often decorate vegetable stands with pyramids of mustard or cress. These are grown on cones of damp moss which have been rolled in the seed and then kept damp by being placed in a dish of water.

To grow these two crops as a practical salad, use seed-trays or any similar container. When grown together, the cress should be sown three days earlier than the mustard. Allow 20g ($\frac{3}{4}$oz) of mustard and 15g ($\frac{1}{2}$oz) of cress to a full-sized normal seed-tray. Try to spread the seed evenly as you sow it. Slide the box into a plastic bag and keep it in a temperature of 18°C (65°F), lower at night. Once germinated, the seedlings should be uncovered and kept in a light place. Once the leaves have expanded, the crop can be cut with scissors. The same soil can be used twice for this purpose. Some people cover the soil with a tissue, dampen it and then sow the seeds to keep the crop free of soil.

Sprouting vegetables are highly nutritious and grow quickly in jars or in specially designed sprouters.
From left to right: Mustard and cress, alfalfa, sunflower, soya, oats, mung – ready to eat and at the half-way stage – rye and wheat.

INDEX

Acknowledgments

The publishers would like to thank:

GEEST HORTICULTURAL GROUP LTD
World's End Nurseries
Jack Beanstalk Chelsea
Clarke and Spears
Tokonoma bonsai
Brian and Wilma Rittershausen (orchids)
Clifton Nurseries
Tropical Plants
Holly Gate Nurseries Ltd (cacti)
The Royal Horticultural Society, Wisley
for so kindly supplying the plants used in the
photography of this book.

We would also like to thank the following
companies for providing materials and
equipment:
C. H. Branham Ltd (plain white pots)
Casa Pupo (decorative white pots)
C. Rassells Ltd
The Craftsmen Potters' Association
Crayonne
David Mellor

The Humidifier Co. of Wembley Park
and Marks and Spencer Ltd.

Illustrator: **Nicolas Hall.**

The publishers would like to thank the following
organizations and individuals for their kind permission to reproduce the photographs in this book:

A-Z Botanical Collection Ltd 65 below right, 71, 75
above, 86 left, 96, 131 right, 139 below left, 153
below left, 177; Bernard Alfieri 93 inset; Heather
Angel/Biofotos 144 above left, 151, 155, 178; Peter
Black 172–173; Pat Brindley 26 above left, 55
above left, 64 above right, 66 above centre, 73
below right, 76 above, 88 right, 92 above, 98 left,
106–107 below, 109 left, 111 right, 116, 117, 120,
123 left, 124, 130, 139 above left, 152, 153 above
left, 161, 164 below right, 165 above left, 176, 179
above right; P. R. Chapman 160, 163, 165 below
left; Bruce Coleman Ltd (Eric Crichton) 80 left, 92
left; John Cowley 142 below right; Eric Crichton 81
right, 174, 175; Mary Evans Picture Library 158,
171, and inset; Iris Hardwick Library 106 below
left, 153 below right, 154; G. E. Hyde 26 below left;
David Hoy Publishing 69; Bill McLaughlin 37, 137;
Ian McLean 54–55 below, 64 above centre; John

Moss 157; Ann Ronan Picture Library 134; Dieter
Schact 89; Harry Smith 26 centre, 29 above right,
52, 53, 54, 56, 62 below left, 77 below right, 91
above, 102 right, 106 above right, 109 right, 114
left, 121 below right, 131 left, 136, 138, 139 below
right, 153 above right, 164 above right, 179 below
right; Spectrum Colour Library 48, 67 above, 144
above right, 162; Sutton Seeds Ltd 82; Michael
Warren 55 right, 65 below left, 78, 88 left, 122
right, 128 above, 143, 144 below, 159; Elizabeth
Whiting and Associates 43 inset

Special Photography by:
Melvin Grey 45, 135; **Paul Kemp** 141; **Spike Powell**
41 above centre and right, 142 above right; **Peter
Rauter**, Stylist: **Sonya Fancett** 2–3, 4–5, 9, 10, 11,
16–17, 18, 19, 21, 22–23, 32–33, 38–39, 40, 41
below right, 42 inset, 42–43, 44, 47, 50–51, 57,
58–59, 60–61, 62 above left, 63, 64 below, 66 below
centre, 67 below, 68–69, 70, 72, 73 below left,
74–75, 76–77, 78–79, 80–81, 83, 84, 85, 86–87,
90–91, 91 below, 93, 94–95, 97, 99, 100–101,
102–103, 104–105, 107 right, 108, 110–111,
112–113, 114–115, 117 below, 118–119, 122 left,
125, 126, 127, 128–129, 132–133, 146–147, 148,
167, 169, 180–181, 183, 184–185; **John Sims** 28,
29, 30, 46, 98 right, 121 above right, 123 right

THE HOUSEPLANT CARE NOTEBOOK

January

February

March

April

THE HOUSEPLANT CARE NOTEBOOK

May

June

July

August

THE HOUSEPLANT CARE NOTEBOOK

September

October

November

December